SECOND EDITION

A FIELD GUIDE TO THE

GRAND CANYON

More than 4 million people visit the Grand Canyon each year, and all of them should take this book along. By using Whitney's well-organized and easy-to-use field guide, you will come away from this geologic wonder with a fuller appreciation of the complex world you have visited.

—*Arizona Highways*

D0981534

SECOND EDITION

A FIELD GUIDE TO THE
GRAND CANYON

Stephen R. Whitney

THE
MOUNTAINEERS

Published by
The Mountaineers Books
1001 SW Klickitat Way, Suite 201
Seattle, Washington 98134

First edition by William Morrow & Co. 1982
Second edition by The Mountaineers Books: first printing 1996, second printing 2001, third printing 2003, fourth printing 2005, fifth printing 2007, sixth printing 2008, seventh printing 2010

Distributed in the United Kingdom by Cordee, www.cordee.co.uk

Manufactured in China

Edited by Kris Fulsaas
Maps by Nick Gregoric
All illustrations by the author
Cover design by Watson Graphics
Book design and layout by Nick Gregoric

Cover photograph: Grand Canyon National Park, view over canyon at sunrise
© Donovan Reese, Tony Stone Images

Library of Congress Cataloging-in-Publication Data
Whitney, Stephen, 1942–
    A field guide to the Grand Canyon / Stephen R. Whitney. — 2nd ed.
      p. cm.
    Includes bibliographies and indexes.
    1. Natural history—Arizona—Grand Canyon—Guidebooks. 2. Grand Canyon (Ariz.)—Guidebooks. I. Title.
QH105.A65W44 1996
  508.791'32—dc20   96–22642
                                              CIP

ISBN (paperback): 978-0-89886-489-2
ISBN (ebook): 978-1-59485-350-0

Contents

Introduction

On first viewing the Grand Canyon, few visitors are immediately able to grasp and appreciate the scene spread before them. The forms are unfamiliar, the scale too outrageous. The landscape is so unlike any other that it suggests, if not an alien world, at least the very edge of the one we know. In some sense the spectacle simply does not register in the brain. The eye records, but the mind looks away. The geologist Clarence Dutton, writing in the late nineteenth century, called the Grand Canyon "a great innovation in modern ideas of scenery" and said that "its full appreciation is a special culture, requiring time, patience and long familiarity for its consummation." This book is offered as an aid to acquiring that special culture.

This volume is first and foremost a field guide, a handy, compact reference for the person who wants to identify and learn something about the rocks, landforms, plants, and animals of the Grand Canyon. Part I, The Canyon Environment, provides information on geography, climate, geologic history, and plant and animal distribution. The geographic area covered by this guide includes the canyon and its adjacent rims from Nankoweap Valley west to Grand Wash Cliffs.

Part II, The Plants, contains descriptions and illustrations of numerous common ferns, wildflowers, cacti, shrubs, and trees found at the Grand Canyon. Though grasses, sedges, rushes, and nonflowering plants other than ferns are important elements in the Grand Canyon flora, they have been excluded for reasons of space and because they are of less interest to most visitors.

Part III, The Animals, covers mammals, birds, reptiles, amphibians, and butterflies.

Each account of a plant or animal begins with its common name, followed by its scientific name in italics. Many people feel uncomfortable using scientific names, which are derived from Latin and often seem difficult to pronounce. Yet common names, though pronounceable and easy to remember, pose even greater problems. Many plants and animals have several common names. Others have none at all. Two unrelated organisms may even share the same common name. Scientific names avoid such confusion because each name applies to one and only one species.

Each scientific name has two parts. The first part names the genus to which an organism belongs; the second names the species. Members of a single species are mutually fertile but are incapable of breeding with members of other species. (There are exceptions, but they need not concern us here.) Several closely related species make up a genus (plural genera). Several related genera constitute a family.

For example, the pine family is represented at the Grand Canyon by the following genera: *Pinus* (pine), *Abies* (fir), *Pseudotsuga* (Douglas-fir), and *Picea* (spruce). The genus *Picea* is represented locally by two species: *Picea engelmannii* (Engelmann spruce) and *Picea pungens* (blue spruce). Thus, the scientific name for a species not only separates it from all other species, but also indicates those among the others to which it is closely related.

The common and scientific names used in this guide match those used in the following checklists, which are available on the Grand Canyon National park Web site at http://www.nps.gov/grca/naturescience <http://www.nps.gov/grca/naturescience> :

- Grand Canyon Vascular Plant List
- Grand Canyon Vertebrate Animals Species List

Other useful checklists that can be downloaded from the Grand Canyon National Park Web site include the following:

- Amphibians of Grand Canyon NP
- Birds of Grand Canyon NP
- Colorado River Plant List
- A Field Guide to the Special Status Plants of the Grand Canyon, Parts One, Two, and Three
- Fishes of Grand Canyon NP
- Grand Canyon Exotic Plant List
- Grand Canyon Invertebrate Species Collection
- Grand Canyon Non-Vascular Plants
- Grand Canyon Potentially Invasive Weed List
- Grand Canyon Threatened and Endangered Species List
- Mammals of Grand Canyon NP
- Reptiles of Grand Canyon NP

Although the taxonomic status of some groups of plants and animals has undergone revision since the above sources were published, no attempt has been made to reflect these revisions, which are of little or no interest to the average reader.

This guide contains descriptions and illustrations of more than 500 species or genera of plants and animals. Even so, space limitations make it impossible to include every species found at the Grand Canyon. Those selected for this guide are primarily the more common and more easily identified types. Where a genus contains two or more species so similar that an untrained observer will find it difficult or impossible to separate them in the field, the genus is often represented only by the most common or widespread species. In several cases, however, two or more species are illustrated or briefly described.

The publications listed in the Suggested References at the back of this book include books for general reading as well as works that supply more detailed information than could be included in this guide. Though a number of technical monographs were consulted in the preparation of this book, most are not widely available and therefore are not cited in the lists of references.

Abbreviations used in the species descriptions are listed in Table 1.

Table 1.
Abbreviations Used in Species Descriptions

Abbreviation	Meaning
Abun.	Abundant within normal range
Aquat.	Aquatic habitats
Bor.	Boreal Life Zone (Canadian and Hudsonian zones of the North Rim)
Can.	Canyon (that is, below the rims)
Cf.	Confer, see
Com.	Common within normal range
Diam.	Diameter
Flr(s).	Flower(s)
For.	Forest (pine, fir, or spruce)
Gorge	Inner Gorge
Grass.	Grassland
Ht.	Height
Irreg.	Irregular in occurrence; present in some years but not others
Lgth.	Length
L Son.	Lower Sonoran Life Zone
Lvs.	Leaves
N Rim	North Rim
Res.	Resident year-round
Ripar.	Riparian (that is, streamside) habitats
S Rim	South Rim
Scrub	Desert scrub
SN Rims	South Rim and North Rim
Spr.	Spring
Sum.	Summer
Tran.	Transition Life Zone
U Son.	Upper Sonoran Life Zone
Uncom.	Uncommon within normal range
var.	Variety
Vis.	Visitor to the area; does not breed in area
Win.	Winter
Wood.	Woodland (pinyon-juniper or oak)

Please note: All plants and animals within the boundaries of Grand Canyon National Park are fully protected by law, and may not be disturbed in any way, including the collecting of seeds or remains. Violators are subject to citation and/or prosecution.

On Behalf of the Grand Canyon

All visitors should leave the Grand Canyon and its inhabitants as little disturbed by our passage as possible. Certain habitats by their very nature are extremely fragile and require our special care. These include the Grand Canyon's various desert habitats as well as the park's wetlands and meadows. In desert habitats, scarce water, high temperatures, and thin soils together create exceptionally harsh conditions for plants. As a result, vegetation once destroyed may require years, or decades, to recolonize an area. In meadows and wetlands, boots can churn the soil into a black muck.

To help preserve these habitats, visitors should stay on established trails, avoid trampling vegetation, and refrain from tramping across, or camping on, meadows or fragile desert soils. It is also important not to cut across switchbacks, as the resulting erosion not only undermines the trail, but destroys trailside plants.

Collecting specimens of any kind, including samples of rocks, is forbidden in Grand Canyon National Park. The conscientious visitor will also avoid doing so in areas outside the park. This guidebook concentrates on external field marks that can be ascertained readily without resort to handheld specimens. Species that cannot be thus distinguished are treated generically and are best identified by genus or family alone. To molest or destroy an organism simply to learn its name is inexcusable in most situations.

Wildlife presents a special problem for visitors. Most people seem to lose all sense in the presence of wild animals, behaving toward them as they do toward their pets. The importance of leaving all wild animals alone cannot be stressed too much. By encouraging campground animals to approach us or to take handouts of food, we disrupt their diet and behavior, degrade their dignity, and increase the danger of injury to ourselves by causing the animals to overcome their innate distrust of humans. The potential danger posed by large, unpredictable mammals such as bears should be apparent to anyone—though it demonstrably is not—but even cute little chipmunks and squirrels can and do inflict painful bites. Many rodents, bats, and other mammals also may carry various diseases, such as rabies, and pests, such as ticks and fleas. It is particularly important not to handle young animals because you may injure them or cause their parents to abandon them. You may also invite serious injury to yourself.

Many visitors discover that their trip to the Grand Canyon becomes a richer, more enjoyable experience when they take the time to get acquainted with the plants and animals that live there. Treating the park's inhabitants with caution and sensitivity will assure that they are around to greet the unborn generations of visitors to follow.

PART I

THE CANYON ENVIRONMENT

1

The Grandest Canyon

Among the earth's great river gorges the Grand Canyon is unmatched in its overall vastness, topographic complexity, striking landforms, and range of colors. Other canyons may equal or surpass it in one or another of these attributes, but none combines them all on such a colossal scale or in such harmonious proportion. And none is so perfectly situated for the purpose of displaying these qualities to utmost advantage. If the Grand Canyon were flanked by mountains, its impact would be diminished. As it is, the gently rolling plateaus that form its rims make the gorge appear, if possible, even deeper, wider, and more rugged than it is.

The Grand Canyon is 277 miles long. Distances across the canyon range from 4 to 15.5 miles, the average being 10. From rims 6000 to 8500 feet above sea level, the canyon walls drop 3500 to 6000 feet to the Colorado River, which flows through the narrow, winding Inner Gorge within the larger chasm. The prominent horizontal rock strata exposed in the canyon walls provide dramatic counterpoint to the vertical dimension. Their various colors, ranging through the entire spectrum, combine in the eye to create the glowing red-orange hue that suffuses the canyon.

Rather than plunging directly to the river, the walls drop in a series of cliffs, slopes, and terraces that reflect the varying degrees of hardness of the strata. Dissecting the walls and scalloping the rims into alternating amphitheaters and promontories are countless side canyons that branch and rebranch off the Inner Gorge like the limbs of a tree. Separating the canyons are ridges eroded into lines of mesas, buttes, and pinnacles that elsewhere would be major peaks, but in the Grand Canyon are nearly lost in the surrounding immensity.

The upper portion of the Grand Canyon—known as Marble Canyon—begins at Lees Ferry, where the Colorado River leaves the younger rocks of Glen Canyon to plunge into the older strata of the Marble Platform. Although this nearly level desert plateau is 2000 to 3000 feet lower than the Kaibab Plateau to the west, the two are formed of the same sequence of rocks, which drop from the Kaibab in a great plunging fold called the East Kaibab Monocline. Marble Canyon

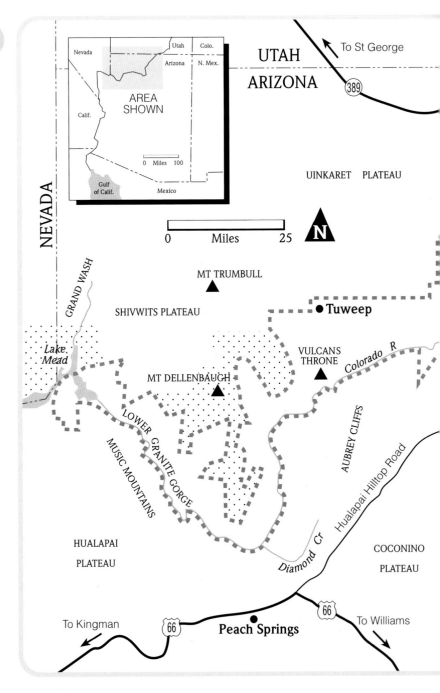

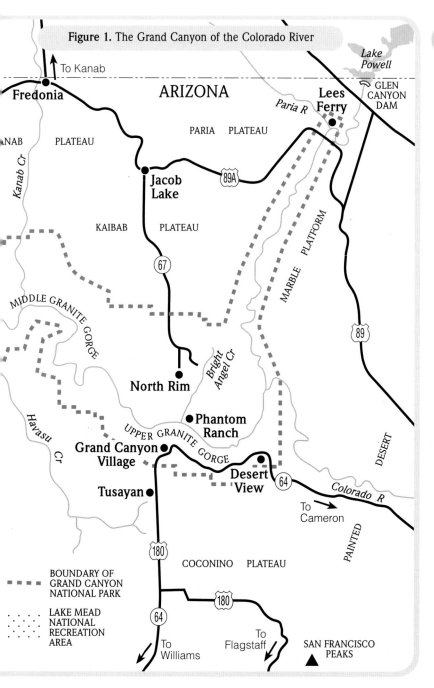

Figure 1. The Grand Canyon of the Colorado River

is a twisting corridor roughly 2000 feet deep and from less than a mile to about 4 miles across. Fifty miles south of Lees Ferry, just above the mouth of Nankoweap Creek, which enters the river from the west, the canyon abruptly widens to about 8.5 miles across. Though Marble Canyon technically extends southward another 10 miles to the confluence of the Colorado and Little Colorado Rivers, it is upstream at Nankoweap that the Grand Canyon first assumes the scale and grandeur for which it is famous.

For most of its length, the South Rim of the Grand Canyon is formed by the Coconino Plateau, which covers about 3500 square miles. From the canyon's edge, it extends south to the base of the San Francisco Peaks and Bill Williams Mountains. From Desert View it stretches west for some 75 miles to Diamond Creek. From there west to the Grand Wash Cliffs, the South Rim consists of a narrow upland called the Music Mountains. The limestone surface of the Coconino Plateau is gently undulating, with elevations ranging from 6000 to 7500 feet above sea level. The plateau is highest near Grandview Point, east of Grand Canyon Village, on the South Rim.

West of the Marble Platform, four plateaus—the Kaibab, Kanab, Uinkaret, and Shivwits—form the North Rim of the Grand Canyon. The Kaibab Plateau is the highest and easternmost of the four. Elevations on the Kaibab range between 7500 and 8500 feet along the canyon rim and increase to just over 9200 feet a few miles north. Its limestone surface has eroded into gentle ridges, shallow basins, and draws.

On the west, the Kaibab drops about 1000 feet to the Kanab Plateau, which is cut in half by the huge gorge of Kanab Creek. The Kanab is separated from the Uinkaret Plateau on the west by the lava-filled Toroweap Valley, which once extended down to the Colorado River but now ends abruptly at the brink of the Inner Gorge, some 3000 feet above. Perched on the brink, overlooking the gorge and visible from the river, is the picturesque cinder cone called Vulcans Throne.

This portion of the Grand Canyon has a different profile from that of the more familiar eastern section. Near Toroweap, the outer cliffs are steeper and less broken by slopes than is the case below Grand Canyon Village. The cliffs drop 2000 feet to a broad inner terrace called the Esplanade, which is 5 to 6 miles across. The Inner Gorge, which cuts through the Esplanade, is less than a mile across, but features vertical cliffs 3000 feet tall.

West of the Toroweap Valley, the Uinkaret Plateau attains a general elevation of about 6000 feet, but its surface is covered by numerous cinder cones and lava flows. The highest cone is Mount Trumbull, which rises to more than 8000 feet above sea level. On the west, the Uinkaret drops to the Shivwits Plateau, the lowest and westernmost step on the North Rim staircase. Like the Uinkaret, the Shivwits Plateau is crowned by scattered volcanic cones, the highest of which is 6690-foot Mount Dellenbaugh. The Shivwits ends on the west at Grand Wash Cliffs, which overlook Lake Mead and the Mohave Desert.

The Colorado Plateau

The Grand Canyon plateaus are located at the southwestern corner of the Colorado Plateau, which covers some 13,000 square miles in northern Arizona, northwestern New Mexico, western Colorado, and eastern Utah. The Colorado Plateau is not, as the name might suggest, a single vast tableland, but rather a geologic province comprising numerous individual plateaus of varying elevation. A geologic province is a geographic region whose various rock formations and landforms are united by a common history that sets them apart from those in adjacent regions. The Colorado Plateau, for example, is bordered on the south and west by the Basin and Range Province and on the north and east by the Rocky Mountain Province.

Elevations on the Colorado Plateau range from 5000 feet to about 12,700 feet above sea level. Its surface has been dissected by rivers into a maze of plateaus and gorges. Here and there, mountain ranges rise abruptly from the plateaus. Scattered throughout the province are isolated buttes and mesas plus the oddest assortment of landforms found anywhere on the planet. No section of the country can boast of more outstanding scenery. Found in the province, in addition to the Grand Canyon, are Zion Canyon, Bryce Canyon, Cedar Breaks, Glen Canyon, Rainbow Bridge, the Canyonlands, Capitol Reef, Arches, Four Corners, Mesa Verde, Petrified Forest, the Painted Desert, San Francisco Peaks, Oak Creek Canyon, and a host of other wonders.

Most of the Colorado Plateau rests atop thousands of feet of sedimentary rocks, which form sequences of often nearly horizontal strata. Most of these rocks originated as sediments deposited in ancient seas, which repeatedly advanced and retreated over the region. Later, the strata rose thousands of feet along geological faults. In the process the rocks were often broken, bowed upward, or gently folded, but their original sequence was rarely disturbed. Today, the rocks are laid open to view by the deep canyons that dissect the region and by the relative sparseness of soil cover and vegetation. As a result, the Colorado Plateau provides geologists with an unsurpassed record of much of the earth's history.

North of the Grand Canyon, the strata have been eroded into a giant staircase of cliffs and tablelands culminating in the Markagunt and Paunsagunt

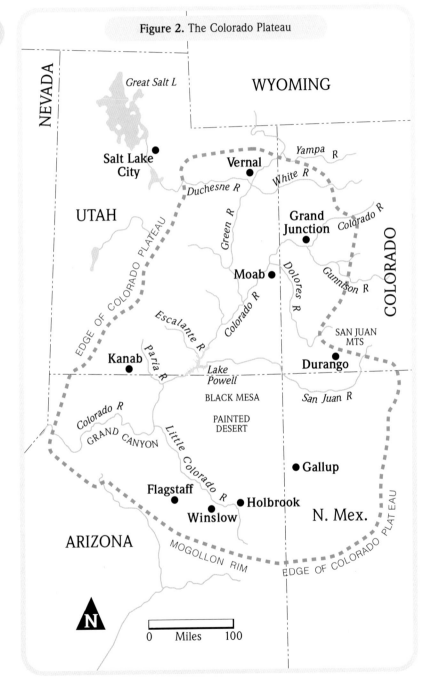

Figure 2. The Colorado Plateau

Plateaus of southern Utah, both of which top 11,000 feet elevation. The Vermilion Cliffs extend along the Utah–Arizona border from the Kanab Plateau east to near Lees Ferry. They continue beyond the river under the name of the Echo Cliffs, which curve southward to parallel the course of Marble Canyon.

Sixty miles south of Lees Ferry, the Little Colorado enters from the southeast through a narrow, steep-walled gorge cut through the Painted Desert. The desert ends abruptly at the sheer cliffs flanking the eastern end of the Grand Canyon. From Desert View north to the Little Colorado River, these cliffs form the Palisades of the Desert. Northward to Nankoweap Canyon they are called the Desert Facade.

About 50 miles south of Desert View rise the San Francisco Peaks, which culminate in 12,670-foot Humphreys Peak. This ancient volcano is the highest point in Arizona and one of the highest in all the Colorado Plateau region. The mountains rise more than 5000 feet above the surrounding lands, where lava flows cover more than 3000 square miles. From the San Francisco Peaks, the Colorado Plateau extends southward to the Mogollon Rim, which cuts across central Arizona into western New Mexico.

The Colorado River

The Colorado River, as originally named, began in southeastern Utah at the confluence of the Grand and Green Rivers. The Green originates in the Wind River Range of Wyoming, the Grand at Middle Park in the Colorado Rockies. In 1921, at the request of the Colorado state legislature, Congress redesignated the Grand River the Colorado. The Green River, a coequal partner in the Colorado River system, was thereby reduced to the status of mere tributary. But that's politics, not geography.

The Colorado River—both Grand and Green—is the major river of the American Southwest and one of the great rivers on the continent. From its headwaters in the middle and southern Rockies it flows 1440 miles to the Gulf of California. Along the way it has cut through more mountain barriers—among them the Grand Canyon plateaus—than any other river in North America. It drains about 244,000 square miles in the states of Wyoming, Colorado, Utah, Arizona, New Mexico, Nevada, and California. Its major tributaries are the Yampa, White, Gunnison, Dolores, San Juan, and Gila Rivers.

When Friar Francisco Garcés first saw the river in 1776, he named it the Rio Colorado, or "Red River," because its waters were stained reddish brown by the tremendous loads of sediments swept downstream. A visitor to the Grand Canyon today will instead likely see a green river, fed by clear, cold water released from Lake Powell, just upstream from Lees Ferry. This huge reservoir lies behind Glen Canyon Dam, which was completed in 1963. Before the dam, the river carried 380,000 tons of sediment on an average day through the Grand Canyon. Today, the daily average is only 40,000 tons, with all the sediments contributed by tributary streams such as the Little Colorado and the Paria. The balance of the sediments that once would have flowed through the Grand Canyon are now trapped behind Glen Canyon Dam. As a result, profound changes have occurred to the environment along the river corridor.

In the clear, cold waters of the new Colorado River, exotic species of fish, including several species of trout, began to flourish. At the same time, native fish such as the Colorado squawfish and humpback chub, which were already threatened by earlier introductions of carp and catfish, declined precipitously in the new environment. The native species, most of which were found only in the Grand Canyon and had become highly adapted to its specialized riverine environment, were unable to compete with more aggressive and less specialized newcomers. The growing trout population, along with the improved visibility provided by the clear water, began to attract bald eagles, which first appeared in the winter of 1985–1986 and have returned regularly since.

Glen Canyon Dam also eliminated the annual spring and summer floods that once swept through the Grand Canyon. The spring floods, derived mostly from the melting snowpack high in the Colorado Rockies, transported mainly coarse sand and tended to scour the river channel. The summer floods, resulting from high-desert thunderstorms, tended to deposit sediments rather than erode the channel, and generally laid down as much new materials as were carried away in the spring. With the elimination of these floods, the annual cycle of scour and fill has been replaced by a more or less steady regime in which finer particles are carried downstream, while coarser materials are dropped along the shore. In addition, fans of debris have built outward from tributary canyons, constricting river flow and creating steeper, more dangerous rapids littered with boulders.

Another marked effect of the elimination of annual floods was the development at the water's edge of a new plant community dominated by the tall exotic shrub tamarisk. Between 1963 and 1983, this community flourished undisturbed. Formerly, plant growth at the water's edge, in what is known as the "scour zone," had consisted only of short-lived plants that were able to germinate, flower, and disseminate their seeds in the months between summer floods and those of the following spring. With the elimination of the floods, the former scour zone was invaded by plants that formerly had been restricted to a belt higher and farther from the river. The increase in cover and food provided by this new vegetation attracted insects, lizards, toads, small birds, and mammals.

These creatures in turn supported larger populations of predators.

By 1983, vegetation along the river seemed to be progressing toward a new, more or less stable state. Then, disaster struck. Lake Powell had been slowly filling for two decades and by the summer of 1983 was near the brim. The Bureau of Reclamation, which manages the dams along the river, allowed the water to rise that high partly to guarantee supplies in the event of drought, partly to maximize profits from power generation, and partly to appease Upper Basin states, which wished to keep as much of "their" water as possible from flowing downstream to thirsty consumers in Arizona and California. Unfortunately, the bureau had not thought through the possible consequences of maintaining the lake at full capacity. When a combination of abundant spring rain and snow in the Upper Basin filled all reservoirs to capacity, the die was already cast. The bureau had no choice but to release the excess through the canyon, which it did in June 1983. In one month of flooding, after twenty years of stability, more than half the newly established vegetation along the river was destroyed. Beaches upstream from Phantom Ranch were severely damaged, and hundreds of thousands of tons of accumulated sediments and beaches were washed downstream.

Although annual floods were a natural occurrence prior to the completion of Glen Canyon Dam in 1963, a deluge on the scale of the 1983 flood was only destructive. Over the next decade, growing concerns about the future of the Grand Canyon river corridor culminated in the passage of the Grand Canyon Protection Act of 1992. This act required the Bureau of Reclamation to develop a plan to manage Glen Canyon Dam in such a way as to enhance, rather than destroy, the riverside environment downstream and to prepare an environmental impact statement describing the impacts of its plan.

One of the management strategies specifically enabled by the Grand Canyon Protection Act is the use of controlled flooding to emulate the hydrological regime that existed in the canyon prior to 1963. Such floods formerly scoured the riverbed and, as they receded, deposited the resulting sediments as sandbars along the banks. The flooding kept the sandbars free of vegetation and prevented cobble deposits at the mouths of tributaries from narrowing the river. As part of its research into the feasibility and effectiveness of implementing annual controlled floods through the canyon, the Bureau of Reclamation, in cooperation with the U.S. Geological Service and the National Park Service, and with the blessing of environmental groups concerned about the future of the canyon, maintained a flow of some 45,000 cubic feet of water through the canyon during the period. Results from the flood were disappointing because beaches that gained sand in the few weeks following the release lost what they had gained over the next 3–4 years. A second, slightly smaller release of water in 2004 has produced more promising results, but long-term prospects remain uncertain.

At the western end of the Grand Canyon the waters of Lake Mead drown the Colorado River at Separation Rapids, now gone, about 35 miles upstream from Grand Wash Cliffs. The lake began to form in 1936, following the completion of Hoover (or Boulder) Dam downstream in Black Canyon. Proposals for building two additional dams in the Grand Canyon itself were beaten back by conservationists in the mid-1960s, though political pressure to build the lower dam continues. As a result, the Colorado River remains free flowing, if regulated and diminished, in its passage through the Grand Canyon.

From Lees Ferry to Grand Wash Cliffs, the river drops 2200 feet in roughly 280 miles. It alternately flows through long, deep pools and short, steep rapids. River depths vary from 6 to 110 feet, the average being about 20. The water is deepest in major pools and in holes at the foot of rapids. The rapids comprise only 10 percent of the river's length, but account for half its total drop. They are spaced an average of about 1.5 miles apart and are most often located at the mouths of tributary canyons.

Climate

The climate of the Grand Canyon is similar to that of Arizona as a whole. Precipitation (see Table 2) is scant to moderate, with roughly equal amounts falling in summer and winter. Relative humidity is generally low. Clear skies are the norm. Winds are usually gentle to moderate. Air temperatures vary greatly between summer and winter, with as much as 50°F separating the seasonal extremes. Fall is usually mild and clear, with little or no precipitation. Spring also brings many clear, mild days, though snow often falls in April, sometimes in May, even on the South Rim.

Within this overall pattern, diverse topography and the considerable difference in elevation between the rims and the river have produced a variety of local climates. As a rule, air temperature drops and precipitation increases with elevation, so that the rims are significantly cooler and more humid than the bottom of the canyon. Because southern exposures receive more sunshine throughout the year than north-facing slopes, the former tend to be warmer and drier than the latter at any given elevation.

Precipitation

Average annual precipitation at the Grand Canyon varies from fewer than 10 inches in the Inner Gorge to nearly 30 inches on the Kaibab Plateau. The North Rim receives considerably more precipitation in winter than summer, but the South Rim and canyon receive roughly equal amounts in each season. The

Table 2.
Precipitation and Air Temperature at the Grand Canyon

Mean precipitation in inches	Phantom Ranch Inner Gorge (el. 2570')	Grand Canyon Village, South Rim (el. 6950')	Bright Angel Ranger Station, North Rim (el. 8400')
January	0.68	1.35	3.05
April	0.53	1.00	1.62
July	0.87	1.50	1.88
October	0.67	1.07	1.43
Annual	8.39	14.46	22.78
Yearly Snowfall	0.2	64.9	128.7
Mean daily temperature in degrees F			
January max.	56.3	41.4	37.8
January min.	36.3	19.6	19.5
April max.	82.1	60.2	52.9
April min.	55.5	31.4	31.4
July max.	106.1	84.7	77.1
July min.	77.7	54.0	46.3
October max.	84.9	64.9	58.6
October min.	59.2	37.2	31.6

(Data from Sellers and Hill: *Arizona Climate*, 1974)

average rainfall in the Inner Gorge for the period from May through October is about 4.5 inches. In 1968, Phantom Ranch recorded less than 4 inches for the entire year.

Winter storms move eastward into the Grand Canyon region from the Pacific Ocean. They typically last up to several days, bringing gentle snow showers to the rims and upper canyon, and light rains to lower elevations. The amount of winter precipitation received at the Grand Canyon varies greatly from year to year in both amount and frequency of occurrence. In wet years a succession of storms may cross the region at weekly intervals. In December 1966, an unusually warm Pacific storm dropped some 14 inches of rain on the Kaibab Plateau over a 3-day period, but such deluges are extremely rare.

On the Kaibab Plateau the average annual snowfall exceeds 125 inches. From early November to May, up to several feet of snow usually block roads leading to the North Rim. Grand Canyon Village, on the South Rim, is about 1500 feet lower than the North Rim Lodge and accordingly receives about half as much snow, or about 60 inches in an average year. Most snow falling on the South Rim remains on the ground for only a few days, though small patches may linger for much of the season in cool, shaded locations, particularly in places just below the rim where the low winter sun does not reach. Less than an inch of snow falls in the Inner Gorge during an average year.

After April, the incidence of Pacific storms drops sharply. From then until the onset of summer thunderstorms in mid-July, the Grand Canyon receives little or no precipitation, making May and June the driest months. Rainfall during this period ranges from about 0.5 inch in the Inner Gorge to 1.5 inches on the North Rim. A second, less severe season of drought occurs in the fall.

From mid-July to mid-September—the monsoon season—thunderstorms may occur almost every afternoon over the Grand Canyon. During the summer, warm tropical air from the Gulf of Mexico enters the region from the southeast. As it moves northward across Arizona, it is forced up and over the Mogollon Rim. In the process the air cools, and its moisture condenses to form puffy cumulus clouds. Over the Grand Canyon this incoming air is borne even higher by powerful thermals rising off the sun-baked canyon walls. As a result the clouds gather, thicken, and pile up to form massive thunderheads. The resulting thunderstorms tend to begin in mid- to late afternoon and last about a half-hour. By shortly after sundown the clouds usually have dissipated. On rare occasions these storms may deliver an inch or more of rain, though lesser amounts are the rule. About one year in seven, tropical storms from the Gulf of California, to the southwest, move into Arizona during the summer. Often lasting several days, these storms account for the region's heaviest rainfall.

Air Temperature

Average daytime high temperatures during the summer range from the low to middle 70s on the Kaibab Plateau to more than 100°F in the Inner Gorge. Daytime highs on the Coconino Plateau for this period are typically in the middle 80s. Average nighttime temperatures during the summer drop to the low 40s on the Kaibab Plateau, the low 50s on the Coconino Plateau, and the high 70s in the Inner Gorge.

During the first two weeks in July, before the onset of summer storms, air temperatures in the Inner Gorge frequently exceed 115°F during the day. Temperatures in excess of 100°F have been recorded for every month from April through October. Beginning shortly after sunrise, the nearly black cliffs lining the gorge heat up rapidly to temperatures over 120°F. Throughout the day and continuing until well after sunset, the cliffs radiate this stored heat like the walls of a brick oven. Visitors unaccustomed to such heat are well advised to avoid the Inner Gorge during the summer.

Average daytime high temperatures during the winter range from the middle 30s to low 40s on the Kaibab Plateau, low to middle 40s on the Coconino Plateau, and high 50s to low 60s in the Inner Gorge. The coldest periods come during winter snowstorms, when cold, moist Pacific air aloft overlies a layer of even colder Arctic air at the surface. The latter air mass is borne into the region from the Great Plains. At such times, nighttime lows on both rims may plummet to below zero. Normally, winter lows range in the middle teens on the Kaibab Plateau, in the high teens to middle 20s on the Coconino Plateau, and in the middle 30s in the Inner Gorge.

2

The Geologic Story

he rock formations exposed in the walls of the Grand Canyon comprise the most remarkable geological record found on earth. Nowhere else does such an ancient, extensive, and largely undisturbed sequence of rocks outcrop over such a vast area. The oldest rocks in the canyon are the schist and gneiss that form the dark cliffs of the Inner Gorge. Extending to a depth of perhaps 25 miles, these metamorphic rocks are about 2 billion years old, among the more ancient exposed rocks on the planet. Above them lie sequences of younger, sedimentary rocks, ranging in age from 1.2 billion to 220 million years old. Of these the most prominent and widely outcropping are the limestones, sandstones, and shales that make up the striking horizontal bands visible on the upper canyon walls. These formations accumulated layer upon layer during successive advances and retreats of the sea that occurred between 570 million and 220 million years ago. Since one layer had to be in place before the next could form on top of it, the rocks decrease in age from river to rims.

The Fossil Record

Accumulating sediments may include the remains of plants and animals. These remains are incorporated in the resulting rocks as fossils. Most fossils consist of skeletal remains, though softer tissues, such as leaves, may leave their imprint before decaying. Samples of fossils found in the rocks of the Grand Canyon are shown in Figures 6, 8, 9, 11, 12, 14, 15, and 17.

Fossil-bearing strata are of particular interest to geologists because they provide samples of the types of plants and animals that existed when a particular body of rock was formed. Fossils also provide clues to the origin of their host rocks. For example, if a formation contains the remains of marine organisms, it must have formed on the seafloor. Fossils therefore indicate to some degree the types of environments that existed in a particular region in times past. Since sedimentary strata originate as a succession of deposits laid down over a certain span of time, the fossil record helps geologists to develop a picture of how the landscape of a particular region evolved during that interval.

Because each type of organism exists on the earth only for a finite period of time, its fossil remains will be found—if at all—only in rocks of that period. A fossil-bearing rock may contain a variety of organisms whose geologic ranges overlap, but those yet to appear or already extinct will not be present. By comparing the associations of plants and animals present in various rock strata, geologists are able to correlate the age of one formation with that of another.

Geologic Time

The geologic time scale shown in Table 3 is based both on recognized rock and fossil sequences throughout the world, and on absolute dates obtained by measuring the decay products of radioactive elements contained in various minerals and then calculating the age of the minerals from known rates of decay. This technique, known as radiometric dating, works for igneous rocks, which form from the cooling and solidification of molten rock, or magma, but not for sedimentary rocks, which most often are made up of the weathered fragments of older rocks. Sedimentary strata that include layers of lava or volcanic ash, representing volcanic episodes during the period in which the sediments were deposited, can be dated by using radiometric methods to determine the age of the volcanic materials. If such sedimentary strata also contain fossils, otherwise undatable strata elsewhere can be dated by comparing their fossils with those of the dated rocks. Most of the sedimentary rocks of the Grand Canyon have been assigned approximate dates by this method.

The geologic time scale divides the history of the earth into four eras. The Precambrian era covers the awesome gulf of time from the consolidation of the earth's crust, about 4.5 billion years ago, to the appearance of the first well-developed suites of fossils, about 570 million years ago. In the Grand Canyon the Precambrian era is represented by the metamorphic rocks of the Inner Gorge and by the tilted sedimentary rocks making up the Grand Canyon Supergroup, which outcrops intermittently in the eastern end of the canyon.

The Paleozoic ("ancient life") era extends from 570 million to 225 million years before the present. It was during this era, when life began to proliferate in the sea and later move onto the land, that the sediments forming the prominent horizontal strata of the upper canyon walls were deposited. The Paleozoic is divided into seven periods, most of which are represented by one or more rock formations in the Grand Canyon. Characteristic fossils of this era include various marine organisms and, in later periods, insects, amphibians, reptiles, ferns, and seed-bearing plants.

28

Table 3.
Geologic Time Scale for the Grand Canyon

Rock Formation	Years Before Present	Epoch	Period	Era
Recent volcanic rocks, stream deposits, and slide materials	10,000–present	Holocene	Quaternary	
	2.5 million–10,000	Pleistocene		
	9–2.5 million	Pliocene		Cenozoic
	25–9 million	Miocene		
	40–25 million	Oligocene	Tertiary	
	60–40 million	Eocene		
	70–60 million	Paleocene		
No formations	135–70 million		Cretaceous	
No formations	180–135 million		Jurassic	Mesozoic
Moenkopi Formation (Red Butte, Cedar Mountain)	225–180 million		Triassic	
Kaibab Formation	250 million			
Toroweap Formation	255 million			
Coconino Sandstone	260 million		Permian	
Hermit Shale	265 million			
Supai Group	285 million		Pennsylvanian	Paleozoic
Redwall Limestone	335 million		Mississippian	
Temple Butte Formation	350 million		Devonian	
No formations	500–400 million		Silurian and Ordovician	
Muav Limestone	515 million		Cambrian	
Bright Angel Shale	530 million			
Tapeats Sandstone	545 million			
Grand Canyon Supergroup	1200 million			Precambrian
Vishnu Complex				

The Mesozoic ("middle life") era extends from 225 million to 65 million years ago. During this time, additional strata were deposited in the Grand Canyon region, but later were almost completely removed by erosion. To see rocks of this area, you have to leave the Grand Canyon proper for nearby areas where they were not stripped away. Mesozoic rocks outcrop in the Vermilion Cliffs and Echo

Cliffs to the north and east of the Grand Canyon and are the major strata exposed over the greater part of the Colorado Plateau. Near the Grand Canyon, however, these rocks outcrop only on Cedar Mountain, east of Desert View, and on Red Butte, south of Grand Canyon Village. Geologists estimate that 4000 to 8000 feet of sandstone and shale have been removed to expose the Paleozoic rocks beneath. When these now-departed Mesozoic rocks were deposited, tropical forest and coastal swamps covered the Grand Canyon region, and dinosaurs ruled the earth.

The Cenozoic ("recent life") era began 65 million years ago and continues today. It is represented in the Grand Canyon mainly by lava flows and cinder cones found near Toroweap Valley, in the western Grand Canyon, and from there west to Lake Mead. There are no Cenozoic volcanic rocks in the eastern Grand Canyon. Deposits of travertine are the only sedimentary rocks of this era to occur within the canyon. By the dawn of the Cenozoic era, the Grand Canyon region began to be uplifted, as part of the major mountain-building episode that created the Rocky Mountains. As a result of this uplift, the Mesozoic rocks covering the Grand Canyon region were entirely eroded away, and the underlying and now exposed Paleozoic strata were raised to their present elevation.

The youngest Paleozoic rocks exposed in the walls of the Grand Canyon had been around more than 220 million years by the time the canyon itself was created, about 3.8 million years ago. If the 2 billion years that have elapsed since the creation of the metamorphic rocks of the Inner Gorge were telescoped into a single day, each minute would represent about 1.4 million years. If the schist formed at 12:01 A.M. of that day, the Paleozoic era began about 6:00 P.M. and ended three hours later. Shortly after 1:00 P.M. the Mesozoic rocks were eroded away and the Paleozoic strata were uplifted. The Grand Canyon itself originated about 11:58 P.M. The entire span of human existence has occurred in the final minute before midnight.

Recognizing Canyon Landforms

A river deepens its channel principally by scraping and gouging its bed. Its tools are the cobbles and boulders swept along by the current. As a river cuts downward, it exposes canyon walls to the forces of weathering and erosion, which waste them back from the water's edge to form a V-shaped gorge.

The profile of the Grand Canyon, however, is not a simple V, but consists of a giant staircase of cliffs, slopes, and terraces (see Figure 3). This sequence of landforms reflects the different rates at which the various strata are eroded. Sandstone, limestone, and schist are hard, resistant rocks and therefore weather slowly to form cliffs. Softer shales wear away to slopes. Broad terraces such as the

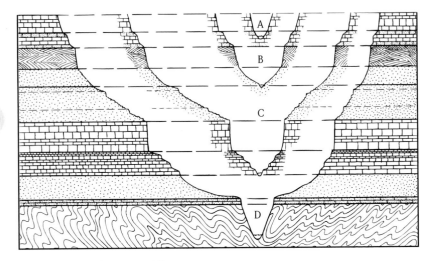

Figure 3. Cliffs, Slopes, and Terraces.
The Grand Canyon began as a narrow V-shaped gorge (A). Chemical and mechanical weathering wore back the walls at varying rates, depending on the hardness of each layer of rock, producing a sequence of cliffs, slopes, and terraces. At the same time, the Colorado River cut more and more deeply through the surface of the gorge (B and C). Together, river cutting and weathering of the canyon walls produced the characteristic stair-step profile of the Grand Canyon (D). Millions of years from now, the Grand Canyon will have been worn down to a broad river valley.

Esplanade and Tonto Platform occur where shales have been almost entirely stripped away from more resistant rocks below.

Weathering is the process whereby the elements—heat, cold, running water, frost, and ice—break down rocks into sediments. Weathering may be either chemical or mechanical. Chemical weathering occurs when moisture seeping into rocks chemically alters their minerals, dissolving some, breaking down others to form clay.

Since carbonate minerals are soluble in water, rainwater seeping into limestone slowly hollows out caverns and underground channels. Numerous caves formed in this way are evident in the Redwall cliff. Runoff seeping into fractures in the Redwall eventually weathers the rocks to a point where large sections may no longer adhere to the rest of the cliff. Resulting rockfalls leave niches or panels in the cliff. The deep alcoves, or embayments, that scallop the Redwall are produced over long periods by successive rockfalls.

Chemical weathering rapidly weakens the bonds uniting the microscopic particles of silt and clay that make up shale. At some point a shale formation becomes so unstable that it is no longer able to support overlying strata of more resistant rocks. As a result the undermined cliffs slump downward along with the shale, producing a landslide. Massive landslides are historically rare in the Grand Canyon, but have nevertheless occurred with regularity throughout its geologic history. The most spectacular example can be seen in Surprise Canyon, where two cliff blocks with a total volume of about one cubic mile slid 1500 feet. Small slides are fairly common, though there is little chance of actually witnessing one.

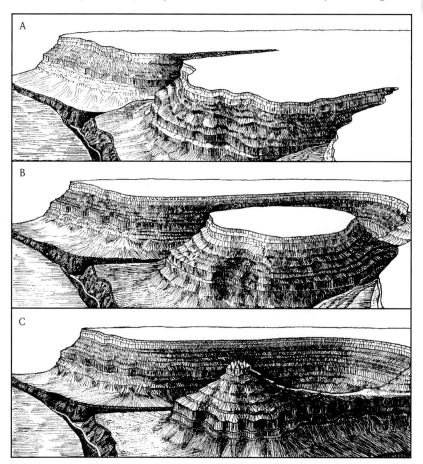

Figure 4. Evolution of Temples and Amphitheaters.
(A) A hypothetical section of the North Rim into which tributary streams have cut a pair of side canyons. The portion of the rims between the canyons forms a promontory. (B) Continued headward erosion by the streams, coupled with weathering of the canyon walls, cuts off the promontory from the rim, producing an isolated plateau. (C) Erosion of the plateau produces a temple, which is connected to the rim by a low saddle. The heads of the side canyons now form broad amphitheaters.

Landslides are the chief mechanism by which the Grand Canyon cliffs have worn back to their present positions. The canyon's spectacular width, then, is due primarily to the occurrence of soft shale strata between harder layers of rock. If the shales were not present, the canyon would probably be a much narrower, V-shaped gorge like that carved by most rivers.

The chief form of mechanical weathering is frost riving. During the winter, when freezing temperatures are common in all but the deepest parts of the canyon, and are not unknown there, frost forms in cracks and crevices and slowly wedges the rocks apart. The wedging occurs because water expands as it freezes. When the frost melts, the crevice contracts a bit. Alternating hot days and cold nights also cause the rocks to expand and contract. If soils form in a crevice and plants become established, their roots help pry the rocks farther apart. Moist soils covering crevice surfaces also provide suitable conditions for chemical weathering. Though such processes operate slowly, they ultimately cause rock fragments to be dislodged from the cliffs. If a cliff is densely fractured, mechanical and chemical weathering in conjunction may cause an entire section to collapse all at once. Fallen debris accumulates at the base of a cliff to form a steep apron called a talus slope.

Had the Colorado River been the only stream at work, the Grand Canyon would not be so wide or complex as it is. But as the river cut downward, tributary streams draining the rims simultaneously cut a host of side canyons. In the process they exposed new areas of cliff to weathering. The ridges separating the side canyons were eroded to produce the Grand Canyon's magnificent buttes, or "temples."

Since a side stream cannot erode its channel below that of the river, the growth of side canyons proceeds in a headward, that is, upstream, direction. In other words, the tributary streams cut back into the canyon walls, scalloping the rims into an alternation of recesses and promontories. The large amphitheaters that have formed at the heads of many side canyons were produced by slides and rockfalls.

The recesses in the North Rim are cut back more deeply than those in the South Rim partly because the former receives more precipitation. As a result, its streams are more vigorous and are thus able to excavate their canyons more rapidly. Moreover, the Kaibab Plateau tilts toward the Canyon, while the Coconino Plateau slopes away from it. Consequently, North Rim streams flow into the canyon, South Rim streams do not.

Because there are few permanent tributary streams in the Grand Canyon, the great majority of side canyons were carved by seasonal torrents, flash floods generated by rains. Flash floods constitute the single most important agent of erosion in arid regions, especially in steep, rocky terrain. The bare cliffs and sparsely vegetated slopes of the Grand Canyon shed enormous amounts of runoff following a storm. The waters rapidly funnel into side canyons and from there down to the river. In the process they transport huge amounts of rock debris from the sides to the bottom of the canyon. The river uses the rocks weathered from the cliffs to scour its channel yet more deeply, and thus the cycle of canyon formation comes full circle.

Recognizing the Rocks

Table 3 lists the Grand Canyon rock formations that correspond to each period and era. Geologists define a rock formation as any body of rock sufficiently distinct from others around it that its geographic location can be shown on a map. A formation is named, if possible, for its principal rock type—limestone, granite, schist, basalt, whatever—and for the place where it was first formally recognized and described. Thus, Redwall Limestone refers to the nearly pure limestone formation exposed in the Grand Canyon's Redwall cliff. A formation containing prominent exposures of two or more types of rock is simply given a geographic name. The Grand Canyon's Kaibab Formation, for example, consists mostly of limestone, but also contains beds of sandstone and lesser units of shale.

Several related formations are sometimes lumped together in groups. The Grand Canyon's Unkar Group, for example, includes formations of shales, sandstone, limestone, and volcanic rocks, all of late Precambrian age. The Unkar Group, Chuar Group, and Nankoweap Formation together constitute the Grand Canyon Supergroup, which designates all formations of late Precambrian age found in the canyon.

With a little practice, just about anyone can learn to recognize the principal rock formations of the Grand Canyon. They exhibit a number of features that can be discerned readily by any observer who takes the time to examine the rocks closely. Some formations are so distinctive that they can be recognized at a glance, even from the canyon rims. The most important features to look out for are as follows:

- **Stratigraphic position.** Where does the formation occur in the sequence of rocks? What formations lie above and below it? See Figures 7, 10, 13, and 16, plus the descriptions of individual formations in the section Grand Canyon Rock Formations later in this chapter.

- **Geographical location.** Because formations of the Grand Canyon Supergroup, as well as certain others, are found only in certain parts of the canyon, it is necessary to know where each formation occurs. General locations are mentioned in the formation descriptions in the

34

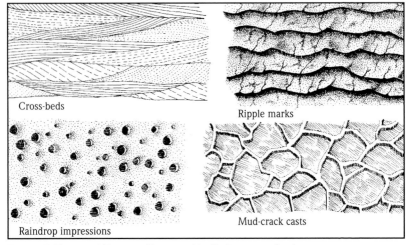

Cross-beds

Ripple marks

Raindrop impressions

Mud-crack casts

Figure 5. Erosional Features Preserved in Sedimentary Rocks.
Such features provide clues to the environment in which the rocks were formed. Cross-beds result from the deposition of overlapping sediments by water or wind. Ripple marks typically form in response to shallow-water currents of the type found in tidal flats. Ripple marks in the Coconino Sandstone were produced by winds blowing across the surface of dunes. Raindrop impressions indicate that the sediments were deposited on land. Mud-crack casts indicate deposits were made in shallow water that evaporated, exposing the sediments to the sun.

next section. The best source of information for the eastern Grand Canyon is the Geologic Map of Grand Canyon National Park, Arizona, copublished by the Grand Canyon Natural History Association and the Museum of Northern Arizona.

- **Rock type.** Is the rock limestone, schist, basalt, sandstone, or what? Brief descriptions of the major rock types in the Grand Canyon immediately follow this list. See Grand Canyon Rock Formations later in this chapter for the types of rock occurring in each formation.

- **Texture and structure.** Is the rock fine-grained, coarse-grained, or somewhere in between? Is it foliated (aligned in thin, wavy sheets) or bedded (made of thick, horizontal or tilted layers)? Are the beds sequential or overlapping?

- **Erosional features.** Does the formation erode to form a cliff, slope, ledge, or some combination thereof? For information on the erosional characteristics of each rock formation, see Grand Canyon Rock Formations later in this chapter.

- **Thickness.** Formations differ in thickness, and a single formation typically varies in thickness from one place to another. For information on the thickness of each formation, see Grand Canyon Rock Formations later in this chapter.

- **Color.** The color of the rock is often an important aid to identification. For information on the color of each formation, see Grand Canyon Rock Formations later in this chapter.

- **Fossil remains.** Each formation is characterized by the presence or absence of certain fossils. Some formations have no recognizable fossils whatsoever. For illustrations of some of the more common fossils, see Figures 6, 8, 9, 11, 12, 14, 15, and 17. For information on the fossils found in each formation, see Grand Canyon Rock Formations later in this chapter.

Types of Rocks

Geologists classify all types of rocks into three basic groups: metamorphic, sedimentary, and igneous. Representatives of all three types occur in the Grand Canyon.

Metamorphic Rocks

The dark schists and lighter gneisses of the Grand Canyon's Inner Gorge are examples of metamorphic rocks, which form through the alteration, or metamorphosis, of other rocks. The process is associated with mountain building, when the earth's crust is brutally buckled and folded. During such episodes, deeply buried rocks are subjected to enormous compression and extraordinarily high temperatures. In the process, the minerals forming the rocks undergo dramatic changes in chemical composition and structure, producing entirely new minerals, even though the rocks themselves remain solid. In response to compression the new minerals usually assume the form of thin flakes aligned in bands perpendicular to the direction of force. Metamorphic rocks are commonly said to be foliated because they break apart in thin leaves along these planes.

The various types of metamorphic rocks—schist, gneiss, slate, marble, quartzite, and others—depend on the nature of the original rocks and the degree of metamorphosis to which they were subjected. Schist, the most common type in the Grand Canyon, is distinguished by its narrow, wavy bands of mica flakes. Dark and fine-grained, it is derived from such materials as shale, fine sandstone, and volcanic rocks. Gneiss, the second most common type in the canyon, forms great wandering intrusions within the schist. Usually derived from granite and related rocks, gneiss is distinguished by its lighter color, coarser texture, and broad, highly contorted bands of quartz and feldspars, which alternate with thinner, darker bands of mica.

Sedimentary Rocks

The great majority of rocks exposed in the Grand Canyon are limestone, sandstone, or shale. Such rocks originate as accumulations of sediments, which include weathered rock particles, organic remains, and chemical precipitates. Sediments are most commonly transported and deposited by streams, but they may also be worked by winds. Limestones, as a rule, originate on the seafloor from debris slowly settling from above. Whatever the mode of deposition, sedimentary deposits accumulate in essentially horizontal beds. Sediments become compacted as additional materials pile on top of them. At the same time, water seeping through the particles deposits mineral cements that bind the particles together. When sediments become so compacted and cemented that they will break rather than crumble, they are sedimentary rocks.

Many sandstones and shales in the Grand Canyon exhibit cross-beds of the sort produced when shifting stream or tidal currents deposit sediments in overlapping layers. The enormous wedge-shape cross-beds in the Coconino Sandstone, however, are the preserved remains of ancient sand dunes. Ripple marks produced by winds or currents are also evident on the surface of many strata. Some of the sediments must have lain above water for a time because the rock surfaces are now pocked with shallow raindrop impressions or fractured into networks of mud cracks. For such features as ripple marks, raindrop impressions, and mud cracks to have been preserved, the sediments must have been little disturbed and, later, gently covered by other materials.

Limestone mainly consists of calcium carbonate, a mineral abundant in seawater and present in the shells of marine animals. Most limestones originate in deep ocean waters, but a common type known as dolomite forms in shallow tidal flats through the chemical alteration of normal limestone. In this process, magnesium replaces some of the calcium in calcium carbonate to produce calcium-magnesium carbonate, the mineral dolomite. Dolomites are rather common in the Grand Canyon.

Though the vast majority of limestones are of marine origin, freshwater forms are not uncommon. Since calcium carbonate and dolomite are soluble in freshwater, limestone formations are typically riddled with caverns hollowed out by underground streams. The many springs in the Grand Canyon occur where such streams finally emerge at the base of limestone formations. Their waters are typically saturated with carbonate minerals, which form deposits of travertine, the type of limestone that composes stalactites and stalagmites. Travertine deposits are widely scattered through the Grand Canyon, but are most spectacular along Havasu Creek. Precipitation of carbonate minerals from the water, which originates in the Kaibab Limestone of the Coconino Plateau, has produced terraced pools dammed by semicircular dikes of travertine. The cliffs adjacent to the water-falls along the stream are hung with bizarre travertine curtains where windblown spray has evaporated from the rock surface.

Limestones are usually fine-textured and light-colored, whites and grays predominating. The limestone of the Redwall cliff is actually gray, but has been stained by iron oxides washed down from the overlying Supai Group. Limestones are commonly rich in marine fossils.

Sandstone, as one might guess, is derived from sand, the smallest type of rock particle visible to the naked eye. Sands may consist of almost any mineral, but quartz and feldspars are most common. Sandstones are fine- to coarse-grained and come in a wide range of colors, depending on their constituent minerals. They usually originate as stream deposits in shallow coastal waters or floodplains. They also accumulate in desert basins fed by landlocked streams. The Coconino Sandstone of the Grand Canyon consists of petrified sand dunes that were piled up by the wind.

Shale originates as deposits of clay, silt, or mud (a blend of silt and clay). Geologists distinguish between mudstone, siltstone, and other types, but in this guidebook all are simply called shale. Shale is extremely fine-grained, with particles so minute that they are invisible even under a hand lens. When weathered, shale breaks into small, thin chips or flakes. Most shales originate as stream deposits in deeper coastal waters, floodplains and river deltas, and large, deep lakes. Like sandstone, shale comes in various colors, but in the Grand Canyon it is mostly bright red from abundant iron oxides present in the rocks. Because of its soft texture, shale erodes to form slopes rather than cliffs or ledges.

Conglomerate and breccia consist of gravels (rock fragments larger than sand) embedded in a matrix of finer particles, either sands or muds, sometimes limestone. Conglomerate gravels are rounded, indicating stream action. Breccia gravels, however, retain their angularity. Some breccias are of volcanic origin, while others form from rocks crushed along geological faults or where slide debris is buried by finer sediments. Conglomerates and breccias are fairly common in the Grand Canyon, and in places form extensive outcrops.

Igneous Rocks

Igneous rocks originate from the cooling and solidification of magma, which forms deep within the earth. If the magma erupts on the surface as lava or pyroclastic ("fire broken") materials, such as volcanic ash, it forms volcanic rocks such as basalt, andesite, and rhyolite. If the magma cools deep within the earth, it solidifies to form granite and similar coarse-grained igneous rocks, which may later be exposed by erosion of overlying rocks. Igneous rocks of intermediate texture form when magma cools just below the surface of the earth. One such rock, diabase, is chemically related to basalt but coarser in texture. Diabase occurs in dikes and sills running through the tilted strata of the Unkar Group.

John Wesley Powell, on his first expedition through the Grand Canyon, named the river corridor Granite Gorge for its extensive outcrops of crystalline rocks. The name has stuck, but remains a misnomer, for these rocks are mostly schist and gneiss. The gneiss, however, originated as granite intruded into the surrounding schist. Later, it too was metamorphosed to produce the light-colored foliated rocks exposed in the cliffs. Here and there among the metamorphic rocks are dikes and sills of unaltered granitic rocks called aplite if fine-grained, and pegmatite if coarse-grained.

Volcanic rocks are scarce in the eastern Grand Canyon but common from near Toroweap Valley west to Lake Mead. Most are basalt, a dark, extremely fine-grained volcanic rock that originates as highly fluid lava. Lava flows have occurred on the Uinkaret and Shivwits Plateaus and have filled Toroweap Valley, Prospect Canyon, and Whitmore Wash. Cinder cones composed of pyroclastic materials are scattered over both the Uinkaret and Shivwits Plateaus; Vulcan's Throne, at the foot of the Toroweap Valley, is one of these cones.

Grand Canyon Rock Formations

This section summarizes the principal features of each of the major rock formations occurring in the Grand Canyon. The formations are described in reverse order from that found in most geologic discussions, which begin with the oldest rocks and proceed forward in time to the most recent. Because most visitors to the Grand Canyon encounter these rocks from the youngest on the rims to the oldest along the river, this order seemed most useful for the present purpose. For a chronological account of the rocks, beginning with the oldest, see the following section, The Story in the Rocks.

Nowhere in the canyon will a visitor walking from rim to river encounter all of the formations described in this section. The descriptions that follow apply mainly to the formations as they appear in the eastern Grand Canyon, from Nankoweap Canyon south to below Desert View and west to Havasu and Kanab Canyons. Most of the formations continue westward, but change somewhat in their composition and appearance. The ranges of thickness given for each formation pertain to their occurrence throughout the entire Grand Canyon.

Paleozoic Rocks

Kaibab Formation (Kaibab Limestone). Mostly fine-grained, thick-bedded, sandy limestone, with a bed of sandstone beneath and minor units of sandstone

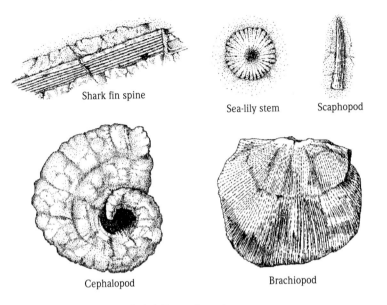

Shark fin spine

Sea-lily stem   Scaphopod

Cephalopod   Brachiopod

Figure 6. Fossils of the Kaibab Formation.

and shale above. Forms the surface of the Kaibab and Coconino Plateaus. Color: cream to grayish white. Thickness: 300 to 400 feet. Fossils: brachiopods, corals, mollusks, sea lilies, worms, and fish teeth. Erodes to form a cliff.

Toroweap Formation. Similar in composition and structure to the Kaibab Formation. Color: pale yellow and gray. Thickness: 250 feet. Fossils: marine

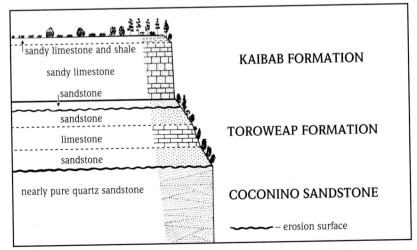

sandy limestone and shale

sandy limestone

sandstone

KAIBAB FORMATION

sandstone

limestone

sandstone

TOROWEAP FORMATION

nearly pure quartz sandstone

COCONINO SANDSTONE

〰〰〰 – erosion surface

Figure 7. Kaibab Formation, Toroweap Formation, and Coconino Sandstone.

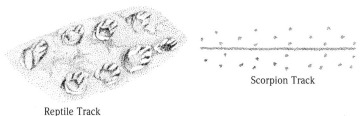

Scorpion Track

40   Reptile Track

Figure 8. Fossils of the Coconino Sandstone.

fossils like those of the Kaibab Formation. Erodes to form a sequence of ledgy cliffs and slopes. From the rims of the Grand Canyon, the Toroweap Formation is easily recognized as the vegetated slope between the Kaibab cliff above and the massive Coconino cliff below.

Coconino Sandstone. Fine-grained quartz sandstone with large, prominent, wedge-shaped cross-beds. Color: white or cream. Thickness: 65 to 350 feet. Fossils: tracks of scorpions, insects, and lizards. Erodes to form a massive cliff.

Hermit Formation. Extremely fine-grained shale, with mud cracks and raindrop impressions. Color: deep red. Thickness: 100 to more than 900 feet. Fossils: conifers, ferns, and other plants; tracks of amphibians and reptiles. Erodes to form a slope. In the western Grand Canyon, the soft Hermit Formation has been stripped off the underlying Esplanade Sandstone to form the terrace known as the Esplanade.

Supai Group. Geologists have given the name *Supai Group* to three mixed shale and limestone formations capped by a sandstone formation, all of late

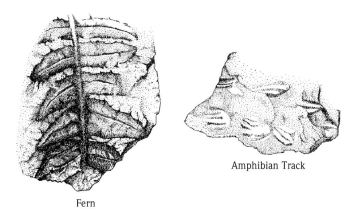

Amphibian Track

Fern

Figure 9. Fossils of the Hermit Formation.

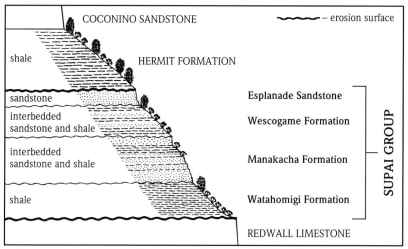

Figure 10. Hermit Formation and Supai Group.

Pennsylvanian and early Permian age. These formations are the Esplanade Sandstone, Wescogame Formation, Manakacha Formation, and Watahomigi Formation. Throughout the eastern and central Grand Canyon, the shales predominate, forming so-called "redbed" slopes. In the western Grand Canyon, the sandstones and limestones increase in prominence. The Supai Group represents a complex assortment of water- and wind-borne deposits accumulating mostly on a coastal plain.

Esplanade Sandstone. Fine- to medium-grained, cross-bedded sandstone separated by thin layers of mudstone. Color: mostly deep reddish brown from iron oxides washed down from the overlying Hermit Shale. Thickness: 200 to more than 800 feet. Fossils: tracks, remains of miscellaneous terrestrial flora and fauna. Erodes to form a cliff broken by ledges and slopes.

Wescogame Formation. Sandstone interbedded with red mudstone and, in the western Grand Canyon, limestone. Color: deep reddish brown. Thickness: 100 to 200 feet. Fossils: tracks, remains of various terrestrial flora and fauna. Erodes throughout much of the canyon to form a basal cliff topped by a slope.

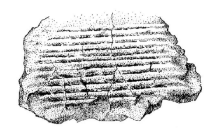

Figure 11. Horsetail Rush from the Supai Group.

Manakacha Formation. Predominantly fine- to medium-grained, cross-bedded sandstone with thin beds of mudstone and limestone. Color: deep reddish brown. Thickness: less than 150 feet to more than 300 feet. Fossils: tracks, remains of various terrestrial flora and fauna. Erodes throughout much of the canyon to form a basal cliff topped by a slope.

Watahomigi Formation. Mostly mudstone and siltstone, interbedded with limestone and dolomite. Color: mostly reddish brown. Thickness: 100 to 300 feet. Fossils: tracks, remains of various terrestrial flora and fauna. Erodes to form a pair of redbed slopes separated by a limestone ledge that sits directly atop the Redwall cliff.

Surprise Canyon Formation. Scattered lenses of sandstone, mudstone, and limestone debris deposited in shallow valleys, collapsed caves, and sinkholes in the upper surface of the Redwall Limestone. Color: highly varied, ranging from yellow to dark gray, reddish brown, and purple. Thickness: 60 to 400 feet. Fossils: marine invertebrates, including corals, brachiopods, echinoderms, bivalves, trilobites, cephalopods, and shark teeth, as well as abundant plant spores and microfossil invertebrates. Rock debris eroded from Redwall Limestone also includes fossils from that formation. Erodes to form cliffy slope between Redwall Limestone and Supai Group's Watahomigi Formation.

Redwall Limestone. Nearly pure marine limestones and dolomites. Upper surface shows depressions caused by erosion prior to the deposition of the Supai Group. Color: light gray, stained bright red by iron oxides washed down from above. Thickness: 500 to 800 feet. Fossils: abundant marine fossils, including sea lilies, corals, brachiopods, trilobites, clams, snails, fish, and algae. Erodes to form the massive red cliff (referred to as the Redwall cliff) just above the Tonto Platform. Riddled with caves and often featuring deep alcoves.

Temple Butte Formation. Gnarly, sugary-textured freshwater limestone of intermittent occurrence, mostly in the eastern Grand Canyon. Color: purplish. Thickness: less than 100 feet, thickening westward. Fossils: armored plates of a primitive freshwater fish; few other identifiable

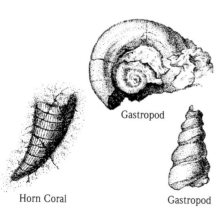

Gastropod

Horn Coral

Gastropod

Figure 12. Fossils of the Redwall Limestone.

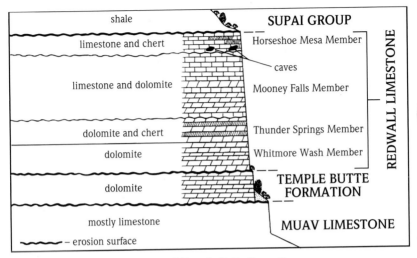

shale	**SUPAI GROUP**
limestone and chert	Horseshoe Mesa Member
	— caves
limestone and dolomite	Mooney Falls Member
dolomite and chert	Thunder Springs Member
dolomite	Whitmore Wash Member
	TEMPLE BUTTE FORMATION
dolomite	
mostly limestone	**MUAV LIMESTONE**
⌇ – erosion surface	

REDWALL LIMESTONE

Figure 13. Redwall Limestone and Temple Butte Formation.

organisms. Erodes to form a cliff. Deposited in stream channels cut into the underlying Muav Limestone. In the western Grand Canyon, the formation consists of continuous beds of gray or creamy dolomite forming massive cliffs hundreds of feet high.

Muav Limestone. Fine- to medium-grained marine limestone, with cavities, passages, and some springs. Interbedded with minor units of sandstone, shale, and conglomerate. Color: mottled gray. Thickness: 136 to 827 feet. Fossils: sparse, but include numerous species of trilobites and some brachiopods. Erodes to form a cliff with sandstone ledges and shale recesses.

Bright Angel Shale. Extremely fine-grained mudstone shale, interbedded with thin units of siltstone, sandstone, and sandy limestone. Color: greenish. Thickness: 270 to 450 feet. Fossils: trilobites, brachiopods, hyolithes, and the trails of various marine animals. Erodes to form a gentle slope. Bright Angel Shale has been nearly stripped away from the underlying Tapeats Sandstone to form the broad terrace of the Tonto Platform.

Tapeats Sandstone. Medium- to coarse-grained sandstone with scattered conglomerate deposits near the base and extensive cross-bedding. Color: dark brown. Thickness: 100 to 325 feet. Fossils: trilobite trails. Features widespread ripple marks. Erodes to form the cliff at the brink of the

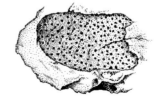

Figure 14. Bony plate from the Temple Butte Formation.

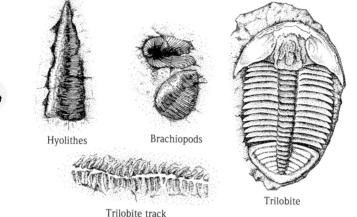

Hyolithes

Brachiopods

Trilobite

Trilobite track

Figure 15. Fossils of the Tonto Group.

Tonto Platform. In the western Grand Canyon, forms a cliff along the river. Sits atop tilted Precambrian strata of the Grand Canyon Supergroup in the eastern Grand Canyon and atop the early Precambrian Vishnu Schist and related rocks in the western Grand Canyon.

Late Precambrian Rocks— The Grand Canyon Supergroup

The Grand Canyon Supergroup consists of tilted sedimentary strata of late Precambrian age. Their tilting represents a period of faulting, folding, and subsequent

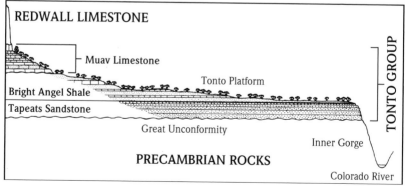

Figure 16. The Tonto Group.

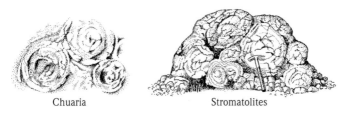

Chuaria   Stromatolites

Figure 17. Fossils of the Grand Canyon Supergroup.

erosion that occurred after their deposition but before that of the overlying Paleozoic strata. The strata outcrop over a wide area in the eastern Grand Canyon from Nankoweap to Hance Rapids at the mouth of Red Canyon. From there westward they occur intermittently, often in side canyons. The Grand Canyon Supergroup includes the Sixtymile Formation, Chuar Group, Nankoweap Formation, and Unkar Group.

> *Sixtymile Formation.* Medium-grained sandstone with breccia and minor units of shale, which were deposited in a terrestrial environment during a period of faulting. Outcrops only in Awatubi and Sixtymile Canyons and as cap rock on Nankoweap Butte. Color: tan to buff. Thickness: 120 feet. Erodes to form a ledgy cliff.

Chuar Group. The Chuar Group includes the Kwagunt and Galeros Formations. Together, these two formations represent deposition in a succession of shallow marine and coastal environments.

> *Kwagunt Formation.* Shale and limestone, with a thick sandstone bed at the base of Carbon Butte. Color: red to purplish. Thickness: up to 2218 feet. Fossils: stromatolites (the oldest fossils found in the Grand Canyon) and Chuaria. Features mud cracks, ripple marks, and raindrop impressions. Erodes to form a ledgy slope. Outcrops from Nankoweap Canyon south to Chuar Canyon on the west side of the river.

> *Galeros Formation.* Interbedded limestone, shale, and sandstone. Color: ocher to yellow-green. Thickness: 570 to 4272 feet. Fossils: stromatolites. Features ripple marks and raindrop impressions. Outcrops from Nankoweap Canyon south to Basalt Canyon, on the west side of the river.

> *Nankoweap Formation.* Coarse-grained, thick-bedded sandstone, with some cross-bedding and mud cracks. Color: white, brown, and purple. Thickness: 330 feet. Erodes to form a cliff. Outcrops in Nankoweap Canyon and below Desert View.

Unkar Group. The Unkar Group is a series of gently tilted sedimentary and igneous rocks that outcrop at isolated locations in the eastern Grand Canyon. The most extensive of these outcrops occurs in the easternmost canyon, from below the confluence of the Little Colorado River to Hance Rapids. Sizable outcrops also occur near Phantom Ranch. The oldest Unkar Rocks were deposited along the western edge of the North American continent some 450 million years after the formation of the underlying Vishnu Complex. The Unkar Group includes the Cardenas Lava, Dox Formation, Shinumo Quartzite, Hakatai Shale, and Bass Formation.

Cardenas Lava. Basaltic and basaltic-andesitic lava flows interbedded with minor units of sandstone. Color: dark brown to black. Thickness: 785 to 985 feet. Erodes to form the dark cliffs that rest atop the Dox Formation. In addition, dikes and sills of diabase, a basaltic rock that forms when magma cools and solidifies in rock fractures beneath the surface, are scattered throughout the Unkar strata. Whether these dikes and sills derived from the same magma source as the Cardenas Lava, which cooled and solidified on the surface of the earth, is uncertain. The eruption of Cardenas Lava atop the damp sands and muds of the Dox Formation marked the end of the long quiet period in which the Unkar sediments were deposited. Some of the Cardenas Lava flows eroded away before the overlying Nankoweap Formation was deposited.

Dox Formation (Dox Sandstone). Sandstone interbedded with shale. Color: mostly reddish orange to reddish brown, some light tan to greenish brown. Thickness: up to 3122 feet. Features ripple marks and mud cracks. Erodes to form gentle hills and valleys. Outcrops widely below Desert View; scattered outcrops westward, mostly in side canyons.

Shinumo Quartzite. Medium- to coarse-grained sandstone with a thick bed of quartzite (a hard sandstone cemented with silica rather than calcite). Color: purple, red, white, and brown. Thickness: 1132 to 1328 feet. Features some cross-beds. Erodes to form a massive cliff. Scattered outcrops in side canyons west of Escalante Creek, below Papago Point.

Hakatai Shale. Shale with minor beds of sandstone. Often cross-bedded, with ripple marks, raindrop impressions, and mud cracks. Color: vivid red-orange. Thickness: 445 to 985 feet. Erodes to form slopes and benches. Scattered outcrops from Red Canyon west.

Bass Formation (Bass Limestone). Mostly fine-grained limestone interbedded with shale. Color: gray. Thickness: up to 327 feet. Fossils: stromatolites. Features ripple marks. Erodes to form a ledgy cliff. Scattered outcrops from Mineral Canyon west. Includes the Hotauta Conglomerate, which lies in channels eroded in the underlying Vishnu Schist.

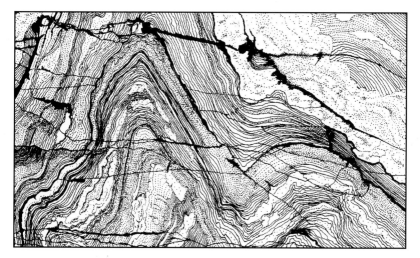

Figure 18. Vishnu Schist, showing the numerous wavy bands characteristic of foliated metamorphic rocks. These rocks form under conditions of enormous heat and pressure such as occur during episodes of mountain building.

Early Precambrian Rocks

Vishnu Schist. Mostly foliated mica schist. Also includes Zoroaster Gneiss, Elves Canyon and Trinity Gneisses, quartzite units, dikes and sills of aplite and pegmatite, and other materials. Color: schist is dark gray to nearly black, with numerous wavy bands; gneiss has broader, wavy bands and is pink or light gray. Thickness: about 800 to 1500 feet. Erodes to form steep cliffs. Outcrops in the cliffs of Lower, Middle, and Upper Granite Gorge, but the rocks extend to unknown depths.

The Story in the Rocks

About 2 billion years ago, the Grand Canyon region lay beneath an ancient sea. Rivers draining a nearby landmass dumped tons of silt and clay in the area. Smaller amounts of sand were also deposited, and layers of limy mud accumulated on the seafloor. From time to time, offshore volcanoes covered the sediments with layers of lava and volcanic ash. For tens of millions of years these materials accumulated to a depth of 5 miles, and consolidated to form shale interbedded with minor layers of limestone and sandstone. With the addition of further sediments, these rocks were buried perhaps 10 miles below the earth's surface. Then, about 1.7 billion years ago, the buried strata were buckled and folded as the land rose to form a mountain range comparable to today's Rocky Mountains. In the process, intense heat and pressure altered the rocks to form the Vishnu Schist of the Inner Gorge. At the same time, great plumes of molten rock intruded into the surrounding schist, cooling at depth to form granite. This rock was then metamorphosed along with the shale to form gneiss, the other major type of rock today exposed in the Inner Gorge.

The crystalline rocks of the Grand Canyon's Inner Gorge are part of what geologists call the Precambrian Basement Complex, the foundation on which the North American continent rests. On top of them lie the mostly horizontal Paleozoic strata that form the major part of the cliffs, slopes, and terraces of the Grand Canyon. At the time these rocks were formed, the Grand Canyon region lay near the equator. Since their formation, the region has moved 2000 miles northward to its current position, and the rocks have been uplifted thousands of feet to form the high plateaus flanking the canyon. At the same time, North America has rotated somewhat in a counterclockwise direction.

North America's migration northward occurred because the earth's crust, rather than being fixed in place, like the skin of an orange, floats on the semimolten rock of the earth's upper mantle. The crust is composed of several large plates, which fit together like a mosaic but slip around the globe like a loose sock. The continents ride around on top of these plates, most of which also include large areas of seafloor. A few of the plates, including the vast Pacific Plate, consist mostly or entirely of seafloor. The North American Plate includes the entire North American continent, as well as the western half of the North Atlantic.

Seafloor crust consists mainly of dark, molten basalt, which wells upward along undersea rift zones. One such zone, the Mid-Atlantic Ridge, extends from near Iceland southward down the middle of the Atlantic Ocean nearly to Antarctica. The northern half of the Mid-Atlantic Ridge forms the boundary separating the North American Plate on the west from the Eurasian and African Plates on the east. Continental crust consists mainly of granitic rocks, which solidify deep within the earth and are later uplifted by mountain building and exposed by erosion.

Plates move away from mid-ocean rift zones and collide along continental margins. When a plate bearing oceanic crust meets a plate bearing lighter, more buoyant continental crust, the oceanic plate dives beneath the continental plate in a process called subduction. When the diving plate reaches sufficient depth, tens of miles beneath the surface, heat and pressure become so intense that the basaltic crust melts, forming plumes of magma that buoyantly rise and intrude into the overlying rocks. Volcanic mountain ranges, such as portions of the Andes and Cascades, form where the magma rises to the surface. If the volcanoes develop offshore, volcanic island chains such as the Aleutians and Japanese archipelago result. Granitic rocks form when the magma cools and recrystalizes in place, miles beneath the surface. When two plates bearing continental crust collide, or when the diving seafloor catches on the lip of the continent, the crust on both plates often buckles upward along the shared boundary, forming mountain ranges such as the Alps and Himalayas. Despite major mountain-building episodes in the nearby Rocky Mountains and, to the west, in the Sierra Nevada and ranges of the Great Basin, the Grand Canyon region experienced only modest uplift and relatively little deformation. This stability over hundreds of millions of years, combined with the work of the Colorado River, is responsible for the remarkable preservation of rock sequences in the Grand Canyon.

Even so, breaks in the record do exist. Such breaks, known as unconformities, occur during periods when regions are subjected to erosion, which not only removes contemporary deposits but may eliminate traces of older, underlying rock formations as well. Several unconformities occur in the strata making up the walls of the Grand Canyon. The earliest, known as the Precambrian Unconformity, represents a period of about 500 million years that passed between the formation of the Vishnu Complex and its burial beneath the now-tilted Bass Formation, the oldest in the Unkar Group. During this vast stretch of time, the mountains that had formed in Vishnu time eroded gradually to form a low plain. Streams carved channels across the plain and filled these channels with the gravels and other sediments that today form the Hotauta Conglomerate.

In thinking about the evolution of today's continents, it is important to remember that at various times over the past 2 billion years, continental landmasses have been both larger and smaller than they are today and both closer and more far-flung. In Precambrian times, when the oldest rocks in the Grand Canyon were formed, North America in its present form did not exist. Instead, the landmass that would become North America was one of a number of smaller sub-continents that over time moved together and coalesced into larger units. Continents grow as they collide with plates bearing islands or other continents. Some terranes, as geologists call them, are nearby volcanic island chains, which are drawn into the continent as the intervening seafloor is swallowed up. Other terranes may be larger units that have moved thousands of miles before finally slamming into a continent. Much of the west coast of North America accumulated in this way.

About 1.2 billion years ago, whatever terrane would become the Grand Canyon region subsided and was invaded by the sea. Marine algae, the earliest forms of life known to have existed in the Grand Canyon region, secreted calcium carbonate, which combined with silts and clays washed in from nearby lands to form limy muds. These later became the Bass Formation. At times the sediments must have lain in a shallow, tidal-flat environment, for the limestone includes dolomite and is interbedded with thin units of shale on which ripple marks are apparent. Fossils from this time include small discs of crushed and carbonized organic matter (Chuaria) and thinly laminated mounds (stromatolites) thought to consist of limy secretions of mat-forming marine algae. These fossils are the oldest in the Grand Canyon and are a prelude to the great bursting forth of life that would occur at the opening of the Paleozoic era.

During late Precambrian time, the sea must have advanced and retreated over the region many times. The sandstones and shales that form the remainder of the Grand Canyon Supergroup are often cross-bedded and bear ripple marks, features that suggest a coastal floodplain or river-delta environment. Some of the rocks also have raindrop impressions and mud cracks, indicating that they were not continuously submerged. The mud cracks also suggest a hot, arid climate for at least part of the time.

Midway through the late Precambrian, lavas erupted on the seafloor and basaltic magma intruded into the upper rock strata. Subsequent eruptions poured lava and ash onto the land. Evidence of this activity is preserved in the form of the basaltic cliffs and diabase intrusions of the Cardenas Lavas.

Following this volcanic activity, the Grand Canyon region continued to alternate between marine and coastal environments. Evidence is provided by the beds of shale, sandstone, and limestone that comprise the Chuar Group. Many of these rocks exhibit raindrop impressions, ripple marks, cross-bedding, and mud cracks.

Toward the end of the late Precambrian, the strata of the Grand Canyon Supergroup were tilted and uplifted along faults trending north and northwest to form another mountain range. Like the one before it, this range eroded away. Erosion removed as much as 15,000 feet of rock, leaving a low plain covered with rugged hills as much as 1200 feet high. The Vishnu Schist formed the surface of the plain, and the scattered outcrops of tilted late Precambrian rocks formed the hills.

This landscape was gradually submerged beneath a sea advancing from the west. Sands were deposited over the region, burying both the plain and the hills. These sands are preserved today in the Tapeats Sandstone, and the boundary between it and the Precambrian rocks beneath marks the Great Unconformity, which represents a colossal break in the record of between 600 million and 1.4 billion years. The Great Unconformity occurs throughout the Grand Canyon, but is especially striking below Desert View where the Tapeats Sandstone sits directly on top of the tilted strata of the Unkar Group.

The Paleozoic Era

The Paleozoic era extends from 570 million to 225 million years before the present. Although primitive life forms, such as the stromatolites found in the Grand Canyon's late Precambrian strata, had appeared on earth before this time, the Paleozoic era marked an explosion in both the number and complexity of life forms, which proliferated over the course of 350 million years to fill virtually every available niche on the lands and in the seas. Geologists divide the Paleozoic era into seven periods: Cambrian, Silurian, Ordovician, Devonian, Mississippian, Pennsylvanian, and Permian. All but the Silurian and Ordovician periods are well represented in the Grand Canyon, whose layer-cake strata form the best exposed and most complete record of the Paleozoic era on the planet.

At the beginning of the Paleozoic era, the Grand Canyon region lay near the equator, receiving sediments from a shallow sea. This low-lying coastal and near-shore environment characterized the Grand Canyon region throughout the entire Paleozoic era, during which time the region subsided between 1.5 and 2 miles, as layer after layer of rocks were piled one atop the other. At the same time, several intervals of uplift and erosion so nearly balanced the rates of accumulation and subsidence that the elevation of the region fluctuated within only a few hundred feet of sea level over much of that vast stretch of time. All together, the Paleozoic rocks of the Grand Canyon form a sedimentary stack about 1.6 miles thick, sitting atop Precambrian continental bedrock some 25 miles thick.

The Cambrian period is represented in the Grand Canyon by three distinct formations: Tapeats Sandstone, Bright Angel Shale, and Muav Limestone. The Tapeats Sandstone represents the remains of the beaches and tidal flats that lined this sea, along with submarine deposits that extended seaward for tens of miles in water up to about 100 feet deep. The sands are commonly cross-bedded and exhibit ripple marks and trails made by trilobites, all of which suggest a shallow, clear-water environment. The sands were deposited on deeply eroded coastal and near-shore submarine terrain characterized by hills and valleys with local relief as great as 800 feet.

As the sea continued to advance eastward over the region, layers of mud, silt, and fine-grained sand were deposited in mostly deeper waters atop the Tapeats Sandstone. These sediments today comprise the Bright Angel Shale. They were covered in turn by deep-water deposits of the Muav Limestone. The origin of conglomerate deposits interbedded in the limestone is uncertain, though they almost certainly were deposited in a shallow subtidal environment.

In mid-Cambrian time the sea retreated westward and remained there for perhaps 150 million years. During this time—the Ordovician and Silurian periods—the Grand Canyon region was uplifted, and erosion removed much of the accumulated rock, exposing the Muav Limestone. In Devonian time, the sea returned. Stream channels cut in the surface of the Muav Limestone were filled with Temple Butte Formation. To the west, thick beds of dolomite formed in shallow tidal flats. The presence of fossilized plates of a primitive freshwater fish in the Temple Butte Formation suggests that the channels represent ancient stream meanders in an estuarine or river-delta environment.

During the following tens of millions of years, the Devonian sea retreated, and the exposed land was uplifted and then eroded to a level plain. During this time, North America was growing westward and southward as successive island chains, rafting northward and eastward on what geologists have named the Farallon Plate, after the Farallon Islands off San Francisco, slammed into the continent.

Then, in Mississippian time, the sea advanced and retreated three times over the region. The nearly pure limestones deposited during these advances today form the massive Redwall cliff. The Mississippian seas were rich in life, leaving an abundance of marine fossils in the Redwall.

The retreat of the third and final Mississippian sea exposed the surface of the Redwall Limestone to profound weathering in a warm, humid tropical environment. Abundant rains fed both surface and underground streams. The surface streams gradually filled with sediments ranging from gravel to small boulders. The underground streams carved caverns in the Redwall Limestone, and sinkholes formed where the roofs of the caverns collapsed. The deposits that collected in both the surface valleys and the sinkholes together form the Surprise Canyon Formation, which occurs as thin, scattered lenses of rock debris on the surface of the Redwall.

The low, highly weathered limestone topography that produced the Surprise Canyon Formation is an example of what geologists call Karst topography, after a region in Yugoslavia. Caverns, sinkholes, and underground streams are typical of Karst topography, which can be seen on the Kaibab Plateau and, less dramatically, on the Coconino Plateau.

During Pennsylvanian time, the area now occupied by the eastern and central Grand Canyon was a low, arid coastal plain bordered on the west by a shallow sea and on the east by low coastal uplands. Toward the end of the Pennsylvanian period and extending into the Permian, the plate carrying Central America and South America slammed into the southern margin of North America, and the resulting crumpling, deformation, and uplift of the crust created high mountain ranges, including the Uncompahgre Uplift to the northeast of the Grand Canyon. Streams carried sediments eroded from the uplift into the

Grand Canyon area, where they were deposited as sand and mud along the shore. Over millions of years, as the sediments continued to wash into the area, the sea advanced and retreated numerous times. During times of retreat, wind-blown sand formed sizable areas of dunes along the shore, while stream-borne silt and mud accumulated on tidal flats and in channels and lagoons. During times of advance, the sea overran and reworked many of these deposits, while marine organisms drifted to the bottom to form beds of limestone and dolomite. The resulting layers of shale, limestone, and sandstone today form the Supai Group.

The sandstone cap of the Supai Group suggests that the sea was retreating by Permian time. After a period of erosion, the Grand Canyon region once again formed a vast floodplain. Rivers draining lands to the north and east deposited thick layers of mud over the region. This mud today forms the Hermit Shale. Preserved in the shale are mud cracks, raindrop impressions, and the tracks of amphibians and reptiles. Fossil seed ferns and other land plants suggest a semiarid environment.

As the Permian period progressed, the climate became increasingly arid until desert conditions prevailed over the region. Winds piled up a vast sea of dunes—or "erg" in the language of geologists—like that found today in the Sahara Desert of North Africa. These dunes, along with the tracks of reptiles that scurried over their surface, are preserved in the Coconino Sandstone. The shape of the ancient dunes can be seen today in the enormous wedge-shape cross-beds of this formation. The sands are nearly pure quartz. Viewed under a hand lens, the grains are seen to be rounded and minutely pitted, giving them a frosty appearance. The pits were probably produced by collisions with other particles during desert windstorms.

In mid-Permian time the desert was twice inundated by advancing seas. The limestones of the Toroweap and Kaibab Formations originated during these advances. The sandstone beds on either side of the limestone record times during each advance and retreat when the region lay along the coast. Both formations contain numerous marine fossils.

The joining of the American continents in late Pennsylvanian and Permian times heralded a long period during which all the major landmasses on the planet gradually moved together to coalesce into a single, vast supercontinent that geologists have named *Pangea,* meaning "entire earth." The Eurasian continent joined to the northeastern margin of North America, and Africa tucked itself into a large curving gap separating the eastern margins of North and South America. Pangea was completed about 240 million years ago, just before the opening of the Mesozoic era, and persisted as a more or less unified landmass for some 100 million years.

About 230 million years ago, as the Paleozoic era was drawing to a close, the *subduction zone* where the Pacific Plate dove beneath North America began to shift eastward, beneath the continent. In response, volcanic and mountain-building activities also moved onshore. The resulting uplift and deformation of the Sevier and Mogollon Highlands to the south of the Grand Canyon banished the sea from the Grand Canyon region and provided the principal source of the thousands of feet of sediments that were deposited over the region during the Mesozoic era.

The Mesozoic Era

The Mesozoic era extends from 225 million to 70 million years before the present. Popularly known as the "Age of the Dinosaurs," the Mesozoic is divided into three periods: Triassic, Jurassic, and Cretaceous. Rocks representing these three periods outcrop widely throughout the Southwest, except in the vicinity of the Grand Canyon, where they were eroded away to expose the underlying Kaibab Formation. The spectacular cliffs, spires, and amphitheaters of Zion Canyon, Bryce Canyon, Monument Valley, Canyonlands, and Arches National Parks, and numerous other picturesque locales northward into Wyoming and eastward into Colorado and New Mexico, were all carved by wind and water from the same Mesozoic strata that long ago were eroded away from the Grand Canyon region. The only Mesozoic rocks found today in the immediate vicinity of the Grand Canyon are small outcrops on Cedar Mountain and Red Butte, both near the South Rim. The contact between the Kaibab Formation and Mesozoic strata is best displayed northeast of the Grand Canyon, where the Echo Cliffs and Vermilion Cliffs rest on the surface of the Marble Platform.

Throughout the Triassic and most of the Jurassic periods, the Grand Canyon region lay at or near sea level, a tropical coastal plain covered with ferns and swampy forests of ginkgo, araucaria, and primitive conifers. Dinosaurs roamed throughout the region in great numbers, and huge carnivorous reptiles plied the coastal waters. Rivers draining the Mogollon Highland, which lay to the south, deposited 4000 to 8000 feet of mud, silt, and sand over the region. The stack of Paleozoic strata gradually subsided as the Mesozoic deposits slowly accumulated.

In late Jurassic time, about 140 million years ago, Pangea, which had remained more or less a single entity for some 100 million years, began to break apart into two masses, fancifully named Laurasia and Gondwanaland, separated by an ever widening body of water known as the Tethys Seaway. Laurasia, which included North America and Eurasia, began to move northward; Gondwanaland, which comprised South America, Africa, Australia, and Antarctica, headed south. At the same time, Laurasia itself began to pull apart, with North America moving northwestward in response to the opening up of the Atlantic Ocean. This movement set off a chain of events that would transform the face of western North America and lead eventually to the creation of the Grand Canyon.

Before the breakup of Pangea and, later, Laurasia, the Farallon Plate had dived deeply into the melting zone along the western margin of North America, where the basalt seafloor crust was consumed by heat. Some of the resulting magma rose to the surface to erupt from ancient volcanoes, such as those that created the Sevier and Mogollon Highlands. Large quantities of magma remained deeply buried, cooling and solidifying to form the vast fields of granite that today are exposed in California's Sierra Nevada, the mountains of Idaho, and the British Columbia Coast Mountains. After the breakup of Pangea and Laurasia, North America began to aggressively override the Farallon Plate, causing the Farallon Plate to dive at a far shallower angle than before. Rather than descending into the melting zone, the seafloor slabs were thrust whole, at shallow angles, directly beneath the continent, where they collided, stacked up, and sheared off, causing some regions to buckle upward and others to collapse, as blocks of continental crust attempted to accommodate the new seafloor arrivals. This "underplating" of the continent, as it has been called, extended eastward to the Great Plains and is responsible for most of the turmoil that produced the Rocky Mountains and the Colorado Plateau.

As the Cretaceous period came to a close, about 70 million years ago, events associated with the rise of the Rocky Mountains caused the Grand Canyon region to bow upward several thousand feet, forming a broad dome known as the Kaibab Upwarp. Eastward compression resulting from the underplating of the continent caused the Precambrian basement rocks to fail, breaking in some places, bending in others to produce the great arching folds called *monoclines,* which formed from reverse movement along the Precambrian faults. Additional faults developed along the monoclines as uplift continued. The monoclines are thought to have formed in late Cretaceous and Eocene times, though exact dates are unavailable.

A major consequence of the late Cretaceous uplift was the wholesale removal of thousands of feet of Mesozoic rocks from the Grand Canyon region west of Aubrey Cliffs. In the western Grand Canyon, the erosion was even more severe, stripping away not only the Mesozoic strata, but Paleozoic formations down to the Muav Limestone. Before the late Cretaceous uplift occurred, the Grand Canyon region lay near sea level. After it was over, the same area lay thousands of feet above sea level, with swift streams carrying the products of erosion northward into accumulation basins in Utah and Nevada. The broad dome of the Kaibab Upwarp was in place, waiting for the handiwork of streams that together would one day create the Grand Canyon.

The Cenozoic Era

The Cenozoic era began about 70 million years ago, marking the end of the dinosaurs and the beginning of a new age dominated by mammals and flowering plants. Pangea had broken up, and the various continents were drifting apart, toward their current positions. North America was pushing northwestward over the Farallon Plate, and the Rocky Mountains were heaving upward in response to the resulting upheaval of the crust. The Grand Canyon region lay thousands of feet above sea level, but so far no single river, the Colorado or otherwise, had managed to cut through the Kaibab Upwarp.

Because the Cenozoic era is the most recent, a greater amount of evidence in the form of rocks and fossils has survived worldwide. In addition, dating techniques increase in both number and reliability as we approach the present. The upshot of all this is that geologists have been able to subdivide the Cenozoic era with far greater precision than preceding eras. Current practice divides the Cenozoic into two periods, the Tertiary and Quaternary, and divides each period into two or more epochs. From eldest to youngest, the Tertiary period comprises the Paleocene, Eocene, Oligocene, Miocene, and Pliocene epochs. The Quaternary period comprises the Pleistocene and Holocene epochs.

Cenozoic rocks are in general poorly represented in the Grand Canyon, consisting mainly of travertine and volcanic deposits, along with scattered deposits of gravel and other rock debris, mainly in the western Grand Canyon. The reason for this paucity of Cenozoic deposits in the Grand Canyon region is the obvious one: that for at least the past 70 million years it has been the source, rather than destination, of sediments. As a result, geologists have had to piece together Cenozoic events in the region, including the creation of the canyon itself, from evidence gathered elsewhere.

Uplift and deformation associated with the birth of the Rocky Mountains persisted into Eocene time, then ceased about 45 million years ago, as the angle of plate subduction again steepened. The deformation and buckling upward of the continental crust as slabs of seafloor were thrust beneath it tapered off, while volcanic activity resulting from the deep melting of the diving slab recommenced.

The most important result of this renewed deep melting of the Farallon Plate was the formation along the west coast of North America of a single vast body of granite, which was uplifted to form a mountain chain stretching from Baja California northward through the Sierra Nevada to the mountains of Idaho. At one time, these mountains, which today form several distinct ranges, were a single mountain chain similar to the Andes. The granitic rocks of which they are made pushed upward through the old continental crust, stretching it westward to form the washboard topography of the Great Basin.

Then, about 30 million years ago, during late Oligocene time, North America entirely overrode the southern section of the Farallon Plate, along with the East Pacific Rise, the zone of upwelling magma that had separated the Farallon Plate on the west from the Pacific Plate on the east. This event brought North America into contact with the Pacific Plate, which was also moving northwestward, albeit at a faster clip than the continent. The onset of movement along this new boundary opened up the Gulf of California, as sections of land pasted to the continent but lying on the East Pacific Plate began to raft northwestward along the newly formed San Andreas Fault. With less resistance from the west, the stretching of the Great Basin increased, as the area due west of the Grand Canyon pushed westward faster than a region to the north, which still met resistance from the remaining remnants of the Farallon Plate. This westward movement broke the connection between the Sierra Nevada and the mountains of Idaho and caused the Great Basin to pull away from the Colorado Plateau.

57

Subsidence associated with the stretching and thinning of the crust on the western side of the Colorado Plateau caused it to tilt down toward the southwest by a full degree. This tilt jacked up the eastern side of the plateau, which experienced increased erosion as a result. Combined with renewed volcanic activity and uplift, the tilt also shifted drainage patterns in the western Grand Canyon, as more rapidly flowing westbound streams cut off and captured older northern drainages. By middle Miocene time, continued stretching of the crust in the Great Basin and renewed uplift along existing faults combined to make the Colorado Plateau a distinct unit.

About 6 million years ago, volcanoes on the Shivwits, Uinkaret and western Coconino Plateaus began to belch lava and ash. Over the next few million years, repeated eruptions from such sources as Mount Trumbull created the spectacular volcanic landforms of the western Grand Canyon. These include extensive basalt flows on the Uinkaret Plateau, lava-filled side canyons, petrified lava falls on the cliffs of the Inner Gorge, basalt columns, the volcanic neck of Vulcan's Forge, and numerous cinder cones, including Vulcan's Throne, at the foot of Toroweap Valley.

Origin of the Grand Canyon

The final chapter in the story of the Grand Canyon—the creation of the canyon itself—is in many respects the most elusive and least satisfying. Despite careful fieldwork and ingenious hypothesis by numerous geologists, the story remains inconclusive. The difficulty is that the eastern Grand Canyon seems to be much older than the western Grand Canyon, making it likely that the two segments were carved at different times by different rivers, which subsequently joined to become the Colorado. Deposits found along the river show its current course to be as old as Oligocene age above the Grand Canyon but as young as latest Miocene or Pliocene age below it. For example, at Grand Wash, where the Colorado River enters Lake Mead, volcanic debris of the Muddy Creek Formation has been dated by radiometric methods to be 6 million years old. These materials lie *beneath* Colorado River gravels, which means that the river's course through Grand Wash was established some time later.

58

Based on current evidence, most geologists have concluded that the Grand Canyon is the product of at least two major streams, which eventually joined to form today's Colorado River. One stream, the argument goes, cut its way across the Kaibab Upwarp, then turned north, flowing in an as yet undiscovered channel across what is now the Shivwits Plateau to drain somewhere in the region now occupied by the Great Basin. A second stream, cutting headward from the newly opened Gulf of California, followed the course of the lower Colorado River, cutting northward and eastward until it met and captured the drainage of the upper stream. When this younger, more vigorous stream finally cut back into the divide separating it from the older river, the latter abandoned its gentler channel and tumbled westward down the new, steeper gorge. Based on the age and sequence of river deposits and other materials, this headwater capture of the upper Colorado River must have occurred some time between 4 and 6 million years ago.

This account of the Grand Canyon's origin would be more satisfying if geologists had uncovered indisputable evidence of the upper Colorado's hypothetical channel northward across the Shivwits Plateau. Gravel deposits on the plateau demonstrate that streams flowed northward across it as recently as 6 million years ago, but whether these channels represent either the ancient Colorado or its tributaries remains unknown.

Also lacking is a convincing explanation of how the Colorado River managed to cut a channel westward across the Kaibab Upwarp, which lies several thousand feet above the Marble Platform to the east. The traditional explanation, first offered in the nineteenth century by John Wesley Powell, suggests that the river was already flowing across the region before uplift of the Kaibab Upwarp occurred, about 70 million years ago. Unfortunately, evidence provided by river deposits demonstrates the age of the upper Colorado to be closer to 40 million years, while that of the lower Colorado is less than 6 million years.

An alternative hypothesis proposed by Edwin McKee, the father of Grand Canyon geology, suggested that before 6 million years ago the ancestral Colorado River flowed south along the eastern base of the Kaibab Upwarp, much as it does today. But instead of swinging westward across the rise, it turned southeastward through the channel now occupied by the Little Colorado River. Meanwhile, a second river, the Hualapai, cut headward into the western flank of the Upwarp, eventually capturing the Colorado River, which was diverted westward along roughly its present course. This act of river piracy would have occurred some time after the deposition of the Muddy Creek Formation about 6 million years ago. Unfortunately for this clever explanation, subsequent evidence has shown that the Colorado River could not have followed a southeastward course through the canyon of the Little Colorado.

A more recent hypothesis suggests that the ancestral Colorado River cut across the Kaibab Upwarp after the land had been uplifted but before erosion had lowered the surface of the Marble Platform. In other words, the river established its channel when the platform and upwarp together formed a continuous surface at roughly the same elevation. Later, erosion lowered the platform by removing several thousand feet of Mesozoic rocks. If this scenario is true, the ancestral Colorado River would have cut through the Upwarp sometime between 25 million and 65 million years ago, possibly leaving the canyon by way of the hypothetical channel northward across the Shivwits Plateau.

All the above hypotheses represent conscientious attempts to explain the origin of the Grand Canyon in the light of available evidence. So far, the rocks have revealed precious few clues, but more are bound to turn up as investigation continues. And while none of the hypotheses is entirely satisfactory in all its details, refinements of one sort or another may be expected in the future.

The forces that produced the Grand Canyon operate at an exceedingly slow pace. But by any measure they have had millions of years in which to work. The rockfalls and landslides that continue to occur indicate that the canyon is growing ever wider. As the Colorado River approaches sea level, it will carve its channel ever more slowly. Yet the walls will continue to waste away. Barring renewed uplift in the region, a broad valley will probably replace the Grand Canyon in another few million years. Enjoy it while you can.

3

Plant and Animal Distribution

lants and animals are neither randomly nor uniformly distributed. Instead, each species is limited to a certain type of habitat and to geographic areas that provide that habitat. Plant habitats are determined mainly by the physical environment, which includes climate, soil, topography, and available water. Animal habitats are governed mainly by the food and shelter provided by various kinds of plants. An association of plants and animals occurring in a particular habitat is called a community.

Through photosynthesis, plants use the energy obtained from sunlight to manufacture carbohydrates from carbon dioxide and water. Animals derive nourishment (energy) from plants or from other animals and perform a variety of services beneficial to plants. These services include pollinating flowers, dispersing seeds, improving soil through burrowing and depositing feces, and controlling the populations of plant-eating animals through predation. Microorganisms break down the remains of both plants and animals into humus from which new plants will spring. Communities, then, are dynamic systems of mutual dependence and accommodation among their members.

From another perspective, communities represent the collective responses of particular associations of plants and animals to their shared physical environments (climate, topography, geology, and soil). Communities and their physical environments together form systems for acquiring, using, and recirculating the energy supplied by the sun. Biologists call such systems *ecosystems* (from the Greek word *oikos,* meaning "household"). Ecology is the branch of biology devoted to the study of ecosystems.

Plant Communities

Since plants are more easily seen than animals and remain in a fixed location, they provide the most convenient means for identifying various communities. The principal plant communities of the Grand Canyon, along with their characteristic plants and animals, are shown in Table 4.

Table 4.
Grand Canyon Plant Communities

Community	Characteristic Plants and Animals
Spruce-Fir Forest (Kaibab Plateau above 8200')	Dominant plants: Engelmann spruce, subalpine fir. Important associates: white fir, blue spruce, quaking aspen. Common animals: red, or spruce, squirrel, Uinta chipmunk, Clark's nutcracker, hermit thrush.
White Fir Forest (Kaibab Plateau: warmer sites above 8250')	Dominant plant: white fir. Important associates: ponderosa pine, Douglas-fir, quaking aspen, greenleaf manzanita, New Mexican locust, Arizona rose, Gambel oak, creeping mahonia. Common animals: mule deer, Kaibab squirrel, Uinta chipmunk, porcupine, hermit thrush, Steller's jay.
Mountain Grassland (Kaibab Plateau: shallow basins above 8400')	Dominant plants: various perennial bunchgrasses. Common wildflowers: mountain dandelions, fleabanes, owlclovers, pygmy lewisia, yarrow, and many others. Common animals: long-tailed vole, northern pocket gopher, mountain bluebird.
Ponderosa Pine Forest (North Rim: 7200–8250'; South Rim: above 7000')	Dominant plant: ponderosa pine. Important associates: Gambel oak, New Mexican locust, cliffrose, Apache plume, mountain mahogany, greenleaf manzanita, big sagebrush, fern bush, rabbitbrush, understory grasses. Common animals: Abert and Kaibab squirrels, golden mantled ground squirrel, porcupine, hairy woodpecker, Steller's jay, mountain chickadee, gray-headed junco, nuthatches.
Pinyon-Juniper Woodland (4000–7300')	Dominant plants: pinyon, Utah juniper. Important associates: rabbitbrush, big sagebrush, fern bush, broom snakeweed, Gambel oak, banana yucca, cliffrose, Apache plume, serviceberry. Common animals: pinyon mouse, desert cottontail, rock squirrel, cliff chipmunk, gray fox, mule deer, pinyon jay, sagebrush lizard.
Blackbrush Scrub (3500–4500')	Dominant plant: blackbrush. Important associates: Mormon tea, desert thorn, bursage, century plant, narrowleaf yucca, various cacti. Common animals: antelope ground squirrel, canyon mouse, desert wood rat, spotted skunk, jackrabbit, coyote, canyon wren, chuckwalla, spiny lizard, gopher snake, common kingsnake.
Mohave Desert Scrub (Inner Gorge below 4000')	Dominant plants: four-wing saltbush, creosotebush. Important associates: century plant, yuccas, Mormon tea, mesquite, ratany, catclaw acacia, various cacti. Common animals: spotted skunk, ringtail, pocket mouse, desert bighorn, canyon wren, collared lizard, whipsnake.
Riparian Woodland (banks of Colorado River and tributary streams)	Dominant plants: tamarisk (river); Fremont cottonwood (tributaries). Important associates: seep-willow, desert willow, true willows, redbud, netleaf hackberry, Arizona walnut (Havasu Canyon). Common animals: raccoon, ringtail, spotted skunk, ducks, spotted sandpiper, Lucy's warbler, American dipper, blue grosbeak, red-spotted toad, tree frog, tree lizard.

61

Most communities are named for their dominant plant or plants, which determine the appearance and structure of the community. Among all the plants found in each community, the dominants are the winners in the competition for resources. These are the plants best adapted for utilizing the resources found in a particular habitat. They even alter the habitat in ways that reduce the ability of some other plants to compete. Some plants may thereby be excluded from a community altogether. Plants able to coexist with the dominants are known as associates.

Rarely is a plant species restricted to a single community. More commonly, a species ranges through several communities, growing wherever suitable habitats exist. Moreover, the dominant species in one community may be an associate in another. A community occurs where the ecological ranges of all its members overlap in response to local conditions.

When the dominant plants are removed from a community by natural or human causes (disease, fire, and logging, for example), the community is replaced by another. Typically, several communities will succeed one another on a disturbed site until the former dominants become reestablished. Since the resulting community will occupy the site indefinitely, barring future disturbance, it is called a climax community.

Animals, like plants, are rarely restricted to a single community. Those which are tend to be small creatures with highly specialized requirements for food, shelter, or both. Predators, omnivores, and large herbivores usually range through several communities. Migratory animals, of which birds are the prime example, move from one place to another as seasonal climatic changes affect their food supply. Cold weather as such is seldom the reason for migration.

Life Zones

In regions such as northern Arizona, where great differences in elevation occur over relatively short distances, the geographic ranges of plants and animals can be conveniently expressed in terms of elevation belts called life zones. These primarily reflect climatic changes that occur with increases and decreases in elevation. Each zone therefore features certain habitats, plants, animals, and communities that are scarce or absent in zones above and below.

The vertical zonation of plants and animals is obvious even to the most casual observer. It is typical of all mountainous regions, including the high plateaus and deep canyons of Arizona and Utah. At the Grand Canyon, for example, belts of desert scrub, woodland, and forest are stacked one upon the other like the rock strata striping the canyon walls.

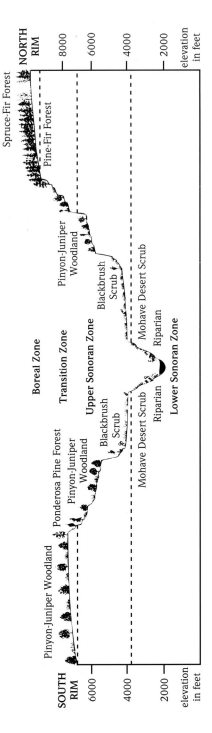

Figure 19. Life Zones and Plant Communities of the Grand Canyon.

The formal concept of life zones originated in the late nineteenth century as a result of studies carried out by American zoologist C. Hart Merriam in the Grand Canyon region. In 1889 Merriam mapped the vegetation belts on the slopes of the San Francisco Peaks, about 50 miles south of the canyon. He attributed such zonation to changes in air temperature with elevation. He went on to suggest that to climb a mountain from desert floor to summit was comparable, in terms of climate, flora, and fauna, to journeying from central Mexico to the Arctic Ocean. To express this correlation, he identified seven life zones for North America: Subtropical, Lower Sonoran, Upper Sonoran, Transition, Canadian, Hudsonian, and Arctic-Alpine. The latter three were called the Boreal zones because they are best developed in the Far North.

All these life zones but the Subtropical and Arctic-Alpine are represented at the Grand Canyon, and the Arctic-Alpine occurs on the summits of the nearby San Francisco Peaks. By Merriam's system, the life zones encountered on a journey from Phantom Ranch to the summit of the Kaibab Plateau are comparable to those occurring from northern Mexico to Hudson Bay.

This observation is true to a degree. Many ecologists contend, and rightly so, that the comparison obscures the significant differences between, say, the desert scrub of the Inner Gorge and that of the Sonoran Desert, or between the spruce-fir forest of the Kaibab Plateau and the boreal forest of Canada. Today, Merriam's life zones are recognized as a pioneering attempt to explain the distribution of plants and animals according to ecological principles. At the same time, they are rather crude categories that obscure more than they illuminate. For this reason, most ecologists now prefer to think in terms of communities, a concept that more closely reflects the complexity in nature and emphasizes the dynamic interrelationship among plants, animals, and their habitats.

Nevertheless, life zones do describe a phenomenon that actually exists in nature. And they provide a useful and reasonably accurate system for discussing the distribution of plants and animals in limited, well-defined areas such as the Grand Canyon or individual mountain ranges. Moreover, since Merriam conceived his system of life zones in northern Arizona, it applies there better perhaps than elsewhere. In this book, both life zones and plant communities are used to indicate the geographic and ecological distribution of plants and animals.

Life zones for the Grand Canyon are as follows:

- **Lower Sonoran Zone.** Inner Gorge below 3500 to 4000 feet elevation. Desert scrub dominated by saltbush or creosotebush.
- **Upper Sonoran Zone.** Inner Canyon and South Rim, 3500 to 7000 feet. Blackbrush scrub, sagebrush scrub, pinyon-juniper woodland.

- **Transition Zone.** Both rims, 7000 to 8250 feet. Ponderosa pine forest.
- **Boreal Zone.** Kaibab Plateau above 8250 feet. Canadian Zone white fir forest on warmer, drier sites; Hudsonian Zone spruce-fir forest on cooler, moister sites. The single term Boreal Zone is used here because the Canadian and Hudsonian forests on the Kaibab Plateau do not form distinct belts, but interfinger according to local topography.

The elevations given above are approximate. As a rule, life zones north of the river occur at somewhat higher elevations than the same zones south of the river. This difference exists because the north wall of the canyon faces south, toward the sun, and therefore is warmer and drier than the south wall, which faces away from the sun.

Zone boundaries do not follow neat contour lines. Instead, lower zones creep upward on hot, exposed ridges, while upper zones extend downward in cool, shady canyons and draws. One notable example from the South Rim is the presence of Douglas-fir in a cooler, moister belt just below the rim, while the same tree is absent from the surface of the Coconino Plateau. The plateau is higher, and in theory should be cooler, but in fact it is not because it receives far more direct sun than areas just below the rim.

Zone boundaries are seldom abrupt. Normally, the transition from one zone to the next is gradual, with certain plants becoming progressively less common while others increase in numbers. Numerous plants (and animals) occur as commonly in one zone as another. So in many places, it is difficult or impossible to assign the vegetation to one zone or the next. Recognizing life zones, however, is merely a useful way to understand the distribution of plants and animals, not an end in itself. Zones, like communities, are human inventions, convenient abstractions that only approximate actual conditions in the natural world. That nature is more complex than our notions of it is cause for celebration, not regret.

PART II

THE PLANTS

4

Ferns and Fern Allies

ferns and fern allies (horsetails, club mosses, spike mosses, and others) have vascular tissue for support and for circulating water and nutrients but, unlike flowering plants, reproduce from spores rather than seeds. Seed-bearing plants, no matter how fernlike they may seem at first glance, are not ferns. The term "fern allies" embraces a variety of spore-bearing vascular plants that differ from true ferns in one way or another.

Though not closely related, ferns and fern allies probably evolved from a common ancestor. They are the oldest vascular land plants in the fossil record, first appearing about 400 million years ago. In the Grand Canyon, fossil ferns have been found in the Hermit Shale. Today there are about 10,000 types of ferns and fern allies, of which about 80 species occur in Arizona and nearly 20 in the Grand Canyon.

This chapter depicts eleven species of ferns found in and near the canyon, including all the common ones and at least one representative of each genus. Many are adapted to growing in cliff crevices, where soil and moisture are more abundant than elsewhere. A few species are largely restricted to seeps, springs, stream banks, or similar moist places. A few, however, thrive in rather arid habitats. Among the cliff-dwelling forms, some prefer or at least grow more abundantly on limestone, a habit that may help to distinguish them from certain other types.

Life Cycle and Reproduction

The life cycle of a fern consists of two distinct stages or generations, each represented by a separate plant. The plants normally called ferns actually represent only the asexual, spore-bearing (sporophyte) generation. Spores are produced in minute cases (sporangia). Clusters of spore cases, called *sori,* are borne on the undersides of leaves. These usually appear during the summer and at first may be covered by a membrane called the indusium. Some ferns lack indusia, however, and instead bear the sori beneath rolled-over leaf margins. Sori may be missing if a plant is too young, the season is wrong, or the leaf is sterile.

Upon maturity, spore cases open slowly, then snap shut, slinging out spores in the process. Borne by the wind, spores that land in suitable places germinate and develop into simple, heart-shaped plants called prothalli (singular prothallus). Smaller than a thumbnail, each prothallus is a self-supporting green plant bearing the male and female reproductive cells. These reproductive cells unite and grow into the plants we know as ferns, thus completing the cycle. Normally, only one fern plant develops from each prothallus. It remains attached to the prothallus, which continues to provide water and nutrients until the young fern is established. Then the prothallus withers away.

Reproduction is essentially the same for fern allies. They do not, however, bear spores on the undersides of their leaves. Scouring rushes bear spores in conelike spikes atop the stems; spike mosses, in special chambers between the leaves; and pepperworts, in individual cases (sporocarps) attached to stalks rising from the base of the plant. Despite these and other differences, ferns and fern allies share the two-stage life cycle consisting of an asexual generation and a sexual generation.

Identifying Ferns

When identifying ferns, pay special attention to the structure of the leaves, the location of the sori, and whether the sori are covered by an indusium or rolled-over leaf margin. If sori are not present, some ferns may be difficult to distinguish. The parts and leaf structure of ferns and fern allies are shown in Figure 20. Species descriptions are limited to features that may be perceived without special training or equipment and without disturbing the specimen plant. These features may not always be sufficient for distinguishing a particular specimen, but they will serve in most cases. Abbreviations used in the species descriptions appear in Table 1.

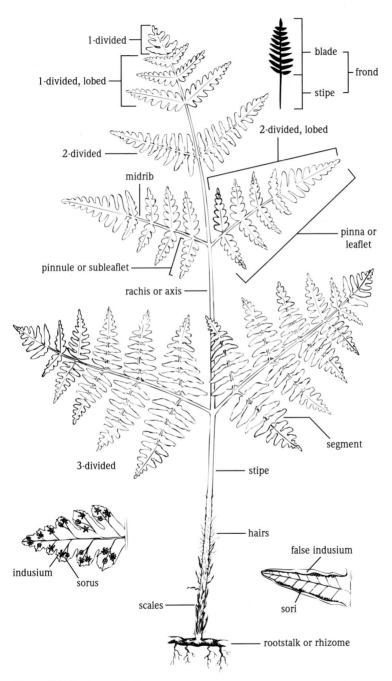

Figure 20. Anatomy of a Fern.

Plate 1

HORSETAILS or SCOURING RUSHES, genus *Equisetum.* Horsetail Family. Com. near streams, ponds, seeps, and springs, and especially along Colorado River. Spores in cone-like spikes at stem tips. Lvs. inconspicuous, forming crownlike sheaths at stem joints. Common Scouring Rush, *E. hyemale,* 8–60" tall, sheaths with 2 dark bands. Smooth Scouring Rush, *E. laevigatum,* 12–40" tall, sheath with 1 dark band. Both have unbranched stems and short spore cones. Field Horsetail, *E. arvense,* 18" tall or less, has both branched (sterile) and unbranched (fertile) stems and longer, slimmer spore cones.

MAIDENHAIR FERN, *Adiantum capillus-veneris.* Fern Family. Com., seeps and springs below 7000'. Fronds to 22" long. Easily identified by fan-shaped subleaflets and black, wiry stems.

WOODSIAS, genus *Woodsia.* Fern Family. Uncom.–rare, moist soil in crevices, on ledges, and among boulders. Two species at Grand Canyon. Mexican Woodsia, *W. mexicana:* fronds 3–14" long, 1–2" wide, 1- or 2-divided, growing in clumps; frond stems pale yellow, smooth or scaly; leaflets mostly offset or alternate, smooth or minutely glandular, toothed or lobed, with teeth ending in delicate hairs. Sori covered by spiderlike membrane. Oregon Woodsia, *W. oregana:* very similar to above, but stems always smooth, brown at base and paler above; leaflets mostly opposite, sometimes alternate; teeth of subleaflets do not end in hairs.

BRITTLE FERN, *Cystopteris fragilis.* Fern Family. Com., Wood., among rocks, near springs. Fronds 2-divided, delicate and thin, mostly or entirely smooth, up to 20" long, 1/4–1/2 as wide, clustered. Sori along veins on undersides of fertile subleaflets, protected by hoodlike membranes.

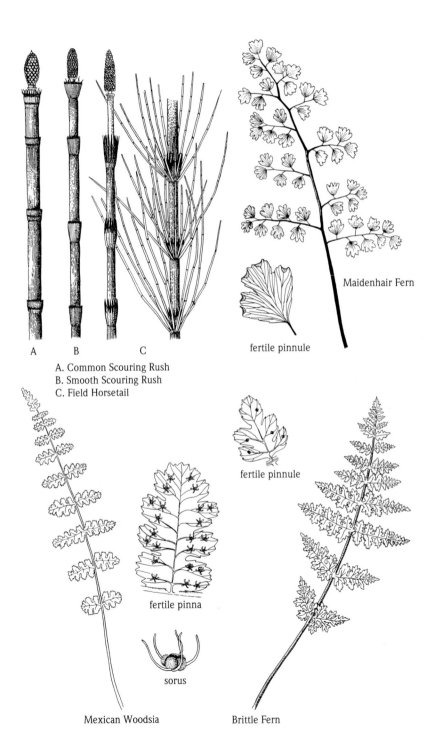

A. Common Scouring Rush
B. Smooth Scouring Rush
C. Field Horsetail

Maidenhair Fern

fertile pinnule

fertile pinnule

fertile pinna

sorus

Mexican Woodsia

Brittle Fern

Plate 2

SLENDER LIP FERN, *Cheilanthes feei.* Fern Family. Com., dry, rocky slopes and cliffs below about 7000'. Fronds to 10" long, 2- or 3-divided, noticeably hairy. Stems brown, scaly at base, otherwise sparsely to moderately white-hairy. Leaflet axes similar, sometimes lighter colored. Usually 6–12 leaflets, opposite or alternate, with long, white hairs above and brownish hairs below.

EATON'S LIP FERN, *Cheilanthes eatonii.* Fern Family. Com., crevices. Fronds to 16" long, 3-divided, with segments sometimes lobed. Stems brown, with closely pressed hairs or scales. Segments with curly white hairs above, dense, rusty hairs below. Sori covered by a single protective membrane.

WOOTON'S LIP FERN, *Cheilanthes wootonii.* Fern Family. Com., nonlimestone crevices. Fronds to 14" long, petioles dark brown, with scales and woolly hairs, not clumped. Blade 3- or 4-divided, with white hairs above and matted rusty hairs and/or scales below. Segments beadlike.

LIP FERN, *Cheilanthes parryi.* Fern Family. Com., rocks and crevices in hot, dry places below 6500'. Fronds 3–6" long, 2-divided and lobed, so hairy they seem like fluffs of cotton. Stems chestnut brown, hairy, with few scales at base. Leaflets covered on both sides with dense hair, usually white, sometimes tan below. The most abundant dry-habitat fern in the park.

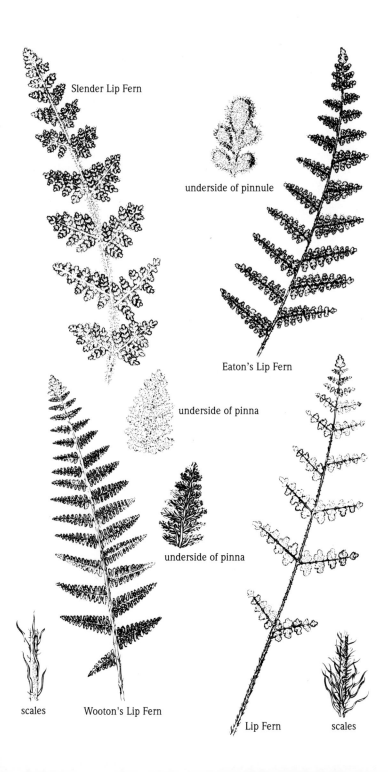

Slender Lip Fern

underside of pinnule

Eaton's Lip Fern

underside of pinna

underside of pinna

scales

Wooton's Lip Fern

Lip Fern

scales

Plate 3

WESTERN BRACKEN, *Pteridium aquilinum.* Fern Family. Com., N Rim, For. openings. Fronds 20–80" long, 2- or 3-divided. Subleaflets smooth or slightly hairy above, densely hairy to downy below. Sori marginal, protected by rolled-over leaf margin.

MALE FERN, *Dryopteris filix-mas.* Fern Family. Uncom., rocky places in cool, moist For. Fronds 24–48" long, 6–12" wide, 1-divided, lobed. Subleaflets parallel-sided, blunt-tipped. Sori nearer midvein than margin. Indusium often has a glandular margin.

WAVY CLOAK FERN, *Astrolepis sinuata.* Fern Family. Com., limestone rocks below 7000'. Fronds 6–18" long, narrowly 1-divided, lobed. Stems white-scaly. Leaflets white-scaly above, white-brown-scaly below, with 3 pairs of lobes. Sori hidden by scales.

JONES'S CLIFF-BRAKE, *Arcyrochosma jonesii.* Fern Family. Uncom., limestone crevices, 3500– 7000'. Fronds 2" long, 2-divided. Stems brown, smooth. Subleaflets smooth, with margins entire or slightly lobed. Sori covered by subleaflet margins.

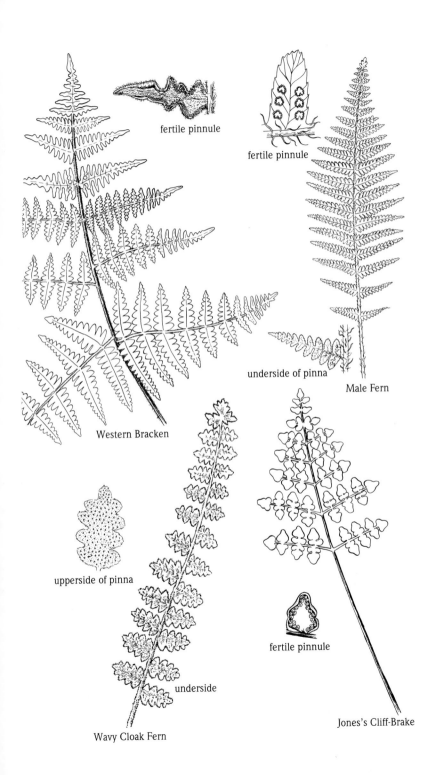

fertile pinnule

fertile pinnule

underside of pinna

Male Fern

Western Bracken

upperside of pinna

fertile pinnule

underside

Jones's Cliff-Brake

Wavy Cloak Fern

5

Flowering Plants

The Grand Canyon, with its varied topography and climate, supports a large flora, which includes some 1400 species of flowering plants. This guide depicts more than 230 of the more common types. For convenient reference, this guide groups them into herbaceous plants, cacti, and trees and shrubs.

The term "wildflower" has no precise botanical meaning, referring in the strictest sense to the bloom of any flowering plants growing outside cultivation. In this guide, flowering plants are divided into three notable groups: herbaceous plants, cacti, and woody plants.

Herbaceous plants are either annual or perennial. Annuals sprout from seed each year and complete their life cycle in a single growing season. Perennials live for several seasons, but are reduced during months of dormancy to persistent underground parts such as bulbs, corms, tubers, rhizomes, or root crowns. Although some perennial herbs die back to woody bases, each year's new growth is herbaceous. In addition to reproducing from seed, some perennials may form new plants through such means as the division of bulbs and corms, the sprouting of tubers, and sprouting along rhizomes (underground stems) or runners (aboveground stems).

Trees and shrubs have woody stems that persist, with or without leaves, from one year to the next. A tree is often defined as a woody plant with a single main stem (trunk) at least three inches in diameter and with a crown of branches reaching to heights of fifteen feet or more. A shrub, therefore, is a woody plant less than fifteen feet tall, with several main stems, most less than three inches in diameter. The distinction is neat in theory but often difficult to apply with certainty in the field. Numerous species of woody plants may grow as either trees or shrubs depending on environmental conditions. In arid regions such as the Inner Canyon, plants that elsewhere typically form trees may be stunted by insufficient moisture. Similarly, some shrubs are naturally shorter than many herbaceous plants, while other shrubs may be dwarfed by hostile environment conditions. To determine whether a small plant is a shrub or herbaceous plant, check its stems. If the stems are all woody, the plant is a shrub, whatever its size.

If the stems are all soft, or very nearly so, the plant is herbaceous.

Different species of cactus grow as trees, shrubs, or both. Cacti have fleshy rather than woody stems, though some have tough, woody bases from which numerous stems may branch. All the cactus species found in the Grand Canyon are normally shrubby.

Plant Adaptations

The dry, scorching summers of the Inner Gorge and the cold, snowy winters of the Kaibab Plateau represent the extremes of climate to be found at the Grand Canyon. Both regimes pose severe challenges to plants, challenges that limit the kinds and numbers of plants able to grow in either place. Those that inhabit these extreme environments have evolved a variety of ingenious strategies for survival. The strategies used by plants for avoiding damage from heat and cold are remarkably similar because the goal in both cases is to minimize heat exchange with the outside environment, the same principle people follow when insulating a home.

Plants in the Inner Canyon must contend with high air temperatures, low humidity, and scant rainfall. If air temperatures are too high, basic metabolic processes slow down or stop. Extreme heat may even cook plant tissues. The usual consequence of hot weather, however, is moisture loss by means of evaporation from leaves and stems. In desert conditions plants are in danger of losing moisture faster than they can replace it from the soil. In effect, the hot, dry air acts as a sponge. Heat and drought, then, are intimately connected in the sense that adaptations to one also usually apply to the other.

Some plants found in desert regions solve the twin problems of heat and drought by growing only in places where these conditions are alleviated to some degree. At seeps, springs, and streamsides, for example, water loss is not a problem. A shady crevice dampened by seepage is also a desirable site. In the Inner Canyon all such places tend to support distinctive plant associations made up of species rare or absent in other situations.

The very sparseness of desert vegetation is itself an accommodation to drought. Plants occupying hot, dry habitats within the canyon tend to be widely spaced in order that each may obtain adequate moisture. Young plants that attempt to invade territories already occupied by older, established plants rarely succeed because the veterans monopolize available moisture.

Most desert wildflowers are short-lived herbaceous annuals that avoid moisture stress by growing only when soils are moist and temperatures mild. As a rule they germinate in early spring following a wet winter. If rains are below normal, however, the seeds may remain dormant for several years. Following germination, the development of roots and shoots is rapid. Flowers and seed are normally produced within a few weeks, after which the plants die. Such short-lived, opportunistic plants are appropriately called ephemerals.

The majority of Inner Canyon plants have adapted to heat and drought by means of special modifications to leaves and stems. These modifications include:

- Reduced leaf surfaces, which minimize moisture loss through evaporation. Cacti have abandoned leaves altogether. Many plants sprout tiny leaves shortly after a rain, quickly shedding them as drought returns.
- Self-pruning, which reduces the number of shoots that must be supplied with water. Many desert shrubs and trees abandon or shed twigs and branches during times of drought.
- Green stems, which enable plants to carry out photosynthesis in the absence of leaves.
- Coated leaves, which reduce evaporative moisture loss. Many desert plants have waxy or leathery leaves as a way to conserve moisture. Coated leaves also reduce damage from ultraviolet radiation.
- Succulence, which enables plants to store moisture in leaves and stems. Cacti are most notable in this regard but are by no means the only desert succulents.
- Summer dormancy, which enables plants to restrict metabolic activities to seasons when temperatures are cooler and moisture is more plentiful.
- Special root systems, which enable desert plants to be opportunistic in exploiting available moisture. Some desert plants have long taproots for securing moisture well below the ground surface. Others have extensive surface roots that allow them to take advantage of even light rains.
- Hair and thorns, which protect desert plants from heat, cold (during winter nights), moisture loss, and tissue loss to herbivores. As a result, most desert plants are densely covered with hairs or thorns.
- Systemic tolerance to heat and drought, which means that most desert plants can carry out basic metabolic processes at temperatures well above and moisture levels well below those tolerable to other plants.

During the winter, plants at higher elevations on the Kaibab Plateau (and to a lesser degree on the Coconino Plateau) are subject to freezing temperatures, cold winds, and snow. The summer growing season is relatively brief and may bring freezing nighttime temperatures. Most plants growing on the plateau are perennials, which become dormant during the winter, but are able to put out new shoots rapidly at the onset of summer. The period of dormancy for most species begins with the cold nights and first snows of autumn. It ends shortly after the snowpack melts, if not earlier.

Perennial herbs die back during the winter to root crowns, bulbs, and other underground parts, in which nutrients are stored to quickly fuel new growth the following year. Trees and shrubs are protected from cold by thick bark and woody tissue. At the onset of cold weather, they begin to reduce the water content of their sap. Like antifreeze, the resins that remain freeze at lower temperatures than water, thus making the plants more resistant to frost damage. Deciduous plants drop their leaves, which would be killed by cold in any case. Conifers and evergreen broadleaf plants have leaves thickly coated with cutin, a waxy varnish that protects them from cold and moisture loss.

Trees and shrubs growing in cold-winter climates typically have flexible limbs that bend rather than break under the weight of snow. The conical form of many conifers permits them to shed snow easily. On steep slopes, young trees are often bent just above the base by the downward creep of the snowpack. The resulting deformation, known as a snow knee, persists in the mature plant.

Seedlings and small shrubs are actually protected by the snow, which covers them with an insulating blanket. If exposed to icy winds, evergreen plants can lose shoots to frost damage, moisture stress, or abrasion by wind-blown snow. Moisture stress occurs because the wind causes evaporation at the leaf surfaces at a time when the ground is frozen and replacement water is therefore unavailable.

Identifying Flowering Plants

Flowering plants, or angiosperms, bear seeds in protective capsules or ovaries. Cone-bearing plants, or gymnosperms, bear naked seeds on the undersides of cone scales or bracts. In order to identify flowering plants, one must often be able to recognize and distinguish various types of flowers, flower clusters, flower parts, and leaves. Closely related species are often distinguishable only by small differences among these features. Botanists have developed a large special vocabulary to describe all of the various parts and characteristics of flowering plants. In the species descriptions in this book, common words have been substituted for technical terms, wherever possible. In some cases, however, there are no popular equivalents and the technical terms have been retained. Before referring to species descriptions, readers should acquaint themselves with the flower and leaf parts and types shown in Figures 21, 22, 23, 24, and 25. The terms used in the species descriptions are defined in words and pictures on each plate. Abbreviations used in the species descriptions appear in Table 1.

Species descriptions contain the following information:

- Common and scientific names and family affiliation.
- Abundance and distribution.
- Overall height of plant expressed in feet or inches. Unless otherwise indicated, a plant is erect or nearly so.
- Stem characteristics.
- Leaf characteristics, including type, shape, texture, margin type, arrangement, and mode of attachment. Unless otherwise indicated, leaf is simple, alternate, entire, smooth, and attached by means of a petiole (the stalk attaching a leaf to a stem).
- Flower characteristics, including type, ovary position, size, number of petals, type of inflorescence, and color variations. Unless otherwise indicated, a flower is regular, has a superior ovary, blooms singly, and lacks significant color variations.
- Blooming season, expressed in months. The period indicated refers to all the plants of that species occurring in the area covered by this book. Moreover, the periods given are for normal years, and some variation may occur.

GENERAL FLOWER PARTS

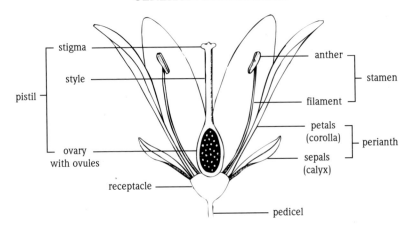

OVARY POSITION

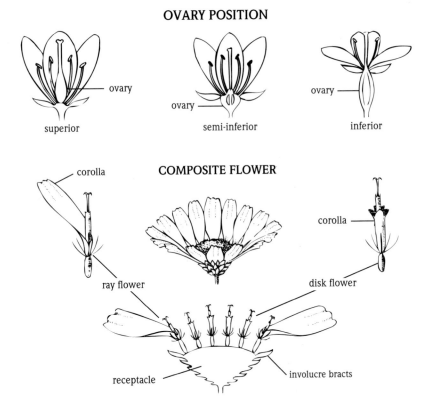

Figure 21. Anatomy of a Flower.

FLOWERS, REGULAR

FLOWERS, IRREGULAR

TYPES OF INFLORESCENCE

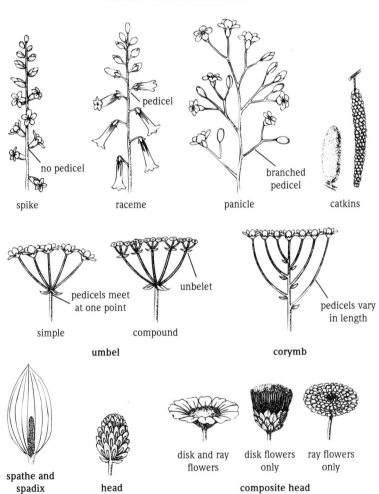

spike

raceme

pedicel

no pedicel

panicle

branched pedicel

catkins

simple

pedicels meet at one point

compound

unbelet

umbel

pedicels vary in length

corymb

spathe and spadix

head

disk and ray flowers

disk flowers only

ray flowers only

composite head

Figure 22. Types of Inflorescence.

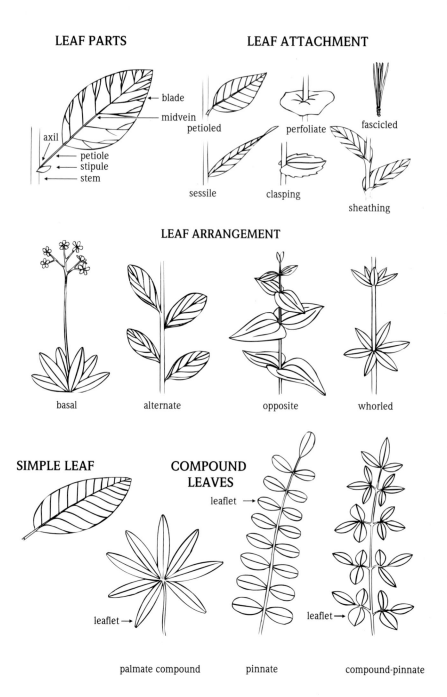

LEAF PARTS

blade
midvein
axil
petiole
stipule
stem

LEAF ATTACHMENT

petioled
perfoliate
fascicled
sessile
clasping
sheathing

LEAF ARRANGEMENT

basal   alternate   opposite   whorled

SIMPLE LEAF

COMPOUND LEAVES

leaflet

leaflet

leaflet

palmate compound   pinnate   compound-pinnate

Figure 23. Anatomy of Leaves.

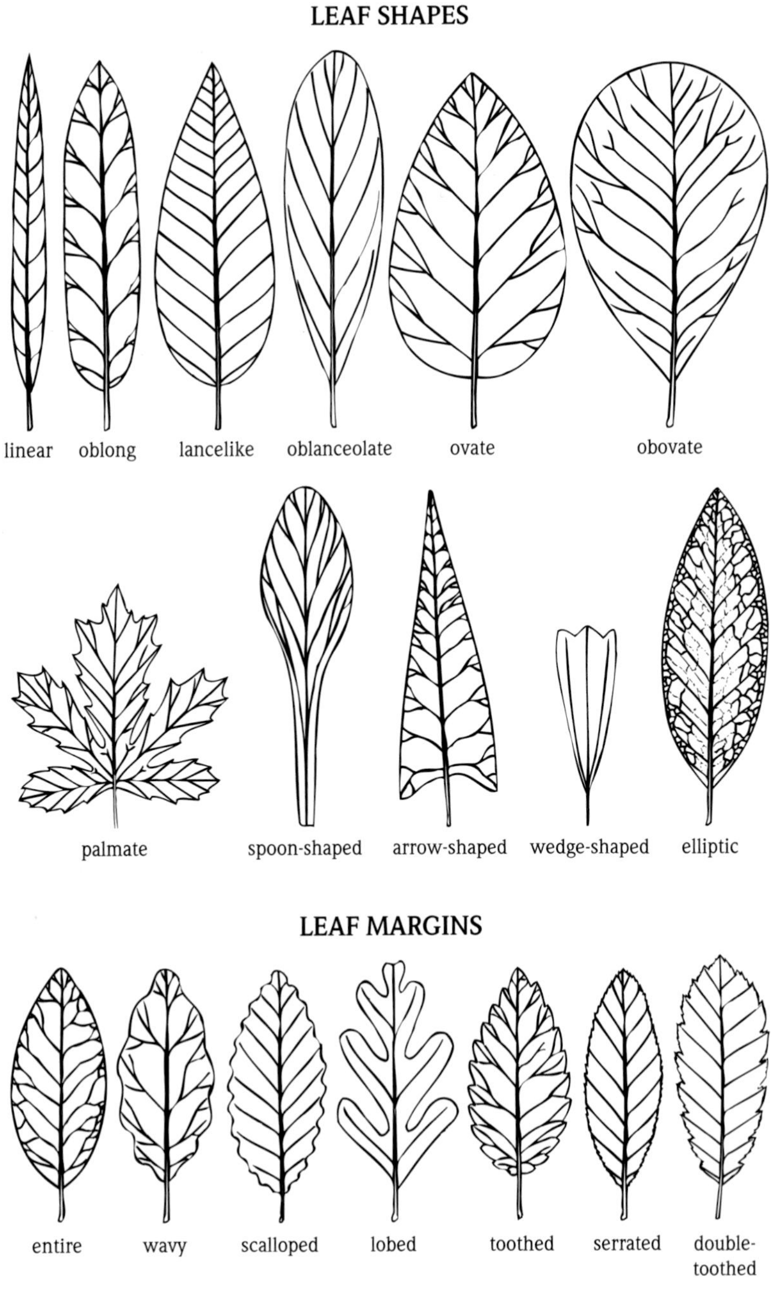

LEAF SHAPES

linear   oblong   lancelike   oblanceolate   ovate   obovate

palmate   spoon-shaped   arrow-shaped   wedge-shaped   elliptic

LEAF MARGINS

entire   wavy   scalloped   lobed   toothed   serrated   double-toothed

Figure 24. Leaf Shapes and Margins.

Herbaceous Plants

Herbaceous plants include all flowering plants that lack woody stems. The Grand Canyon is home to about 650 species of herbaceous plants, of which 130 of the more common and showy types are depicted in this book. Those selected represent most of the important taxonomic groups and include species common to each of the principal life zones and plant communities.

For easy reference, the flowers are grouped by color. Within each color section the plants are grouped by family. Color alone is an unreliable field mark for many species. Some have flowers that change color with age. Others have flowers of different shades, though seldom on the same plant. Some of the plates show both principal color and variations. More often, the variation is only mentioned in the description. It is important to remember that flower and leaf characteristics may be more important than color to proper identification. The color sections are merely convenient places to begin searching. If a plant in question does not appear in one color section, look for similar plants in other sections. Compare them with the specimen plant and read the species descriptions to find out if the flowers vary in color.

Plate 4

SEGO LILY, *Calochortus nuttallii.* Lily Family. Com., SN Rims, dry openings in Wood. and For. Ht. 8–16". Lvs. linear, sparse, mostly basal. Flrs. 1–2" Diam., 3 petals, sometimes lilac or yellow. May–July. Cf. Weakstem Mariposa, Plate 17.

DEATH CAMAS, *Zigadenus elegans.* Lily Family. Com., N Rim, Grass. and damp, rocky places, For. Ht. 8–24". Lvs. linear, basal. Flrs. partly inferior, ½" Diam., 3 petals, in raceme, sometimes yellowish white with or without purple tinge. July–August.

SAND VERBENA, *Abronia elliptica.* Four O'Clock Family. Com., Can., mostly river beaches in dry sand. Ht. 4–20". Stems erect or trailing, sometimes covered with sticky down. Lvs. opposite, oblong, oval, or elliptic, fleshy, ½–2½" long. Flrs. tubular, 5-lobed, fragrant, in heads 2–3" Diam., night-blooming. April–November. One of 3 species of sand verbena in Can., others with pink or reddish Flrs.

MINER'S LETTUCE, *Claytonia perfoliata.* Portulaca Family. Com., Can., moist, shady banks and crevices. Ht. 2–6". Lvs. basal, with 1 perfoliate leaf per stem just below the Flrs. Basal Lvs. variable, 2–8" long, with petioles longer than blades. Perfoliate leaf succulent, ½–2" Diam. Flrs. to ¼" Diam., 5 petals, in loose raceme above perfoliate leaf. January–June.

FENDLER SANDWORT, *Arenaria fendleri.* Pink Family. Com., N Rim, Grass. Ht. 1½–12". Stems glandular-downy, at least below. Lvs. linear, stemless, opposite. Flrs. to ½" Diam., 5 petals, in cyme. April–September. Other sandworts, SN Rims and Can.

PRICKLE POPPY, *Argemone pleiacantha.* Poppy Family. Com., SN Rims, dry, disturbed areas, and Can., along trails. Ht. to 36". Stems and Lvs. prickly. Lvs. stemless, lobed, and spined. Flrs. to 4" across, usually 6 petals. Year-round. Other, very similar species also occur in the area.

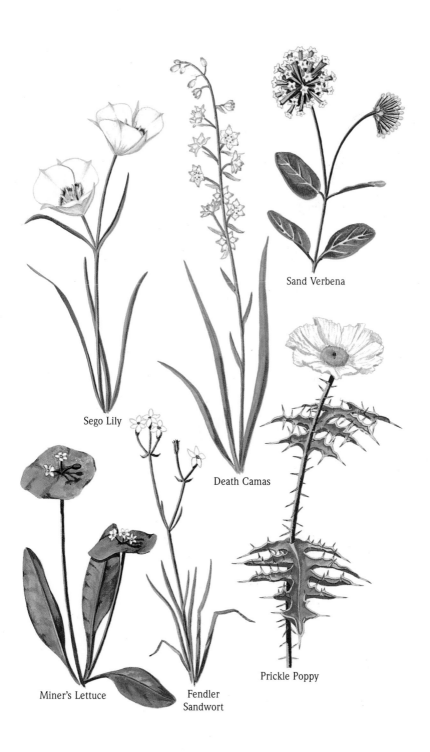

Sand Verbena

Sego Lily

Death Camas

Miner's Lettuce

Fendler
Sandwort

Prickle Poppy

Plate 5

WATERCRESS, *Nasturtium officinale.* Mustard Family. Locally Com., Can., Aquat. Stems floating, creeping, or partly erect. Lvs. pinnate with oval leaflets. Flrs. tiny, 4 petals, in heads to ½" Diam. March–August.

WILD CANDYTUFT, *Thlaspi montanum.* Mustard Family. Com., SN Rims, Wood. and For., and N Rim, Grass. Ht. 6". Lvs. both basal and clasping. Basal Lvs. nearly round, to ³/₄" long; clasping Lvs. tiny, oblong. Flrs. tiny, 4 petals, in racemes. Plants often in dense clusters. March–August.

WILD STRAWBERRY, *Fragaria virginianum* ssp. *glauca.* Rose Family. Locally Com., N Rim, moist, shady places in For. Ht. to 8", erect, but with trailing runners. Lvs. palmate compound, with 3 leaflets, each mostly wedge-shaped, to about 1½" long, smooth above, downy below, with coarse-toothed margins. Flrs. ½–1" across, 5 petals, in cymes on leafless stems. Fruit a tiny strawberry. May–October.

ROCK MAT, *Petrophytum caespitosum.* Rose Family. Com., SN Rims and Can., rocky places. Prostrate mat, 12–24" across. Stems woody toward base: a subshrub. Lvs. wedge- to spoon-shaped, tiny, in tufts. Flrs. numerous, tiny, 5 petals, in spikes to 2" long. June–October.

WHITE CRANESBILL, *Geranium richardsonii.* Geranium Family. Com., SN Rims, conifer For. Ht. to 36". Stems smooth or downy, upper part often glandular. Lvs. opposite, palmately lobed, to 6" Diam., with stiff, flattened hairs, especially on veins. Flrs. to 1" across, 5 petals, with glandular-soft-hairy stems. April–October. Cf. purple cranesbill, Plate 18.

WHITE VIOLET, *Viola canadensis.* Violet Family. Uncom., N Rim, damp, shady places, For. Ht. 6–12". Stems slightly downy. Lvs. heart-shaped, toothed, to 2" across. Flrs. ½–1", 5 petals. May–July.

Watercress

Wild Candytuft

Wild Strawberry

White Cranesbill

Rock Mat

White Violet

Plate 6

EVENING PRIMROSE, *Oenothera caespitosa.* Evening Primrose Family. Com., SN Rims, open areas and roadsides. Ht. to 8", with Lvs. and Flrs. all rising from root crown. Lvs. linear or lance-shaped, margins wavy or cleft, to 6" long. Flrs. to 3" across, 4 petals, becoming pink with age. Each Flr. blooms one night only. March–September. One of several evening primroses found in area. Cf. Tall Yellow Primrose, Plate 10.

FIELD BINDWEED, *Convolvulus arvensis.* Morning Glory Family. An invasive introduced species. Com., roadsides, disturbed areas. Trailing vine with stems 8–48" long, smooth to densely downy. Lvs. variable in size or shape; usually ½–2" long, oblong. Flr. funnel-shaped, ½–2" long, 5 fused petals. May–September. The related Scarlet Starglory, *Ipomoea coccinea,* has bright red Flrs.

WINTERGREEN, *Pyrola picta.* Wintergreen Family. Com., N Rim, For. Ht. 4–10". Lvs. basal, broadly oval, sometimes finely toothed, to 2¾" long. Flrs. small, nodding, 5 petals, in raceme. July–August. One of 4 species in area.

BRISTLY HIDDENFLOWER, *Cryptantha setosissima.* Borage Family. Com., SN Rims, often along roads. Ht. to 36". Stems densely covered with bristles. Lvs. linear/oblong or lance-shaped, to 4" long. Lowest Lvs. form basal rosette. Lvs. also along stem; lower ones with petioles; upper ones without and covered with stiff flattened hairs and bristles. Flrs. ½" Diam., short-tubular, with bristly calyx, in panicle. One of 20 species of hiddenflower in the area. Can. species mostly smaller. May–September.

SACRED DATURA, *Datura meteloides.* Nightshade Family. Com., Can., Scrub. Ht. 20–70". Stems downy. Lvs. egg-shaped, usually with asymmetric base and wavy margins, 2–12" long. Flrs. tubular, 6–10" long, 4–8" wide, night-blooming, turning purple or brown after dawn. April–October. Very poisonous.

DESERT TOBACCO, *Nicotiana obtusifolia.* Nightshade Family. Com., Toroweap area, Can., especially Gorge, dry places. Ht. 8–36". Stems and Lvs. covered with sticky down. Lvs. variable in shape, upper ones without stems, 2" long, 1" wide. Flrs. tubular, 5-lobed. Year-round. Coyote Tobacco, *N. attenuata,* is very similar and replaces the above at upper elevations in Can. and on SN Rims.

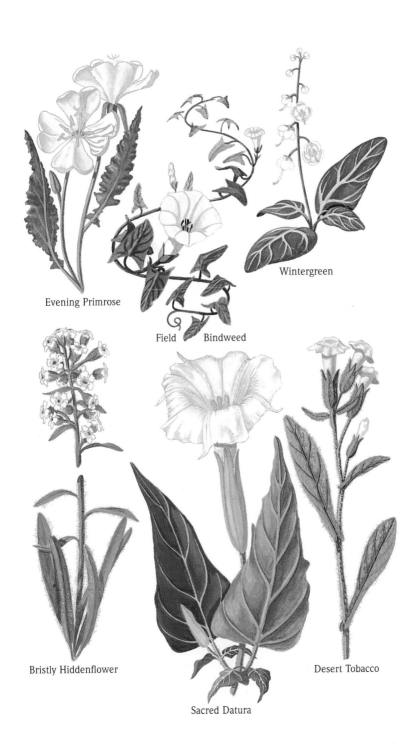

Evening Primrose

Wintergreen

Field Bindweed

Bristly Hiddenflower

Sacred Datura

Desert Tobacco

Plate 7

YARROW, *Achillea millefolium.* Aster Family. Com., mostly N Rim, sunny places. Ht. 10–20". Stems covered with long, soft hairs. Lvs. lacy, finely dissected, 1¼–4" long, ½" wide. Flrs. composite, less than ½" Diam., about 4–8 disk flowers, in dense terminal panicle. May–September.

BABY WHITE ASTER, *Chaetopappa ericoides.* Aster Family. Com., S Rim, Scrub and Wood. Ht. 2½–5". Stems numerous, branching from woody base, covered with stiff, flattened hairs, often glandular. Lvs. about ½" or less, linear or spoon-shaped, hairy. Flrs. composite, about ½" Diam. April–May and August–September. Smallest of several asters in the area. Cf. Mohave and Hoary Asters, Plate 21.

WHEELER'S THISTLE, *Cirsium wheeleri.* Aster Family. Com., SN Rims, pine For. Ht. 16–32". Stems woolly. Lvs. deeply lobed, spiny, sparsely woolly above densely below, to 5" long. Flrs. composite, but with disk Flrs. only, usually pink or purple, sometimes white on N Rim. July–September. Cf. Carmine Thistle, Plate 16.

ROCKY MOUNTAIN PUSSYTOES, *Antennaria parvifolia.* Aster Family. Com., SN Rims, Grass. and For. openings. Mat-forming, 1–6" tall. Lvs. stemless, mostly basal, wedge-shaped, woolly both sides, to ¾" long. Flrs. composite, but with disk Flrs. only, in clustered heads at end of stem. May–August.

TIDY FLEABANE, *Erigeron concinnus.* Aster Family. Com., SN Rims and upper elevations in Can. Ht. 4–20". Stems and Lvs. hairy, sometimes glandular. Lvs. linear, to 4" long, but usually shorter. Flrs. composite with 50–100 rays, 1–1½" Diam., sometimes blue or pink. April–October. Difficult to distinguish from other fleabanes. Cf. Fleabane, Plate 21.

STEMLESS TOWNSENDIA, *Townsendia exscapa.* Aster Family. Com., SN Rims, Wood. Ht. 1–2". Stemless or nearly so. Lvs. basal, linear, with rolled margins, hairy, to 2" long. Flrs. composite, ½–1" Diam., rays sometimes purplish. March–August.

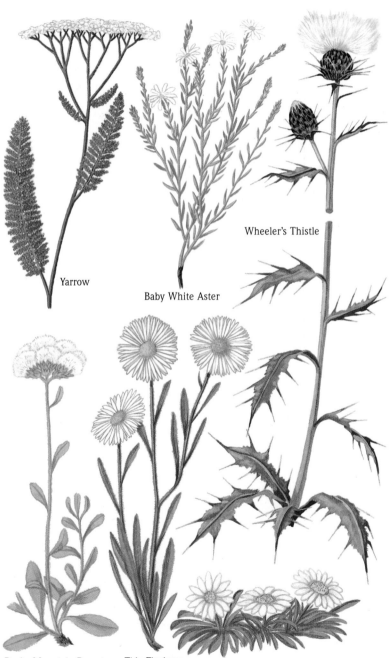

Yarrow

Baby White Aster

Wheeler's Thistle

Rocky Mountain Pussytoes Tidy Fleabane

Stemless Townsendia

Plate 8

DESERT TRUMPET, *Eriogonum inflatum.* Buckwheat Family. Com., Can., rocky places. Ht. to 30". Stems swollen at nodes. Lvs. basal, oblong to nearly round, smooth or short-haired, to 1" long. Flrs. without petals, but with petallike calyx. March–October.

SULFUR FLOWER, *Eriogonum umbellatum.* Buckwheat Family. SN Rims and Can., dry, open places. Ht. 4–12". Stems woolly. Lvs. woolly, spoon-shaped, basal, to 1" long. Flrs. similar to above, but in umbels. June–August.

GOLDEN CORYDALIS, *Corydalis aurea.* Corydalis Family. Uncom., SN Rims and Can., moist places. Ht. 4–16". Lvs. bipinnate with dissected leaflets. Flrs. Irreg., 4 petals, 2 spreading, one of these with spur at base, about ½" long. February–June.

UTAH DEERVETCH, *Lotus utahensis.* Legume Family. Com., N Rim, sunny spots, road-sides, disturbed places; Uncom., S Rim, where it is replaced by the similar Wright Deervetch, *L. wrightii.* Ht. 4–12". Stems and Lvs. downy. Lvs. pinnate or nearly palmate, stemless, with 3–7 narrow leaflets. Flrs. Irreg., about ½" long, 5 united petals. April–August.

YELLOW SWEET-CLOVER, *Melilotus officinalis.* Legume Family. Com., SN Rims, roadsides, disturbed areas; Com., Gorge, along river. Ht. to about 78". Plant bushy. Lvs. compound with 3 leaflets, each wedge-shaped, ½–¾" long. Flowers Irreg., 5 separate petals, ¼" long. May–October. Often grows with White Sweet Clover, *M. alba,* which is similar but has white flowers.

GOLDEN PEA, *Thermopsis rhombifolia.* Legume Family. Com., SN Rims, pine For. Ht. 12–24". Stems nearly smooth to downy. Lvs. compound, with 3 leaflets, each oblong to elliptic, slightly downy, 1–3" long. Flrs. Irreg., 5 united petals, ½–1" long. April–June.

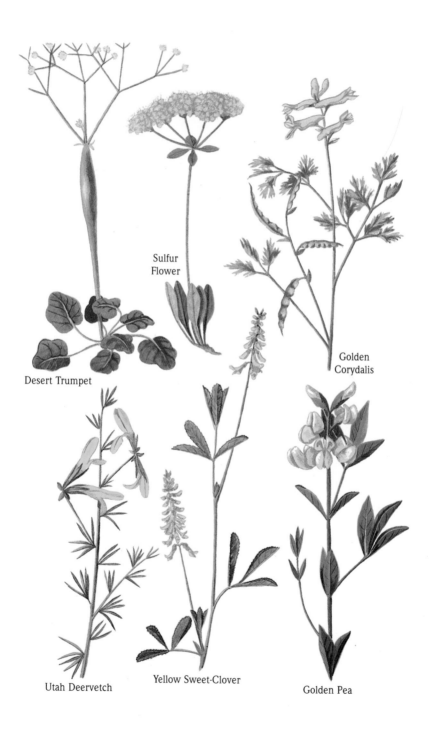

Sulfur
Flower

Golden
Corydalis

Desert Trumpet

Utah Deervetch

Yellow Sweet-Clover

Golden Pea

Plate 9

GOLDEN COLUMBINE, *Aquilegia chrysantha.* Columbine Family. Com., N Rim and Can., Ripar. and moist crevices. Ht. 12–40". Lvs. compound with 3-lobed and cleft leaflets, each smooth or slightly downy below. Flrs. regular, 2–3" long, 5 petals with spurs. April–September. Cf. Red Columbine, Plate 15, and Colorado Columbine, Plate 22.

HEART-LEAFED BUTTERCUP, *Ranunculus cardiophyllus.* Columbine Family. Com., N Rim, Grass.; rare, S Rim. Ht. 6–15". Stems and Lvs. smooth to soft-hairy. Lvs. both basal and alternate. Basal Lvs. heart-shaped, 1½–2" long, with stems. Alternate Lvs. stemless, with linear lobes. Flrs. ¾–1½" Diam., 5 petals. One of several similar buttercups in the area. June–August.

WESTERN WALLFLOWER, *Erysimum capitatum.* Mustard Family. Com., SN Rims and Can. above Gorge, sunny places. Ht. to 32". Stems and Lvs. downy. Lvs. variable in shape and margins, 1½–6" long. Flrs. about ½" Diam., 4 petals, in racemes. March–September.

BLADDERPOD, *Lesquerella intermedia.* Mustard Family. Com., SN Rims, open areas. Ht. ½–7½". Stems and Lvs. covered with star-shaped hairs. Lvs. linear, mostly basal, ½–1½" long. Stem Lvs. similar but smaller. Flrs. about ½" Diam., 4 petals, in racemes. April–August. Cf. Purple Bladderpod, Plate 17.

YELLOW MONKEYFLOWER, *Mimulus guttatus.* Figwort Family. Uncom., Can., limited to moist places in side canyons. Ht. 2–40". Lvs. mostly oval, opposite, usually toothed, with or without stems. Flrs. Irreg., tubular, 5-lobed, about 1" long. March–September. Cf. Crimson Monkeyflower, Plate 16.

YELLOW OWLCLOVER, *Orthocarpus luteus.* Figwort Family. Com., Grass. Ht. 4–15". Stems glandular-hairy. Lvs. narrow, mostly entire, less than ½" long, with glands and minute bristly hairs. Flrs. Irreg., with beaklike upper lip and inflated lower lip, long, in terminal spike. July–September. Cf. Purple Owlclover, Plate 20.

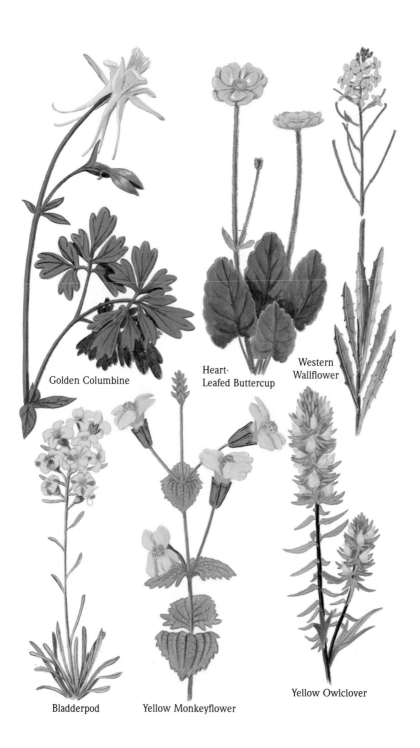

Golden Columbine

Heart-
Leafed Buttercup

Western
Wallflower

Bladderpod

Yellow Monkeyflower

Yellow Owlclover

Plate 10

COMMON MULLEIN, *Verbascum thapsus.* Figwort Family. Com., SN Rims, roadsides and disturbed places, also Wood. and For. Ht. 1–6½'. Stems and Lvs. densely woolly. 1st-year Lvs. basal, oblong to wedge-shaped, 4–10" long. 2nd-year Lvs. on flowering stem, elliptic to lance-shaped, clasping, drooping. Flrs. slightly Irreg., 5 petals, to 1" across, in terminal spike. June–August.

PRINCE'S PLUME, *Stanleya pinnata.* Mustard Family. Com., Can., steep rocky slopes. Ht. 16–60". Stems and Lvs. smooth or downy, with woody base. Lvs 2" long, lower ones deeply divided into lance-shaped segments, upper ones shorter, wedge-shaped, entire or divided. Flrs. about 1" Diam., 4 petals with "claws," in terminal raceme 8–24" long. May–September.

CLIFF CINQUEFOIL, *Potentilla osterhoutii.* Rose Family. Com., SN Rims, rock crevices. Ht. 2–8". Lvs. pinnate with 5–11 glandular-hairy leaflets. Flrs. to ½" across, 5 petals. June–September. One of several species of cinquefoil in the area.

STICKLEAF, *Mentzelia pumila.* Loasa Family. Com., SN Rims and Can., open, sunny, well-drained slopes and flats. Ht. 8–18". Stems rough, woody toward base, twisted, much-branched. Lvs. linear to wedge-shaped, to 1½", with sandpaper texture from stiff, barbed hairs. Flrs. ¾–1½", 10 petals, solitary or a few in cymes. February–October.

TALL YELLOW PRIMROSE, *Oenothera longissima.* Evening Primrose Family. Com., N Rim, roadsides. Ht. 3–10'. Basal Lvs. wedge-shaped, 4–8" long; stem Lvs. shorter, narrowly lance-shaped. Flrs. with long floral tube and 4 petals 1¾" long. Each Flr. blooms one night only, turning red toward morning. July–September. Cf. Hooker's Primrose, below, and Evening Primrose, Plate 6.

HOOKER'S PRIMROSE, *Oenothera elata* ssp. *hookeri.* Evening Primrose Family. Com., SN Rims and Can., moist places, incl. along river. Ht. 2–3'. Stems often reddish. Basal Lvs. wedge- to lance-shaped, margins wavy or toothed; stem Lvs. lance-shaped 2–5" long, nearly stemless. Flrs. similar to above species, but oral tube only 1–2" long. Each Flr. blooms one night only, turning orange-red by morning. July–October. Cf. Tall Yellow Primrose, above, and Evening Primrose, Plate 6.

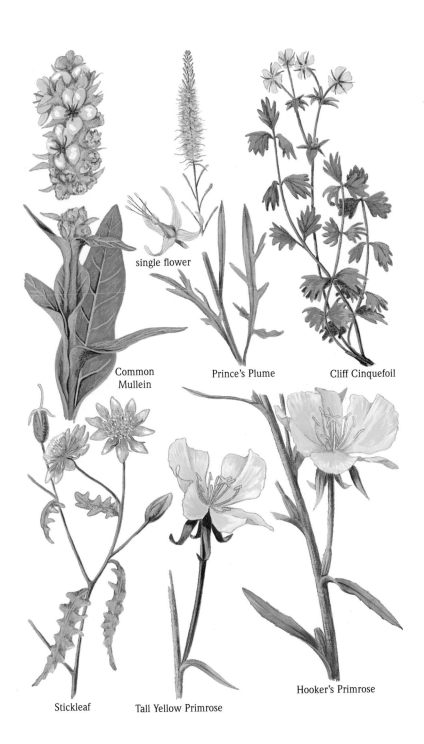

single flower

Common
Mullein

Prince's Plume

Cliff Cinquefoil

Hooker's Primrose

Stickleaf

Tall Yellow Primrose

Plate 11

MENODORA, *Menodora scabra.* Olive Family. Uncom., S Rim, Grass. and Scrub. Ht. to 14". Stems rough. Lvs. ½–1½" long, lower Lvs. egg-shaped, upper Lvs. lance-shaped, both nearly smooth and nearly stemless. Flrs. tubular, ½–¾" Diam., 4-lobed. March–September.

PUCCOON, *Lithospermum multiflorum.* Borage Family. Com., SN Rims, pine For. Ht. 1–2'. Stems hairy. Lvs. linear to lance-shaped, hairy, 1½–2" long. Flrs. tubular, ¼–½" long, in racemes. May–August.

GROUNDCHERRY, *Physalis crassifolia.* Nightshade Family. Com., Gorge, hot, dry flats and talus slopes. Ht. 1–2'. Stems spreading, forming a bushy plant. Lvs. egg-, delta-, or heart-shaped, margins entire or wavy, ½–1½" long. Flrs. bell-shaped, ½" Diam., petals joined. February–October.

ORANGE MOUNTAIN-DANDELION, *Agoseris aurantiaca.* Aster Family. Com., N Rim, meadows. Ht. 4–24". Lvs. basal, linear, oblong, lance- or wedge-shaped, entire or divided, 2–10" long. Flrs. composite, but with ray Flrs. only. Heads ½–1" Diam. The only orange dandelion; Flrs. turn pink or purple with age. June–August. Cf. Pale Mountain-Dandelion, below, and Common Dandelion, Plate 14.

PALE MOUNTAIN-DANDELION, *Agoseris glauca.* Aster Family. Very similar to above, but Flrs. are yellow. Found only on N Rim. On S Rim it is replaced by the yellow Arizona Mountain Dandelion, *A. arizonica.* June.

HAIRY GOLD-ASTER, *Heterotheca villosa.* Aster Family. Com., SN Rims and upper elevations of Can., Wood. and Scrub. Ht. 4–20". Stems may be woody toward base in larger plants. Plants downy. Lvs. linear to wedge-shaped, less than 1" long. Flrs. composite, heads about 1" across. May–October.

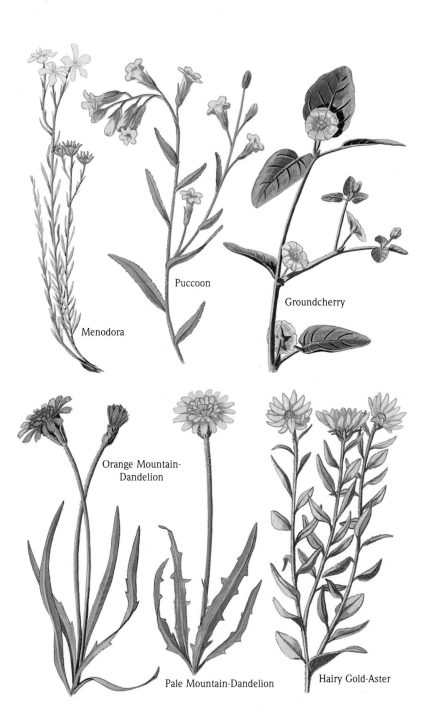

Puccoon

Menodora

Groundcherry

Orange Mountain-
Dandelion

Pale Mountain-Dandelion

Hairy Gold-Aster

Plate 12

YELLOW RAGWEED, *Bahia dissecta.* Aster Family. Com., SN Rims and higher elevations in Can., open, sunny places. Ht. 4–32". Lvs. cleft 2–3 times, somewhat hairy, about 1–2¾" long. Flrs. composite, with 10–15 rays. Heads about 1" Diam. with sticky hairs. June–October.

PARRY TACKSTEM, *Calycoseris parryi.* Aster Family. Com., Tonto Platform and Gorge, Scrub. Ht. 2–12". Stems spreading or semi-erect, with tack-shaped glands on upper halves. Lvs. mostly basal, pinnately divided to entire. Flrs. composite, with ray Flrs. only. Heads about 1–1½" Diam. with tack-shaped glands. March–May.

WESTERN HAWKSBEARD, *Crepis occidentalis.* Aster Family. Com., SN Rims, open areas. Ht. 3–10". Stems and Lvs. densely woolly, somewhat sticky. Lvs. wavy-toothed to deeply divided, with toothed lobes, mostly 4½" long. Flrs. composite, with 5–30 heads per stem, each head about 2" Diam. June–September.

BLANKET FLOWER, *Gaillardia pinnatifida.* Aster Family. Com., SN Rims and Can., open areas. Ht. 4–13¾". Plants with stiff hairs. Lvs. wedge-shaped, pinnately divided or merely lobed and toothed, 1–3" long. Flrs. composite; heads about 1½" Diam. April–November.

CURLYCUP GUMWEED, *Grindelia squarrosa.* Aster Family. Com., S Rim, roadsides and open areas. Ht. 6–40". Lvs. oblong to wedge-shaped, 1–2¾" long, margins finely toothed or entire. Flrs. composite, with heads about 1" Diam., in corymb. June–October. Rayless Gumweed, *G. aphanactis,* is similar but heads lack ray flowers.

BROOM SNAKEWEED, *Gutierrezia sarothrae.* Aster Family. Com., SN Rims and Can., dry, open places. Ht. 4–36". Stems herbaceous, but woody toward base. Plant somewhat rough-textured, with resinous glands. Lvs. linear or nearly so, smooth or hairy, about ¼" long. Flrs. composite, with 3–8 both disk and ray Flrs. Heads small, but numerous in clusters. July–November. *Gutierrezia microcephala* similar, but plant and Flrs. smaller; replaces *G. sarothrae* in the Gorge.

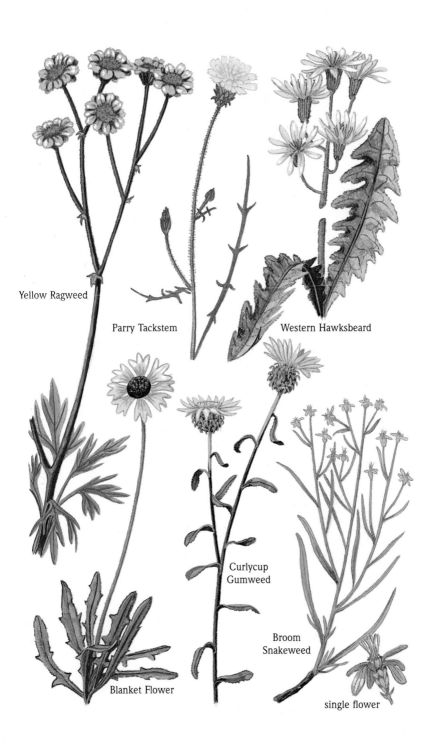

Yellow Ragweed

Parry Tackstem

Western Hawksbeard

Blanket Flower

Curlycup
Gumweed

Broom
Snakeweed

single flower

Plate 13

SPINY GOLDENWEED, *Machaeranthera pinnatifida.* Aster Family. Com., Can., mostly Gorge. Ht. 8–24". Stems smooth or woolly, usually glandular, sprouting from woody base. Lvs. ½–2½" long, linear or spoon-shaped, smooth or woolly, margins usually with bristle-tipped teeth. Flrs. composite, ¾–2" Diam., with spine-tipped bracts. One of several species of goldenweed in the area. January–October.

COMMON SUNFLOWER, *Helianthus annuus.* Aster Family. Com., S Rim and Can., roadsides and open areas. Ht. 1–6½'. Stems covered with numerous, stiff, bristly hairs. Lvs. egg-shaped, 1½–8" long, entire or toothed, lower ones often heart-shaped. Flrs. composite, 2–3" Diam., usually solitary. July–September. The Prairie Sunflower, *H. petiolaris,* is similar but smaller.

HYMENOPAPPUS, *Hymenopappus filifolius* var. *lugens.* Aster Family. Com., SN Rims, open areas. Ht. 4–20". Plants more or less woolly. Lvs. 2-divided, mostly basal, 2–3½" long. Flrs. composite, without rays. Heads less than ½" Diam. May–September.

PERKY SUE, BITTERWEED, *Tetraneuris acaulis.* Aster Family. Com., SN Rims and upper elevations in Can., Wood. and For. openings. Ht. 4–12". Lvs. basal, narrowly lance-shaped, nearly smooth or gray with silky hairs, glandular. Flrs. composite, about 1" Diam., with white-hairy bracts. April–October.

GREENSTEM PAPERFLOWER, *Psilostrophe sparsiflora.* Aster Family. Com., Can. above Redwall and S Rim, Wood. and Scrub. Ht. 14". Stems sparsely soft-haired. Lvs. mostly entire and stemless, to 2¾" long. Flrs. composite, about ½–1" Diam., with small disk and a few broad, 3-lobed rays. April–August.

CONEFLOWER, *Ratibida columnifera.* Aster Family. Uncom., S Rim, open areas. Ht. 10–32". Stems stiff-haired and glandular. Lvs. pinnately divided, stiff-haired. Flrs. composite, large and showy, with thimblelike disk and drooping rays. In some plants Flrs. are purplish brown, Cf. Plate 25. July–November.

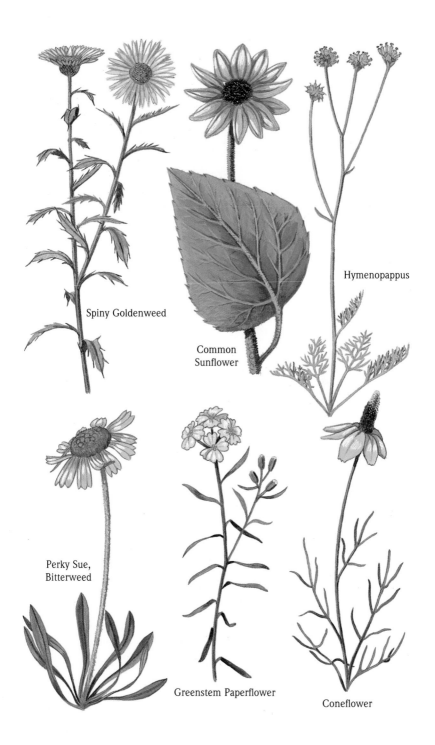

Spiny Goldenweed

Common
Sunflower

Hymenopappus

Perky Sue,
Bitterweed

Greenstem Paperflower

Coneflower

Plate 14

THREADLEAF GROUNDSEL, *Senecio longilobus.* Aster Family. Com., S Rim, often along dry washes. Ht. 12–40". Plant woolly. Lvs. threadlike, some divided into threadlike lobes 1" long or more. Flrs. composite, about ½–1" Diam., with drooping rays. One of several similar species in area. May–September.

TALL GOLDENROD, *Solidago altissima.* Aster Family. Com., SN Rims, Grass. and open areas. Ht. 2–5'. Stems downy. Lvs. lance-shaped, finely serrated or nearly entire, downy below, rough above, to 4¾" long. Flrs. composite, 12–15 in panicle. July–October.

COMMON DANDELION, *Taraxacum officinale.* Aster Family. Introduced species. Com., SN Rims and Can., open places. The familiar dandelion of suburban lawns. Ht. 2–12". Lvs. sharply lobed and toothed, stemless or nearly so, basal, to several inches long. Flrs. composite, but lack disk, about ½–2" Diam. Nearly year-round. Cf. Mountain Dandelions, Plate 11, which have rather different Lvs.

SALSIFY, *Tragopogon dubius.* Aster Family. Com., SN Rims. Ht. 12–36". Lvs. linear, clasping, 1–10" long. Flrs. composite, with long, pointed bracts, but lack disk. Seedlike fruit form round, white dandelionlike heads 2–3" Diam. May–August.

GOLDEN CROWNBEARD, *Verbesina encelioides.* Aster Family. Com., SN Rims and Can. Ht. 12–48". Stems gray-downy. Lvs. lance- to egg-shaped, 1–4" long, toothed, with stiff hairs. Flrs. composite, 1–1½" Diam. April–October.

GOLDENEYE, *Viguiera multiflora.* Aster Family. Com., SN Rims, Grass. and pine For. Ht. 10–40". Stems finely downy or nearly smooth. Lvs. opposite below, alternate above, linear to lance-shaped. Flrs. composite, 8–12 rays, about 2" Diam. July–October.

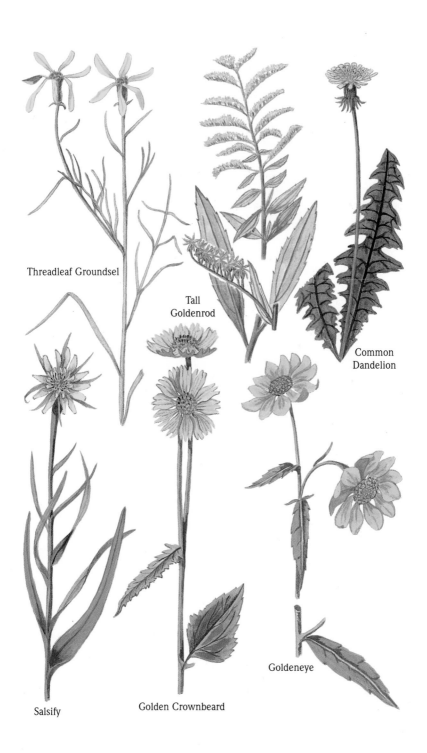

Threadleaf Groundsel

Tall
Goldenrod

Common
Dandelion

Salsify

Golden Crownbeard

Goldeneye

Plate 15

RED COLUMBINE, *Aquilegia triternata.* Columbine Family. Rare, moist places 6000–10,000', notably near Ribbon Falls and in Long Jim Canyon. Ht. 8–24". Stems numerous, slender, sparsely downy, with few Lvs. Lvs. mostly basal, compound, with 3-lobed and cleft leaflets at end of long petiole. Flrs. nodding, about 1½" long. May–October. Cf. Golden Columbine, Plate 9, and Colorado Columbine, Plate 22.

GLOBE MALLOW, *Sphaeralcea parvifolia.* Mallow Family. Com., SN Rims and Can., dry, open places 4000–7000'. Often along roads. Ht. to 40". Stems sprouting from woody crown. Lvs. 6–20" long, broadly egg-shaped to nearly round, unlobed or with 3 shallow lobes, margins toothed, veins prominent. Stems and Lvs. covered with gray hairs. Flrs. about 1" Diam., 5 petals. April–October. One of several quite similar species in the park.

PINEDROPS, *Pterospora andromedea.* Indian Pipe Family. Uncom., SN Rims, For. Ht. 8–40". Stems clammy and downy. Lvs. reduced to small scales near stem base. Flrs. to ½" Diam., urn-shaped, 5-lobed, nodding, in terminal raceme. Plants lack chlorophyll; probably parasitic. June–August.

BUTTERFLY WEED, *Asclepias tuberosa.* Milkweed Family. Uncom., N Rim, pine For. openings. Ht. 12–32". Stems hairy or rough-downy. Lvs. lance-shaped, stemless, margins sometimes rolled under, 1¼–4½" long. Flrs. star-shaped, about ½" Diam., corolla consisting of 5 petallike lobes to which are attached upright hoods, each with a small horn. Flrs. sometimes yellow or orange, in umbels about 3" Diam. Of several milkweeds in area, this is the only one without milky sap. July.

SKYROCKET, *Ipomopsis arizonica.* Phlox Family. Com., N Rim; Uncom. and local, S Rim and Can. just below rim, moist Grass. and pine For. Ht. 6–32". More or less sticky-hairy. Lvs. pinnately divided, 1–2" long. Flrs. tubular, with 5 pointed, petallike lobes flaring to form a star, ¾–1¾" long, color variable, including solid red, pink, and white. April–October.

LONG-LEAVED PAINTBRUSH, *Castilleja linariaefolia.* Figwort Family. Com., SN Rims and Can. above Supai Formation, Wood. and For., dry openings and rocky places. Ht. 12–32" or more. Stems woody toward base, fine-downy to nearly smooth below, somewhat hairy near flowers. Lvs. linear, smooth or slightly downy, clasping, unlobed, ½–3" long. Flrs. Irreg., tubular, beaked, 2" long, sheathed in showy, red, 3-lobed bracts in dense terminal spikes. April–October. One of four paintbrushes in park. Similar Desert Paintbrush, *C. chromosa,* with 5-lobed bracts, is most common paintbrush in Can.

Red Columbine

Globe Mallow

Pinedrops

single flower

color variation

Butterfly Weed

Skyrocket

Long-Leaved Paintbrush

Plate 16

CRIMSON MONKEYFLOWER, *Mimulus cardinalis.* Figwort Family. Com., Can., shady seeps and stream banks. Ht. 10–36". Lvs. oval, opposite, stemless, toothed, 3/4–4 1/2" long. Flrs. Irreg., tubular, 5-lobed, about 2" long. March–November. Only bright red monkeyflower in area. Cf. Yellow Monkeyflower, Plate 9.

UTAH BEARDTONGUE, *Penstemon utahensis.* Figwort Family. Com., Can. above Redwall, Scrub and Wood. among rocks. Ht. 28". Lvs. opposite, oblong to narrowly wedge-shaped, 1/2–2" long, upper ones stemless and clasping. Flrs. nearly regular, tubular, with 5 flared, petallike lobes. Flrs. in panicles. March–May. Cf. two following species and other penstemons on Plates 21 and 24.

FIRECRACKER PENSTEMON, *Penstemon eatoni.* Figwort Family. Com., Can., rocky places. Ht. 12–39". Lvs. opposite, 1/2–4"; lower ones narrowly wedge- or lance-shaped; upper ones egg- or heart-shaped, stemless, clasping. Flrs. Irreg., tubular, with 2-lobed upper lip and 3-lobed lower lip, neither flared. Flrs. in panicles. February–June.

SCARLET BUGLER, *Penstemon barbatus.* Figwort Family. Com., SN Rims and Can., Grass., Scrub, Wood., and For. Ht. 16–55". Lvs. opposite, 1 1/2–4" long; lower ones wedge- or spoon-shaped; upper ones linear or lance-shaped. Flrs. Irreg., tubular, with 2-lobed, unflared upper lip and 3-lobed, flared lower lip. Flrs. in panicles. June–October.

CARDINAL FLOWER, *Lobelia cardinalis.* Bellflower Family. Uncom., Can., moist places. Ht. 12–40". Stems smooth or sparsely downy. Lvs. linear to lance- or egg-shaped, 2 1/2–6" long, smooth or sparsely hairy. Flrs. Irreg., tubular, 1–1 1/2" long, with tube slit down one side nearly to base, with 2-lobed upper lip, 3-lobed lower lip, and united stamens, in spikelike racemes. August–September.

CARMINE THISTLE, *Cirsium rothrockii.* Aster Family. Com., SN Rims and Can. just below rims, open places. Ht. 24" or more. Lvs. deeply lobed and spiny. Flrs. composite, but lacking ray flowers, with spiny bracts. Difficult to distinguish from other red thistles in area. May–October.

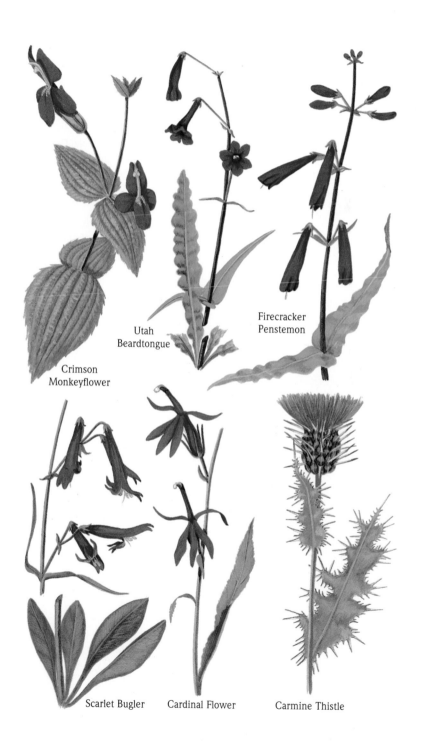

Utah
Beardtongue

Firecracker
Penstemon

Crimson
Monkeyflower

Scarlet Bugler   Cardinal Flower   Carmine Thistle

Plate 17

WEAKSTEM MARIPOSA, *Calochortus flexuosus*. Lily Family. Com., SN Rims and Can., especially Tonto Platform, Scrub. Ht. 6–16". Stems often drooping, bent, or twisted. Lvs. mostly basal, linear, to 8" long. Petals 1¼–1½" long, 3 petals, sometimes white or purple. March–July. Cf. Sego Lily, Plate 4.

TRAILING FOUR O'CLOCK, *Mirabilis oxybaphoides*. Four O'Clock Family. Com., Can., Gorge, and Tonto Platform. Stems trailing, 6–10" long, radiating out from hub of plant, covered with glandular hairs. Lvs. opposite, oval to oblong, ½–1½" long, more or less glandular-hairy. Flrs. Irreg., 3 to a head, together appearing as a single regular Flr. about ¾" Diam., rarely white. Flrs. open before dawn, close by midday. April–October.

COLORADO FOUR O'CLOCK, *Mirabilis multiflora*. Four O'Clock Family. Com., S Rim, roadsides, and Can., rocky places. Ht. 12–40". Stems erect or trailing, forming clumps, sticky or nearly smooth. Lvs. opposite, numerous, broadly oval or oblong, 1–4" long with or without hairs. Flrs. 2" long, 1" Diam., 8–12 in a cluster, 5-lobed, bloom for only 1 day. April–October.

LEWISIA, *Lewisia pygmaea*. Portulaca Family. Com., N Rim, Grass. Ht. 1–2½". Lvs. linear, basal, 1–3" long, fleshy. Flrs. 1–3 per stem. June–August.

PERENNIAL ROCK CRESS, *Arabis perennans*. Mustard Family. Com., SN Rims, Wood., and Can., rock crevices and Gorge. Ht. 6–12". Stems smooth above, covered with forked hairs below. Lvs. mostly basal, wedge- to lance-shaped, toothed or entire, densely downy, upper ones stemless. Flrs. ½" Diam., 4 petals, pink to purple. February–October. One of a half-dozen rock cresses in area.

PURPLE BLADDERPOD, *Lesquerella purpurea*. Mustard Family. Com., Can., especially Gorge. Ht. 4–20". Plant covered with star-shaped hairs. Lvs. mostly basal, oblong to wedge-shaped, to 4" long; stem Lvs. much smaller, stemless. Flrs. nearly ½" Diam., 4 petals, white streaked with purple when young, turning solid purple with age. January–May. Round seed pods distinguish this and other bladderpods from the rock cresses. Cf. Bladderpod, Plate 9.

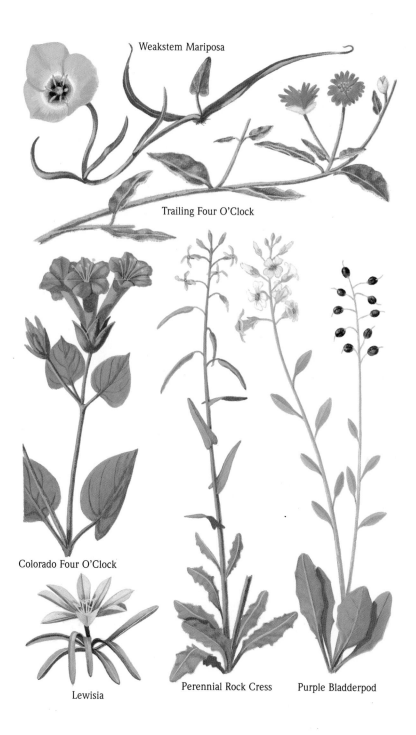

Weakstem Mariposa

Trailing Four O'Clock

Colorado Four O'Clock

Lewisia

Perennial Rock Cress

Purple Bladderpod

Plate 18

LINEARLEAF HEDGEMUSTARD, *Schoenocrambe linearifolia.* Mustard Family. Com., SN Rims, Wood. and For. openings. Ht. 12–40". Stems sprout from somewhat woody rootstock. Lvs. mostly linear and entire, 3/4–3 1/4" long. Flrs. about 1" across, 4 petals, H-shaped, sometimes fading to white or yellow. May–September.

ROCKY MOUNTAIN BEE PLANT, *Cleome serrulata.* Caper Family. Com., S Rim, roadsides and open areas. Ht. 20–40". Lvs. lance- or narrowly wedge-shaped, sometimes finely toothed, 3/4–3 1/4" long. Flrs. 1" Diam., 4 petals, with long stamens, clustered in spherical racemes. June–September. Two other species, both with yellow flowers, also occur at the canyon.

FILAREE, STORK'S BILL, *Erodium cicutarium.* Geranium Family. Introduced species. Com., SN Rims and Can., roadsides and disturbed areas. Prostrate plant with spreading, hairy stems 4–16" long. Lvs. 2-divided, 1 1/4–4" long, radiating from center. Flrs. less than 1/2" across, 5 petals, clustered, with stems glandular-hairy. February–August.

PURPLE CRANESBILL, *Geranium caespitosum.* Geranium Family. Introduced species. SN Rims, pine For. Ht. 4–36". Stems downy, somewhat declining. Lvs. opposite, palmately lobed, 3/4–1 1/2" Diam., covered with flattened hairs. Flrs. to 1" across, 5 petals, with downy stems. May–October. Cf. White Cranesbill, Plate 5.

FIREWEED, *Chanerion angustifolium* ssp. *circumvagum.* Evening Primrose Family. Com., N Rim, open areas. Ht. to 5'. Lvs. lance-shaped, stemless or nearly so, 2–6" long. Flrs. about 1" across, 4 petals, in long, terminal racemes. July–September.

CLIMBING MILKWEED, *Furastrum cynanchoides.* Milkweed Family. Gorge and side canyons, forming dense clumps over rocks and other plants. A vine with stems up to 6' long. Lvs. opposite, linear to oval, 1–2 1/2" long. Flrs. 3/8" Diam., 5 petals, in many-flowered umbels. April–July.

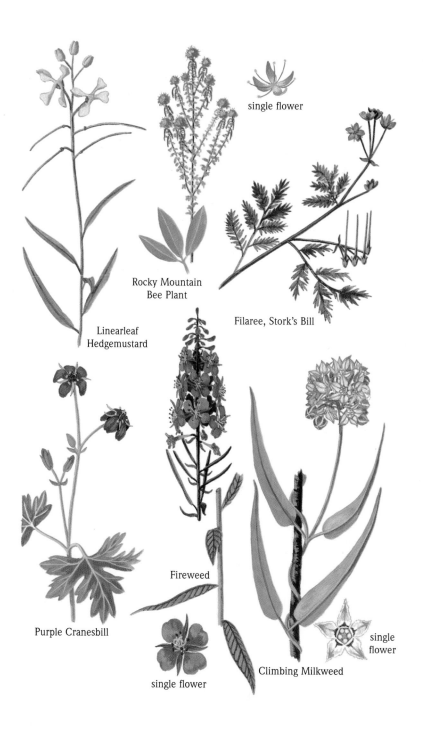

single flower

Rocky Mountain
Bee Plant

Filaree, Stork's Bill

Linearleaf
Hedgemustard

Fireweed

Climbing Milkweed

single
flower

Purple Cranesbill

single flower

Plate 19

SPREADING PHLOX, *Phlox diffusa.* Phlox Family. Com., N Rim, open, rocky places at higher elevations. Mat or cushion plant. Ht. 1–3". Lvs. needlelike, but not stiff or spine-tipped, about ½" long. Flrs. about ½" Diam., often densely covering plant. June–August. Desert Phlox, *P. austromontana,* similar, but with grayish green, sharp, spine-tipped Lvs. It is found in Can. and on SN Rims in open, rocky places. April–August.

LONGLEAF PHLOX, *Phlox longifolia.* Phlox Family. Com., S Rim and upper elevations of Can., Wood. Ht. 2½–12". Stems vary from smooth to downy to glandular-hairy. Lvs. linear, ¾–3" long. Flrs. about ⅝–¾" Diam., 5 petals, sometimes white. April–June.

NEW MEXICAN VERVAIN, *Verbena macdougalii.* Verbena Family. Com., SN Rims, Wood. and Scrub. Ht. 12–32". Stems downy to hairy. Lvs. elliptic to egg-shaped, wrinkled above, hairy-downy on both sides, nearly stemless, 1–3" long. Flrs. tubular, tiny, in dense terminal spikes. June–September.

GOODDING VERBENA, *Verbena gooddingii.* Verbena Family. Can. below 6000', dry places. Ht. 8–18". Stems branched, densely hairy. Lvs. to about 1½" long, mostly 3-cleft, hairy on both sides, tapering to a short petiole. Flrs. tubular, tiny, in dense terminal spikes. Nearly year-round.

CAVE PRIMROSE, *Primula specuicola.* Primrose Family. Uncom., Can., wet seeps. Ht. to 4". Lvs. basal, oblong to lance-shaped, to about 3" long. Flrs. tubular with flared petals, in umbels, about ½" long. Note yellow Flr. tube. May–June.

ALPINE SHOOTING STAR, *Dodecatheon pulcherrum.* Primrose Family. Rare, N Rim, meadows. Ht. 4–16". Lvs. basal, narrowly wedge-shaped, 1–6" long. Flrs. 1" long or less, 4 petals bent backward. June–September.

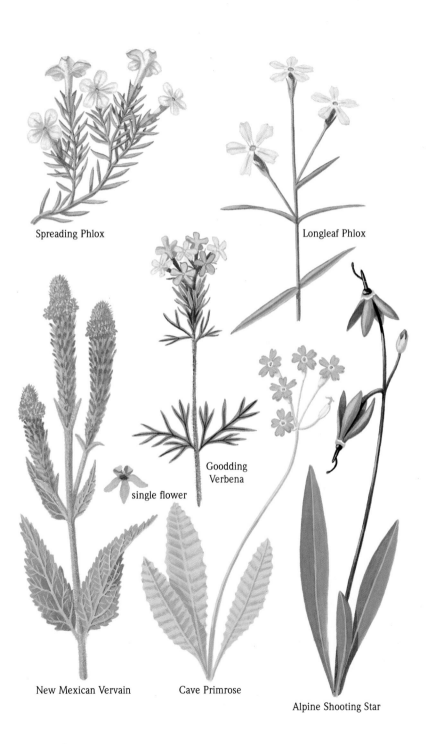

Spreading Phlox

Longleaf Phlox

Goodding
Verbena

single flower

New Mexican Vervain

Cave Primrose

Alpine Shooting Star

Plate 20

SPECKLEPOD, *Astragalus lentiginosus.* Legume Family. Com., widespread. A highly variable species. Ht. 4–40". Stems erect, ascending, or prostrate. Lvs. pinnate, to 7" long, usually with 11–27 leaflets. Flrs. Irreg., to 1" long, pink to purple. March–August. One of numerous locoweeds in the area.

GRASSLEAF PEAVINE, *Lathyrus graminifolius.* Legume Family. Com., S Rim and Can., rocky areas, Wood., and For. A vine with stems several feet long, climbing by means of tendrils. Lvs. pinnate, 1–4" long, terminating in a tendril, with 4–12 leaflets. Flrs. Irreg., about ½" long. Closely related to the garden pea. April–September.

LAMBERT LOCOWEED, *Oxytropis lambertii.* Legume Family. Uncom., S Rim, Grass. and other open areas. Ht. 4–12". Lvs. pinnate, silvery-haired, with 7–17 linear to oblong leaflets. Flrs. Irreg., about ½–1" long. June–September.

TWINING SNAPDRAGON, *Maurandella antirrhiniflora.* Figwort Family. Com., Gorge and side canyons, often on shaded ledges. A vine with trailing or climbing stems to Lgth. of 6½' or more. Lvs. delta- or arrow-shaped or with 3–5 lobes, to 1" long. Flrs. Irreg., about 1" long, tubular with 2-lobed upper lip and 3-lobed lower lip. April–October.

PURPLE-WHITE OWLCLOVER, *Orthocarpus purpureo-albus.* Figwort Family. Com., N Rim, Grass. Ht. 4–16". Lvs. 3-cleft, with linear lobes, stemless or nearly so, 1" long. Flrs. Irreg., to ¾" long, upper lip beaklike, lower lip inflated, in terminal spikes with numerous leafy bracts. Resembles the paintbrushes (genus *Castilleja*). July–September. Often grows with Yellow Owlclover, *O. luteus,* Plate 9.

LOUSEWORT, WOOD BETONY, *Pedicularis centranthera.* Figwort Family. Com., SN Rims, Wood. and For. Ht. ¼". Lvs. basal, pinnately divided with broad, toothed lobes, 2–6" long. Flrs. clustered, Irreg., tubular, 2-lipped, upper lip helmet-shaped, about 1½" long. April–June.

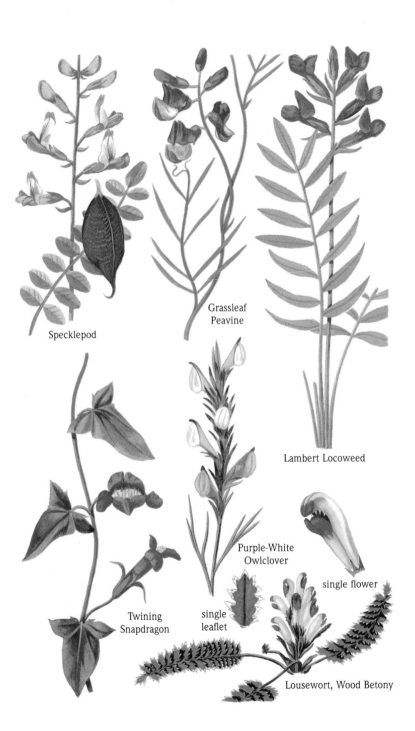

Specklepod

Grassleaf
Peavine

Lambert Locoweed

Twining
Snapdragon

Purple-White
Owlclover

single
leaflet

single flower

Lousewort, Wood Betony

Plate 21

PALMER PENSTEMON, *Penstemon palmeri.* Figwort Family. Com., S Rim and Can., rocky places in Scrub and Wood. Ht. 20–48". Lvs. opposite, oblong to egg-shaped, 1–3" long, upper ones stemless and clasping, forming perfoliate pairs. Flrs. Irreg., inflated, with 2-lobed upper lip, 3-lobed lower lip, 1½" long, in panicles. March–September.

BROOMRAPE, *Orobanche fasciculata.* Broomrape Family. Com., SN Rims and Can., Scrub and Wood. Ht. 2–8". Stems nearly leafless, with Lvs. reduced to tiny, nonfunctional scales. Lacking chlorophyll. Broomrape is parasitic on the roots of sagebrush and other plants. Flrs. Irreg., tubular, 2-lipped, ½–1¼" long. May–August.

MOHAVE ASTER, *Xylorhiza tortifolia.* Aster Family. Com., Can. below Redwall, talus slopes and dry places. Ht. 12–28". Stems slightly hairy or glandular to woolly, rising from woody base. Lvs. linear, oblong or lance-shaped, hairy to woolly, stemless, 1¼–2⅜" long. Flrs. composite, 1½–2½" Diam., numerous, sometimes white or blue. March–May.

HOARY ASTER, *Machaeranthera canescens.* Aster Family. Com., SN Rims and Can., Wood. and Scrub. Ht. 4–16". Stems slightly hairy to nearly smooth. Lvs. linear to lance- or wedge-shaped, sharply toothed, short-stemmed to nearly stemless, to 2" long. Flrs. composite, about 1" Diam., numerous, with downy bracts. May–November.

FLEABANE, *Erigeron formosissimus.* Aster Family. Com., SN Rims, For., shady places. Ht. 4–16". Stems more or less glandular or hairy. Lvs. linear to spoon-shaped, to 2" long, more numerous toward base, upper ones often stemless. Flrs. composite, about 1½" Diam., with 75–150 rays, sometimes pale blue, Cf. Plate 24. June–September.

WIRE LETTUCE, *Stephanomeria minor* var. *minor.* Aster Family. Uncom., SN Rims, dry places 4500–8000', Scrub, Wood., Grass., and For. Ht. 4–20". Stems slender, smooth, branched. Lvs. mostly erect, grasslike, lower ones more or less pinnately toothed or lobed. Flrs. composite, mostly terminal and solitary on branches, with 5 or so rays. May–September.

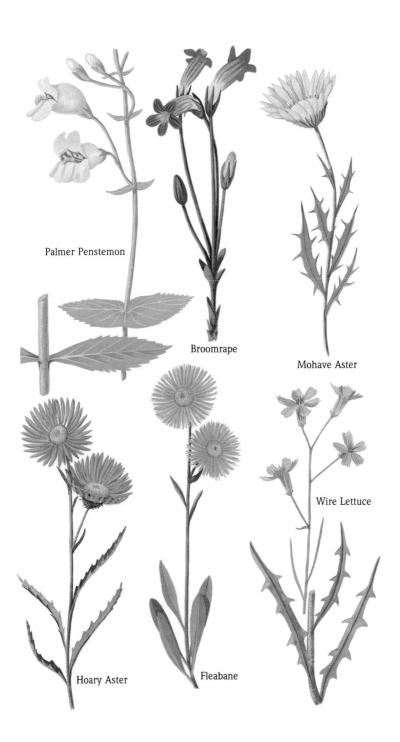

Palmer Penstemon

Broomrape

Mohave Aster

Hoary Aster

Fleabane

Wire Lettuce

Plate 22

COLORADO COLUMBINE, *Aquilegia caerulea.* Columbine Family. Uncom., N Rim, For. and Grass., damp places. Ht. 6–24". Lvs. mostly basal, 2–3 times palmately compound, leaflets deeply lobed. Flrs. regular, 2½–3" long and to 4" Diam., 5 petals with spurs. Petallike sepals normally blue, but may be white. June–July. Cf. Golden Columbine, Plate 9, and Red Columbine, Plate 15.

MONKSHOOD, *Aconitum columbianum.* Columbine Family. Uncom., N Rim, Ripar. Ht. 20" or more. Stems mostly smooth, but downy and often sticky near the Flrs. Lvs. palmate with 3–5 divisions, each cleft and toothed, finely downy to nearly smooth. Flrs. Irreg., to about 1½" long, in terminal raceme, sometimes white, with hood formed by sepals. June–September.

NELSON'S LARKSPUR, *Delphinium nelsoni.* Columbine Family. Com., SN Rims and Can. Ht. 4–20". Stems finely haired to nearly hairless. Lvs. few, palmately lobed, with the lobes segmented, 1¼–2" Diam. Flrs. Irreg., with 1 sepal extended backward to form a spur; upper petals white, inconspicuous, largely replaced by petallike sepals. May–July.

BARESTEM LARKSPUR, *Delphinium scaposum.* Columbine Family. Com., SN Rims and Can., Grass., Wood., and For. Ht. 8–20". Stems leafless or nearly so. Lvs. mostly basal, divided 3–5 times, with divisions lobed or toothed, about 1" Diam. Flrs. similar to those of Nelson's Larkspur, but spur is bronze-tipped and only upper 2 petals are white. March–July.

BLUE FLAX, *Linum lewisii.* Flax Family. Com., SN Rims and Can., Scrub and Wood. Ht. to 36". Lvs. linear, tiny, pressed against stem. Flrs. 1–2" Diam., 5 petals. Dark blue form occurs on N Rim. March–September.

ROCKY MOUNTAIN IRIS, *Iris missouriensis.* Iris Family. Com., N Rim, Grass. Ht. 8–20". Lvs. basal, linear, to 18" long. Flrs. 1½–2" tall, with 3 showy, drooping, petallike sepals, 3 upright petals, and 3 cleft, petallike styles. Ovary inferior, flower stem long, arising from juncture of 2 elongate leaflike bracts. May–September.

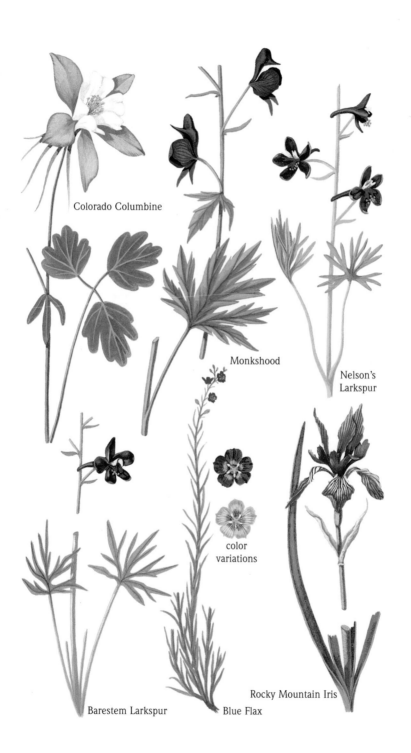

Colorado Columbine

Monkshood

Nelson's
Larkspur

color
variations

Rocky Mountain Iris

Barestem Larkspur

Blue Flax

Plate 23

PHACELIA, SCORPIONWEED, *Phacelia crenulata* var. *corrugata*. Waterleaf Family. Uncom., SN Rims and Can., rocky slopes and gravelly flats, pinyon-juniper Wood. Ht. 20". Stems somewhat hairy and glandular. Plant foul-smelling. Lvs. to 4" long, egg-shaped to oblong, margins wavy to lobed. Flrs. small, densely packed in coiled cymes. March–September.

GRAND CANYON PHACELIA, *Phacelia glechomaefolia*. Waterleaf Family. Com., Can., especially Gorge of western section. Ht. 4–12". Stems sticky-downy. Lvs. oblong to nearly round, entire to scalloped. Flrs. to about ½" long, varying from pale to deep blue or purple. April–June, but only when rainfall is sufficient.

FRANCISCAN BLUEBELLS, *Mertensia franciscana*. Borage Family. Com., N Rim, moist, shady places about 5600', often in spruce-fir For. above 8000'. Ht. 4–40". Lvs. elliptic, to 5" long, sometimes stemless, hairy below. Flrs. tubular, about ½" long, nodding, in cymes, pink in the bud stage. June–September.

PARRY BELLFLOWER, *Campanula parryi*. Bellflower Family. Com., SN Rims, Grass. Ht. 2½–12". Lvs. to 2½" long, lower ones spoon- to wedge-shaped, upper ones shorter, linear. Flrs. bell-shaped, to 1" long, erect or nodding. July–September.

HILL LUPINE, *Lupinus hillii*. Legume Family. Com., SN Rims, For., Wood., and Grass. Ht. usually more than 8". Plant covered with silky hairs. Lvs. palmate-compound, 1–2" Diam.; leaflets narrowly oblong. Flrs. Irreg., about ¼" long, crowded in terminal raceme, sometimes white. May–September. One of numerous lupines in area. Cf. Palmer Lupine, below.

PALMER LUPINE, *Lupinus palmeri*. Legume Family. Com., SN Rims and Can. above 4000', Wood. and For. openings. Ht. 12–18". Stems leafy, densely covered with soft hairs. Lvs. palmate-compound, with elliptic-oblanceolate leaflets about 6–18" long. Flrs. Irreg., about ½" long, in terminal raceme, but less crowded than in Hill Lupine. April–October. Cf. Hill Lupine, above.

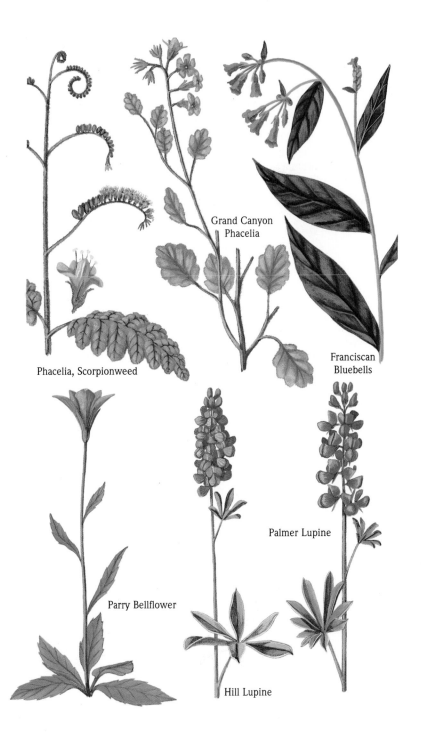

Grand Canyon
Phacelia

Franciscan
Bluebells

Phacelia, Scorpionweed

Parry Bellflower

Palmer Lupine

Hill Lupine

Plate 24

PARRY GENTIAN, *Gentiana parryi.* Gentian Family. Uncom., N Rim, Grass. above 8500'. Ht. 4–16". Stems leafy, often numerous. Lvs. opposite, stemless, egg- to lance-shaped. Flrs. bell-shaped, to about 1½" long. August–September.

BLUE-EYED MARY, *Collinsia parviflora.* Figwort Family. Rare, SN Rims and Can., moist places. Ht. 2–16". Stems usually covered with fine down. Lvs. opposite, linear to egg-shaped, sometimes finely toothed, stemless or nearly so, to 2" long. Flrs. Irreg., less than ½" long, with 2-lobed upper lip and 3-lobed lower lip. February–June.

TOADFLAX PENSTEMON, *Penstemon linarioides.* Figwort Family. Com., SN Rims and Can., Wood. and For. Ht. 2–14". Prostrate, with woody base. Stems more or less downy. Lvs. opposite, linear to wedge-shaped, crowded toward base of stem, to 1" long. Flrs. Irreg., with short, inflated tube, flaring upper and lower lips, about ½" long, in panicles. June–September. Cf. Thickleaf Penstemon, below, and penstemons on Plates 16 and 21.

THICKLEAF PENSTEMON, *Penstemon pachyphyllus.* Figwort Family. Com., S Rim, Wood. and For. Ht. 10–26". Stems covered with fine down. Lvs. opposite, thick, lance- to wedge-shaped, about ½–3" long, upper ones stemless. Flrs. similar to those of Toadflax Penstemon, above, but tube less inflated. April–June. Cf. penstemons on Plates 16 and 21.

SPEEDWELL, *Veronica americana.* Figwort Family. Com., springs and stream banks. Ht. 4–40". Plant somewhat succulent. Stems rising from creeping bases. Lvs. opposite, lance- to egg-shaped, short-stemmed to 3½" long, finely or minutely toothed. Flrs. slightly Irreg., 4-lobed, in racemes. March–December. The similar Water Speedwell, *Veronica anagallis-aquatica,* has stemless Lvs. and is strictly Aquat., growing along the Colorado River and perennial sidestreams.

FLEABANE, *Erigeron formosissimus.* This is the blue phase of the species shown on Plate 21.

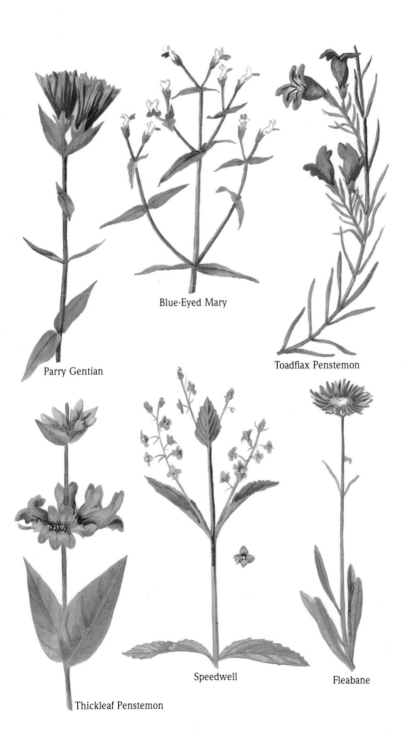

Blue-Eyed Mary

Parry Gentian

Toadflax Penstemon

Thickleaf Penstemon

Speedwell

Fleabane

Plate 25

SPOTTED MOUNTAIN BELLS, *Fritillaria atropurpurea.* Lily Family. Uncom., SN Rims, For. Ht. 24". Upper half of stem leafy. Lvs. narrow, linear, more or less whorled, 1–4" long. Flrs. nodding, to ¾" long, 3 petals. April–June.

SPOTTED CORALROOT, *Corallorhiza maculata.* Orchid Family. N Rim, For. Ht. 8–24". Lvs. reduced to a few tiny sheaths on stem. Flrs. Irreg., about ¾" Diam., distinctly orchidlike. July–September.

GIANT HELLEBORINE, *Epipactis gigantea.* Orchid Family. Com., N Rim and Can., near water. Ht. 8–40". Stems sparsely covered with downy hairs. Lvs. lance- to egg-shaped, clasping, to 8". Flrs. Irreg., about 1½" Diam., distinctly orchidlike. April–July.

GREEN GENTIAN, *Frasera paniculata.* Gentian Family. Com., Can. and SN Rims, 4000–7500'. Ht. to 42". Lvs. opposite, stemless, linear to wedge-shaped, white-margined, to 4" long. Flrs. to ¾" Diam., 4 petals, with 1 fringed gland on each petal. June–September. Desert Green Gentian, *S. albomarginata,* nearly identical but with whorled Lvs., often found in pinyon-juniper Wood.

DEERS EARS, *Frasera speciosa.* Gentian Family. Com., SN Rims, For. Ht. 12–60". Stem solitary, smooth or finely downy. Similar to above species, but stem Lvs. in whorls of 3–7 and corolla lobes have 2 fringed glands. June–September.

CONEFLOWER, *Ratibida columnaris.* Aster Family. This is the brown phase of the species shown on Plate 13.

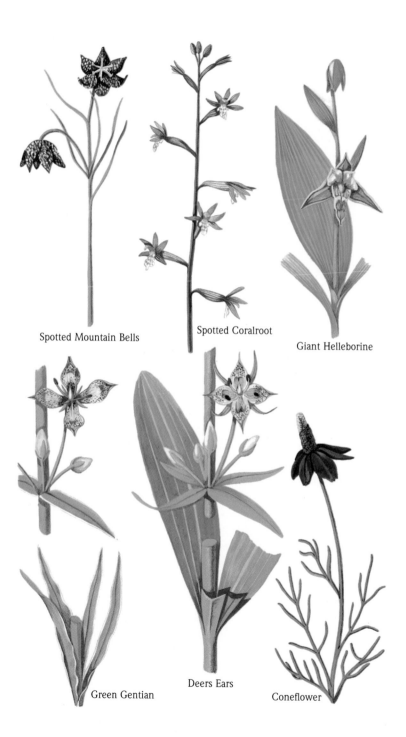

Spotted Mountain Bells

Spotted Coralroot

Giant Helleborine

Green Gentian

Deers Ears

Coneflower

Cacti

Cacti comprise a distinctive family of flowering plants, one not closely related to any other. They are confined almost exclusively to the New World, ranging from southern Canada to Tierra del Fuego. Of some 1500 different species, 60 are found in Arizona and about two dozen in the Grand Canyon. In the following plates, 15 are shown.

Most cacti have fleshy, leafless green stems, but in tropical America the family also includes woody vines, shrubs, and trees with well-developed leaves. Such plants are probably much like those from which typical cacti evolved. Prickly-pears and chollas (genus *Opuntia*) bear tiny relict leaves on new stems, but drop them soon afterward.

In the absence of leaves, typical cacti carry out photosynthesis by means of green, fleshy stems, which also function as reservoirs for water. The waxy coat on the stems inhibits moisture loss. At a distance, cacti may not appear green because of their dense spines, which are actually modified leaves. Spines grow in clusters that typically consist of one or more central spines and numerous, usually shorter radial spines. The spines may be straight or curved; needlelike, barbed, or hooked; smooth or rough. Most cacti bear spines over all or nearly all their stem surfaces. A few have spines only in certain places, and still others are spineless. Since the shape, arrangement and distribution of spines is more or less distinctive for each type of cactus, spines are among the more important features to note when attempting to identify a specimen.

Prickly pears and chollas also bear tiny barbed bristles called glochids (pronounced GLOCK-ids). Unlike spines, these bristles detach readily from the plant. Embedded in the skin, glochids can be more unpleasant than spines and are removed only by means of tweezers. The process is difficult and painful.

Cacti are noted for their exquisite flowers, which are typically large and vividly colored. The blossoms of Grand Canyon cacti are mostly red or reddish purple, less often various shades of yellow. Color variations are common within a single species and even on a single plant. Flowers are regular, with numerous, nearly identical petals and sepals. The pistil consists of an inferior ovary, a single style, and several stigmas. It is surrounded by numerous stamens, which along with the pistil form a conspicuous central cluster.

Spines, glochids, flowers, and new stems sprout from small, well-defined places called areoles. Arranged on stems in spirals, areoles are one of the features that distinguish cacti from other flowering plants. Prickly pears have more or less smooth stems, with areoles well distributed over the entire surface. Stems of other species may either be ribbed or covered with nipplelike bumps called tubercles.

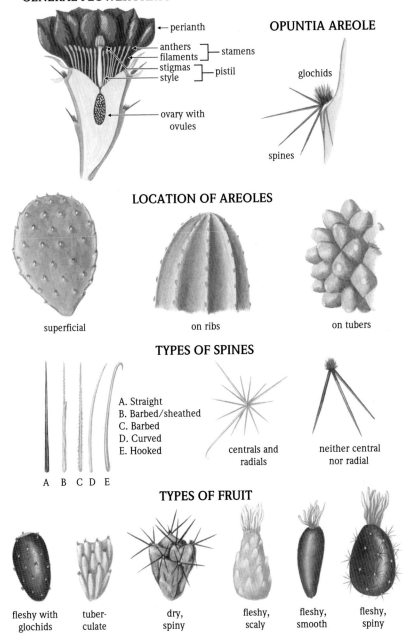

GENERAL FLOWER PARTS

← perianth

anthers
filaments ⎤ stamens
stigmas ⎤ pistil
style

ovary with ovules

OPUNTIA AREOLE

glochids

spines

LOCATION OF AREOLES

superficial

on ribs

on tubers

TYPES OF SPINES

A. Straight
B. Barbed/sheathed
C. Barbed
D. Curved
E. Hooked

A   B   C   D   E

centrals and radials

neither central nor radial

TYPES OF FRUIT

fleshy with glochids

tuberculate

dry, spiny

fleshy, scaly

fleshy, smooth

fleshy, spiny

Figure 25. Anatomy of a Cactus.

Ribbed cacti have areoles spaced along the rib crests. Tuberculate cacti have a single areole atop each tubercle.

Cacti at the Grand Canyon tend to be shrubby, typically forming low mats or clumps. Prickly pears and chollas have branched stems consisting of a series of flattened, globular, or cylindrical joints. Stems of other canyon species are unbranched, solitary, or in clusters, and shaped like globes, barrels, or columns. At the Grand Canyon the number and variety of cacti are greatest within the canyon, where they typically grow in hot, arid places among rocks, grasses, and shrubs. Even so, a few species also occur on both rims, where the climate is somewhat more humid and significantly cooler.

Among the flowering plants, none have proved more difficult to classify than cacti. The distinctions among closely related species are often obscure and variable. Many species hybridize freely in the wild, producing intermediate forms that even professional botanists have difficulty classifying. The beginning student, then, should not be dismayed to encounter forms that do not correspond in all respects with the species described in the following plates. The descriptions apply only to typical adult specimens. Juvenile plants may be quite different.

Enjoy the cactus, but please do not pick flowers and fruits or otherwise remove or deface the stems. All cacti in the park are protected by both federal and state laws.

Plate 26

ARIZONA BEEHIVE CACTUS, *Escobaria vivipara.* Cactus Family. Com., SN Rims and upper elevations in Can., Wood. and For. openings. Stems unbranched, spherical or melon-shaped, to 6½" tall and 3¼" Diam., solitary or clumped, with nipplelike bumps grooved on upper side. Spines straight and stiff: 3 central, to ¾" long, turned up and down; 15–20 radial, to about ¾", spreading. Flrs. to 2½" Diam., pink to magenta. Fruit smooth, to 1" long. June–September.

COTTONTOP CACTUS, *Echinocactus polycephalus* var. *xeranthemoides.* Cactus Family. Rocky places, especially on limestone, below 7000'. Stems 1–12, unbranched, melon-shaped, to nearly 24" tall and 12" thick, with 10–20 ribs, clumped. Central spines curved; radials straight, flattened, stiff, and downy: 3–4 central, to 3" long; 6–8 radial, smaller. Flrs. about 2" Diam., with woolly, scaled tube. Fruit egg-shaped, to 1½" long, woolly, dry, spineless. February–June.

ENGELMANN HEDGEHOG CACTUS, *Echinocereus engelmannii.* Cactus Family. Com., Gorge and Toroweap area, Scrub and rocky places. Stems unbranched, melon- or barrel-shaped, to 12" tall and 3¼" Diam., usually with 10–13 ribs, clumped. Spines needlelike, usually flattened at base, curved or twisted, flexible; 2–6 central, to 3½" long; 6–12 radial, smaller. Flrs. 2" Diam., several per stem. Fruit egg-shaped, about 1³⁄₈" long, spiny until mature, edible and fleshy. February–May.

FENDLER HEDGEHOG CACTUS, *Echinocereus fendleri.* Cactus Family. Upper Can. and SN Rims, Scrub, Wood., and pine For., in openings. Stems unbranched, egg-shaped, to 6" Diam., with 9 or 10 ribs, solitary or in small clumps. Spines slightly up-curved, rigid; 1 central and 9–11 shorter radial spines. Flrs. to 2¾" Diam. Fruit egg-shaped, about 1¼" long, with interlocking spines until mature, edible and fleshy. May–June.

CLARETCUP HEDGEHOG CACTUS, *Echinocereus triglochidiatus* var. *melanacanthus.* Cactus Family. SN Rims and Can., sandy or rocky places above 4000'. Stems unbranched, melon-shaped, to 6" tall and 3¼" Diam., with 5–8 ribs and dense spines; up to 50 stems per clump. Spines straight, stiff; 1–4 central, to 3" long; 5–20 radial, shorter. Flrs. about 1¼" Diam. Fruit nearly cylindrical, edible and fleshy, more or less spiny, to 1¼" long. February–June.

Arizona Beehive Cactus

Cottontop Cactus

Engelmann Hedgehog Cactus

Fendler Hedgehog Cactus

Claretcup Hedgehog Cactus

Plate 27

CALIFORNIA BARREL CACTUS, *Ferocactus cylindraceus.* Cactus Famiy. Com., Lower Can. and Gorge, Scrub. Stems 1–3, unbranched, columnar, 1–3' tall and to 16" Diam., with 20–30 ribs. Central spines 4, more or less flexible and twisted, the lower one often curved downward, 2–3" long; 15–25 radial spines. Flrs. to nearly 2½" Diam. Fruit globular, about 1" Diam., fleshy, scaly. April–May.

FISHHOOK CACTUS, *Mammillaria tetrancistra.* Cactus Family. Gorge. Stems unbranched, oblong, 4–10" tall, 2–3" Diam., with nipplelike bumps; solitary or sometimes clumped. Central spine 1, hooked; at least some curved radial spines straight, slender, about ½" Diam. Flrs. about 1" Diam., often forming a wreath at crown of stem. Fruit smooth, to 1" long and ½" Diam. Seeds black with a distinct brown, corky base. *Mammillaria microcarpa* is at least as Com. in Gorge.

BEAVERTAIL CACTUS, *Opuntia basilaris.* Cactus Family. Com., Gorge and Tonto Platform, Scrub and rocky places. Stems low and spreading, jointed, branched at joints. Pads flattened, about 3–6" long, 2–5" wide, spineless, but with tufts of glochids in areoles. Flrs. 2–3" Diam. Fruit about 1¼" long, egg-shaped, dry and spineless. March–May.

PANCAKE PEAR, *Opuntia chlorotica.* Cactus Family. Rocky walls and ledges, 2000–6000'. Treelike, 3–8' tall, with stout trunk and ascending, jointed branches. Joints or pads flattened, round to broadly egg-shaped, 4–8" Diam. Areoles prominent, bristled and tufted with 3–7 main spines and 15–40 spinelets. Main spines to 1½" long, turned downward. Flrs. to 2½" Diam. Fruit fleshy, nearly globular, to 2" long and 1½" Diam., not spiny. April–June.

GRIZZLY BEAR CACTUS, *Opuntia erinacea.* Cactus Family. Com., SN Rims, especially Tonto Platform and Esplanade, Wood. and Scrub. Stems clumped, to about 6" tall, with 2–4 erect or ascending jointed branches. Joints or pads flattened, round, or oval, to 4" long, densely spiny. Spines 5–8 per areole, longest 1–4", flexible, straight or curved. Flrs. to 2½" Diam., clustered at tip of older stems, pink, magenta, or yellow. Fruit dry, spiny, melon-shaped, to 1¼" long. May–June.

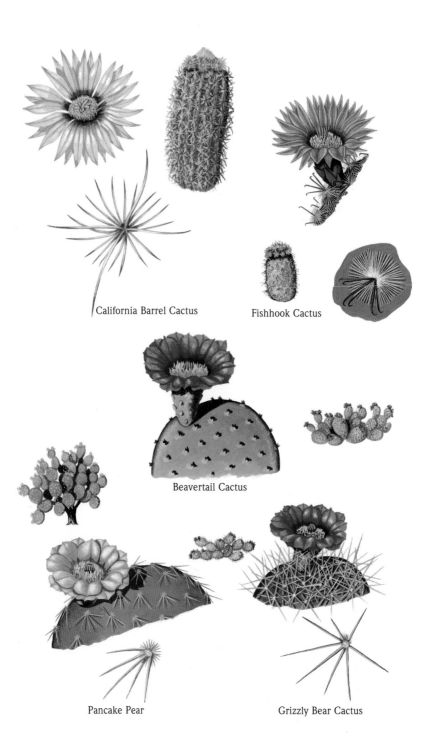

California Barrel Cactus

Fishhook Cactus

Beavertail Cactus

Pancake Pear

Grizzly Bear Cactus

Plate 28

DESERT PRICKLY PEAR, *Opuntia phaeacantha.* Cactus Family. SN Rims and Can., mostly on Esplanade and below, Scrub. Large, spreading cactus with branches of 10 or more joints forming clumps 2–10' Diam. Without a central trunk but growing 2–3 joints high. Joints or pads flattened, egg-shaped, to 10" long, often on edge along the ground. Spines 1–2" long, usually 3 per areole, missing from lower part of pads. Flrs. to 3¼" Diam., sometimes red or pink. Fruit edible, fleshy, spineless, egg- or club-shaped, to 2" long. April–June.

PLAINS PRICKLY PEAR, *Opuntia polyacantha.* Cactus Family. Wood. and pine For. Low, spreading cactus forming mats to 12" high and 12" Diam. Joints or pads flattened, oval, to 4" long. Spines to 3" long, 3–10 per areole, mostly curved downward. Flrs. 2–3 Diam., sometimes magenta. Fruit dry, spiny, about ¾" long. May–July.

WHIPPLE CHOLLA, *Opuntia whipplei.* Cactus Family. Can. Usually mat-forming, to 18" high. Stems jointed, cylindrical, 3–6" long, to ¾" Diam., covered with nipplelike bumps. Spines 7–14, to 1" long, sheathed. Flrs. about 1" Diam. Fruit fleshy, spineless, bumpy, to 1¼" long. June–July.

SIMPSON'S HEDGEHOG CACTUS, *Pediocactus simpsonii.* Cactus Family. Rare, Wood. and For. above 6000'. Stems solitary or few-clumped, unbranched, nearly spherical, 1–8" Diam., with nipplelike bumps. Spines straight and spreading, to ¾" long; 5–8 or more central spines; 15–30 radial spines, shorter. Flrs. sometimes yellow. Fruit dry, smooth, spineless. May–July.

PINEAPPLE CACTUS, *Sclerocactus parviflorus.* Cactus Family. Can., 5000–6000', especially on the Esplanade. Stems usually solitary, but sometimes branching to simulate small clusters, barrel-shaped, to 7" tall, and 3" Diam., with 13–15 ribs crowned with nipplelike bumps. Central spines usually 4, at least one hooked, surrounded by 8–10 radial spines. Flrs. to 2" Diam., greenish yellow to purple or lavender. Fruit to ⁹⁄₁₆" long, scaly with tiny hairs.

Desert Prickly Pear

Plains Prickly Pear

Whipple Cholla

Simpson's Hedgehog Cactus

Pineapple Cactus

Trees and Shrubs

Trees and shrubs are plants with persistent woody stems. About 200 species occur at the Grand Canyon, of which roughly 10 percent are conifers. Trees dominate the woodlands and forests of higher elevations. Shrubs dominate the desert areas of the South Rim and canyon proper. Many plants grow either as trees or shrubs, depending on local conditions. The most important trees and shrubs in each plant community are listed in Table 4. The following plates depict 84 of the more common and conspicuous trees and shrubs at the Grand Canyon.

Unlike herbaceous plants, which tend to catch our attention only when they are in bloom, trees and shrubs are conspicuous whether flowers are present or not. For this reason, woody plants are grouped here according to leaf characteristics, rather than flower color. Within each section, species are grouped by family. Terms used in species descriptions are defined and illustrated in Figures 21, 22, 23, 24, and 25. Readers should take special care to become thoroughly familiar with leaf characteristics.

Plate 29

Leaves Needlelike

WHITE FIR, *Abies concolor.* Pine Family. Com., N Rim, Tran. and Bor.; local, S Rim, just below rim. Tree to 100'. Lvs. 2-sided, 1½–3" long. Cones to 5½" long, erect on upper branches.

CORKBARK FIR, *Abies lasiocarpa,* var. *arizonica.* Pine Family. Com., N Rim, Bor. Tree to 90'. Lvs. similar to those of White Fir. Bark with numerous resin blisters. Cone 2–4" long, erect on upper branches. Branches horizontal or drooping, foliage often extending to the ground.

ENGELMANN SPRUCE, *Picea engelmannii.* Pine Family. Com., N Rim, Bor. Tree to 100'. Lvs. 4-sided, stiff, pointed but not sharply so, to 1" long. Cones 1" long, with thin, papery scales without prickles. Branches often touch ground. Stems of young trees have minute hairs.

BLUE SPRUCE, *Picea pungens.* Pine Family. Rare, N Rim, Bor. Tree to 70' or more. Similar to above, but needles are sharply pointed, bark is more furrowed, cones are larger (to 4" long), and stems of young trees are hairless.

DOUGLAS-FIR, *Pseudotsuga menziesii.* Pine Family. Com., N Rim, Tran. and Bor.; local, S Rim, just below rim. Tree to 80'. Stems look like bottle brushes. Lvs. ³⁄₄–1½" long, 2-sided, twisted at base. Cones usually 2–3" long, hanging rather than upright, with 3-pronged bracts protruding from between the scales.

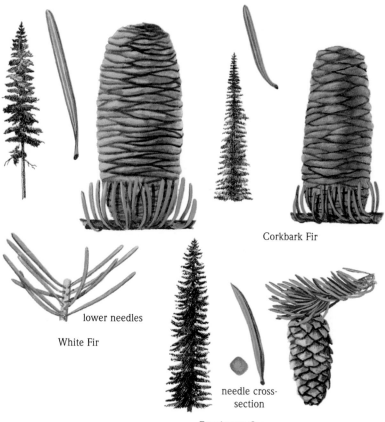

Corkbark Fir

lower needles

White Fir

needle cross-section

Engelmann Spruce

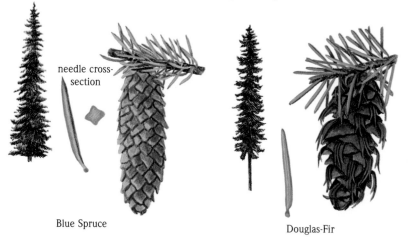

needle cross-section

Blue Spruce

Douglas-Fir

Plate 30

Leaves Needlelike, Awl-shaped or Scalelike

PONDEROSA PINE, *Pinus ponderosa.* Pine Family. Com., SN Rims, Tran. Tree to 100' or more, with open crown of huge, bent branches. Lvs. 5–11" long, in bundles of 3. Cones to 5½" long, armed with out-turned prickles. Bark of mature trees reddish to golden, divided into large vertical plates; bark of young trees black and furrowed.

COLORADO PINYON, *Pinus edulis.* Pine Family. Com., SN Rims and Can., U Son. and Tran., 4000–7000'. Tree to 45', sometimes shrubby. Lvs. to 2" long, in bundles of 2. Cones 2–5" long, with edible seeds. Bark reddish, not plated. Crown usually rounded. Singleleaf Pinyon, *P. monophylla,* similar but needles mostly single and cones somewhat larger. Rare and local in eastern Grand Canyon, but replaces *P. edulis* west of Shivwits Plateau. Where their ranges overlap, these two latter species hybridize.

COMMON JUNIPER, *Juniperus communis.* Juniper Family. Com., N Rim, Bor., For. Sprawling or prostrate shrub forming clumps less than 3' high. Lvs. to 1" long, awl-shaped rather than scalelike as in other local junipers. Cones berrylike, about ¼" Diam.

UTAH JUNIPER, *Juniperus osteosperma.* Juniper Family. Com., SN Rims and Can., 4500–7500', U Son. and Tran., Wood. and For. Tree to 20', often shrubby but usually with a single trunk. Lvs. scalelike, tightly pressed to stems in alternately opposite pairs, margins entire. Cones berrylike, less than ¼" Diam. Fruit 1- to 2-seeded, mealy, blue with whitish bloom, turning reddish brown with age. One-Seed Juniper, *J. monosperma,* similar but fruit smaller, fleshy, turning coppery with age. Rocky Mountain Juniper, *J. scopulorum,* similar to above, but Lvs. smaller with glandular pit; branches smaller and often drooping; confined to the extremities of N Rim promontories.

SALT-CEDAR, TAMARISK, *Tamarix chinensis.* Tamarisk Family. Com., Ripar. Wood. along Colorado River; rare and local, S Rim. Shrub or small tree: Ht. 16'. Lvs. scalelike, less than ⅛" long, densely clustered along stem. Foliage appears feathery. Branches somewhat drooping. Branchlets deciduous in Win. Flrs. tiny, densely clustered in showy terminal spikes. March–August.

Colorado Pinyon

Ponderosa Pine

Singleleaf
Pinyon

leaf arrangement

Common Juniper

single flower

leaf arrangements

Utah Juniper

Salt-Cedar, Tamarisk

Plate 31

Leaves Simple, Alternate and Lobed

GAMBEL OAK, *Quercus gambelii.* Beech Family. Com., SN Rims, Tran., pine For.; also Can. Shrub or small tree to 30', often forming thickets. Lvs. deciduous, variable, to 6" long, though normally shorter on S Rim, oblong, with deep, rounded lobes, smooth above, more or less downy below. Male and female Flrs. in separate catkins on same plant. Acorns about 1" long, with cup enclosing half or more of nut. May. Cf. Gray Oak, Plate 36.

WAX CURRANT, *Ribes cereum.* Saxifrage Family. Com., SN Rims and Can., U Son. through Bor., Wood. and For. Shrub to 6'. Stems spineless. Lvs. deciduous, usually less than 2" Diam., with shallow lobes. Berries red. April–June. Sticky currant, *R. viscosissimum,* is similar but Lvs. more than 2" Diam., with deep lobes, and black berries. Gooseberry Currant, *R. montigenum,* has 3 straight spines at each stem node, bristly purplish Flrs., and bristly berries that are easily removed from stems. Whitestem Gooseberry, *R. inerme,* similar to *R. montigenum,* but Flrs. white or pink and berries difficult to remove. Desert Gooseberry, *R. velutinum,* has yellow berries, and Trumpet Gooseberry, *R. leptanthum,* has black berries.

CLIFFROSE, *Purshia mexicana.* Rose Family. Com., SN Rims and Can., U Son. and Tran., Wood., pine For., and rocky places. Large shrub or small tree to 25'. Lvs. hairless, to ½" long. Flrs. showy, about ½" Diam. Fruit an achene with a white, feathery tail. April–September.

APACHE PLUME, *Fallugia paradoxa.* Rose Family. Com., SN Rims and Can., U Son. and Tran., 3500–8000', dry washes and open places. Shrub to 5', with numerous basal stems. Lvs. hairy, to ½" long. Fruit similar, but with a purple, feathery tail. April–October.

CANYON GRAPE, *Vitis arizonica.* Grape Family. Com., Can., Ripar., in side canyons and near seeps and springs. Vine, sometimes bushy. Stems woolly when young, with shredded bark when mature. Lvs. deciduous, to 3" long, with a tendril opposite each leaf. Flrs. in panicles to 2" long. Grapes black at maturity, edible but tart. April–July.

autumn

Wax Currant   fruit

Gambel Oak   flower   fruit

Cliffrose

fruit

Apache Plume   fruit   flower   Canyon Grape

Plate 32

Leaves Simple, Alternate and Entire

ARROYO WILLOW, *Salix lasiolepis.* Willow Family. Can., Ripar. and most places in arroyos on SN Rims. Usually a shrub, sometimes a small tree to 30'. Lvs. deciduous, to 4" long, entire or nearly so, dark and smooth above, pale and smooth or downy or with whitish bloom below. Male and female Flrs. in erect catkins less than 1" long. February–April. Bebb Willow, *S. bebbiana,* mostly on N Rim, with Lvs. hairy on both sides. Scouler Willow, *S. scouleriana,* similar to Arroyo Willow, but Lvs. broadest toward tip and catkins more than 1" long. Coyote Willow, *S. exigua,* the most Com. species along the river, has entirely smooth, narrow, entire Lvs. Red Willow and Goodding Willow have entirely smooth, toothed Lvs., Cf. Plate 35.

FOUR-WING SALTBUSH, *Atriplex canescens.* Goosefoot Family. S Rim and Can., Scrub, often in saline habitats. Shrub to 2'. Lvs. thick, usually stemless, to 2" long. Flrs. tiny, in leafy spikes or panicles. Fruit a 4-winged achene. April–August.

WINTER FAT, *Krascheninnikovia lanata.* Goosefoot Family. Uncom., S Rim and Can., Scrub, L and U Son. Shrub to 3'. Lvs. and leaf stems densely woolly. Lvs. linear, to 2" long, sometimes in bundles. Flrs. mostly in male and female spikes on separate plants. Seed heads cottony. April–October.

LITTLELEAF MOUNTAIN MAHOGANY, *Cercocarpus intricatus.* Rose Family. Com., SN Rims and just below, rock crevices. Intricately branched shrub to 5'. Lvs. to ½" long with strongly rolled margins. Flrs. tiny, profuse. Fruit an achene with a feathery tail to nearly 3" long. March–April. The less common Curlleaf Mountain Mahogany, *C. ledifolius,* a pine forest shrub, has broader, less tightly rolled Lvs. that are woolly below. True Mountain Mahogany, *C. montanus,* Cf. Plate 36, has flat, partly toothed Lvs.

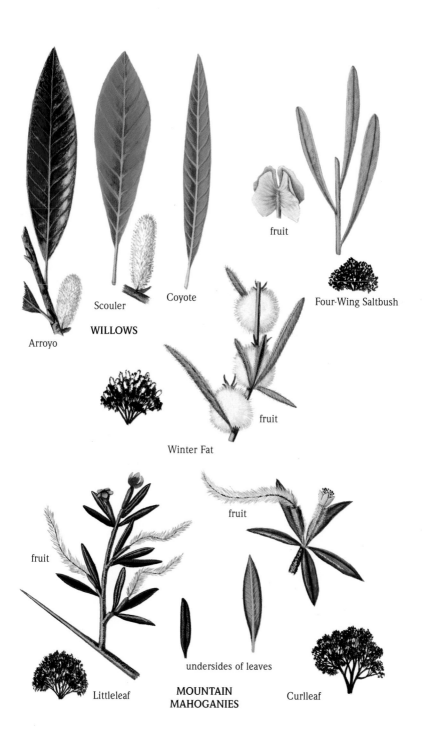

fruit

Four-Wing Saltbush

WILLOWS

Scouler

Coyote

Arroyo

fruit

Winter Fat

fruit

fruit

undersides of leaves

Littleleaf

MOUNTAIN MAHOGANIES

Curlleaf

Plate 33

Leaves Simple, Alternate and Entire

WESTERN REDBUD, *Cercis orbiculata.* Legume Family. Com., Can., Ripar, also near seeps and springs. Shrub or tree to 12'. Lvs. deciduous, glossy, to nearly 4" Diam. Flrs. showy, Irreg., to ½" long, appearing before the Lvs. Seeds in pealike pods persisting through Win. March–May.

GREASEBUSH, *Glossopetalon spinescens* var. *arridum.* Bittersweet Family. Wood. below SN Rims. Shrub to 6½'. Stems spiny. Lvs. to ½" long. Flrs. to ⅛" long. March–June.

BUCKBRUSH, *Ceanothus fendleri.* Buckthorn Family. SN Rims and upper elevations of Can., Wood. and pine For. Shrub to 3', often forming thickets. Branches spiny. Lvs. downy and whitish below, nearly smooth above, ½–1" long. Flrs. about ½" long, in dense racemes. Fruit a small capsule. April–November. Desert Ceanothus, *C. greggii,* has thicker, opposite Lvs. Martin Ceanothus, *C. martini,* lacks spines and is found only on N Rim.

ROUNDLEAF BUFFALO BERRY, *Shepherdia rotundifolia.* Oleaster Family. Com., Can., rocky points on SN Rims. Evergreen shrub to 3'. Young twigs scaly. Lvs. to 1" long, thick, cupped downward, scaly, woolly below. Flrs. tiny, petalless, but with scaly, petallike calyx. Fruit berrylike, sweet and watery, with pale yellow juice when ripe. March–June.

GREENLEAF MANZANITA, *Arctostaphylos patula.* Heath Family. N Rim, Tran. and Bor., For.; also Can. Shrub to 6'. Bark shiny, with peeling or shredding strips. Lvs. to 1½" long and wide, often held vertically. Flrs. urn-shaped, nodding, in panicles with sticky-downy branches. Fruit berrylike. May–June. The similar Pointleaf Manzanita, *A. pungens,* is equally Com. on S Rim, but not very common in areas of greatest visitation.

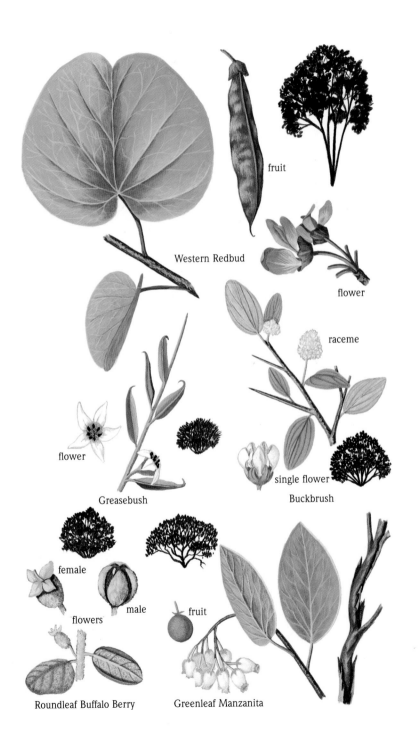

Western Redbud

fruit

flower

raceme

flower

Greasebush

single flower

Buckbrush

female

male

flowers

fruit

Roundleaf Buffalo Berry

Greenleaf Manzanita

Plate 34

Leaves Simple, Alternate and Entire

DESERT THORN, PALE WOLFBERRY, *Lycium pallidum.* Nightshade Family. S Rim and Can., Scrub and Wood., U Son. Shrub to 6'. Branches spiny, sometimes downy. Lvs. to 1½" long. Flrs. to nearly 1" long. Fruits resemble small cherry tomatoes, edible but bitter. April–June. Torrey Wolfberry, *L. torreyi,* and Anderson Desert Thorn, *L. andersonii,* the Com. species of the Gorge, are similar, but have yellow Flrs. with lavender lobes.

RUBBER RABBITBRUSH, *Ericameria nauseosa.* Aster Family. Com., SN Rims and Can., open places below 8000'; along river only in Marble Canyon. Shrub usually to 7', often forming thickets. Twigs densely covered with feltlike hairs. Bark sometimes shredded. Lvs. smooth to woolly, to 2¾" long, aromatic, soon deciduous. Flrs. composite, in densely clustered heads, each about ¼" Diam. July–October. Parry Rabbitbrush, *C. parryi* var. *nevadensis,* is very similar, but has Flr. heads in leafy terminal racemes. Green's Rabbitbrush, *Chrysothamnus greenei,* and Douglas' Rabbitbrush, *C. viscidiflorus,* are very similar white-barked shrubs with persistent dark green Lvs.

BRITTLEBUSH, *Encelia farinosa.* Aster Family. Com., Gorge, Scrub, and rocky places. Rounded shrub to 3'. Lvs. to 3", occasionally toothed, densely silver-haired, often deciduous in dry periods. Flrs. composite, with 1" heads in panicles rising above the Lvs. March–June. Bush Encelia, *E. frutescens,* has solitary heads and hairy flower stalks.

TRIXIS, *Trixis californica.* Aster Family. Com., Can., rocky places below 5000', especially Gorge. Shrub to about 3'. Lvs. to 2", sometimes toothed, margins slightly rolled under. Flrs. composite, 9–14 per head, 2-petaled. April–June.

ARROWWEED, *Pluchea servicea.* Aster Family. Gorge, along river and side streams, especially on sand dunes. Willowlike shrub to 16'. Lvs. to 2" long, silky-haired. Flrs. composite with heads in terminal clusters. March–July.

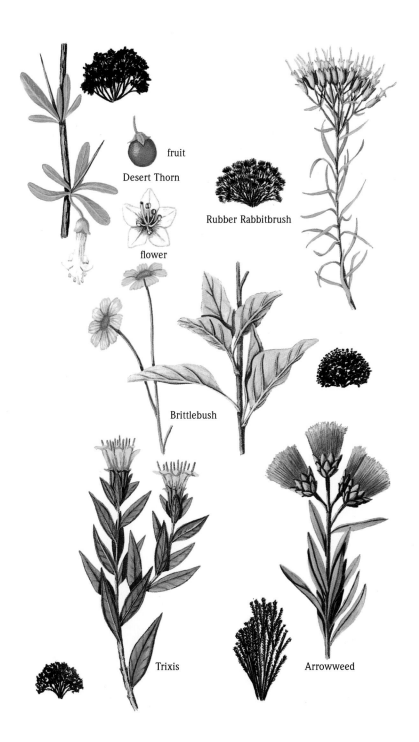

fruit

Desert Thorn

flower

Rubber Rabbitbrush

Brittlebush

Trixis

Arrowweed

Plate 35

Leaves Simple and Alternate, with Toothed or Scalloped Margins

FREMONT COTTONWOOD, *Populus fremontii.* Willow Family. Com., Can., Ripar., along permanent or seasonal tributary streams, but rarely the river. Tree to 50'. Trunk unbranched for half its length or more, branches large and spreading. Bark deeply furrowed on old trees. Lvs. deciduous, to 3" long. Flrs. in drooping male and female catkins. March–May.

QUAKING ASPEN, *Populus tremuloides.* Willow Family. Com., mostly N Rim, Bor.; For. and Grass. margins; rare and local on S Rim. Tree to 40'. Bark white with black stretch marks and warty patches, becoming dark gray and furrowed at base on older trees. Lvs. deciduous, to 2" long, sometimes nearly entire, with flat, twisted stems, causing Lvs. to quake or tremble in the slightest breeze.

RED WILLOW, *Salix laevigata.* Willow Family. Com., mostly Can., Ripar. below 7000'. Tree to near 40'. Bark rough, twigs smooth, yellowish brown or reddish brown. Lvs. deciduous, to 5" long, so finely toothed as to sometimes seem entire, with whitish bloom below. Flrs. in erect male and female catkins that appear with Lvs. Goodding Willow, *S. gooddingii,* is similar, but Lvs. with glandular margins and without whitish bloom below. Cf. willows, Plate 32.

WATER BIRCH, *Betula occidentalis.* Birch Family. Uncom., N Rim, near Bright Angel Spring and Roaring Springs, and in Big Spring Canyon. Shrub or tree to 30'. Lvs. deciduous, to 1½" long. Flrs. in drooping male and upright female catkins. Fruit woody and conelike. June.

KNOWLTON HOP-HORNBEAM, *Ostrya knowltoni.* Birch Family. Com., Can., U Son., along trails. Shrub or tree to 25'. Lvs. deciduous, to 2" long, finely haired below. Flrs. in drooping male and upturned female catkins. Fruit a papery sack containing a single nut. March–April.

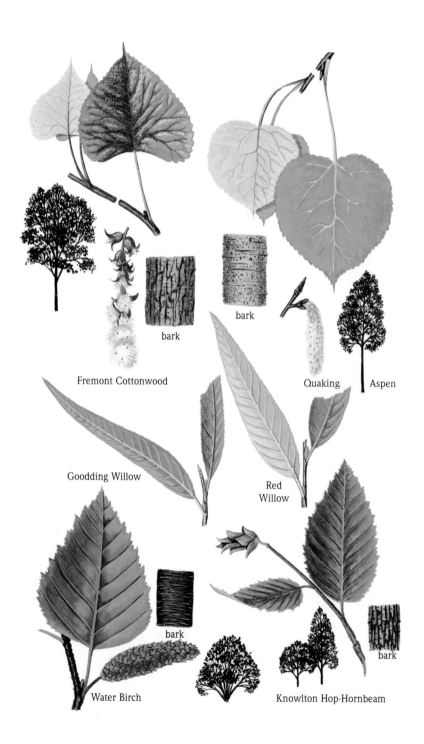

Fremont Cottonwood

Quaking   Aspen

Goodding Willow

Red
Willow

bark

bark

bark

bark

Water Birch

Knowlton Hop-Hornbeam

Plate 36

Leaves Simple and Alternate, with Toothed or Scalloped Margins

GRAY OAK, *Quercus grisea.* Beech Family. Uncom., Can., mostly in side canyons, Scrub and Wood. Tree to 60'. Lvs. entire or partly toothed, finely haired below. Male Flrs. in drooping catkins; female Flrs. in clusters in leaf axils. Acorns to $^3/_4$" long. The more common Shrub Live Oak, *Q. turbinella,* always shrubby and with hollylike Lvs., is dominant on the Esplanade and the rims of the western Grand Canyon. Wavyleaf Oak, *Q. undulata,* a 6' shrub, has wavy toothed Lvs. and is confined to the Can., mostly north of the river and west of Bright Angel Canyon; especially common in the Esplanade Woodland.

NETLEAF HACKBERRY, *Celtis laevigata* var. *reticulata.* Elm Family. Com., S Rim and Can., Ripar. Shrub or tree to 30'. Lvs. deciduous, to $2^1/_2$" long, rough above. Older bark warty. Flrs. small, hairy, solitary or in small clusters. Fruit berrylike, pea-sized, edible but astringent. March–October.

UTAH SERVICEBERRY, *Amelanchier utahensis.* Rose Family. Com., SN Rims and Wood. below rims. Shrub or tree to 15'. Twigs and buds usually downy. Lvs. to $1^1/_4$" long, entire toward base. Flrs. in racemes about 1" long, appearing in Spr. before Lvs., fragrant. Fruit blueberrylike, slightly sweet and edible. April–August.

TRUE MOUNTAIN MAHOGANY, *Cercocarpus montanus.* Rose Family. SN Rims and Can., Wood. and For. Shrub to 10'. Lvs. flat, margins not rolled under, to 1" long or more, more or less hairy on both sides. Cf. Littleleaf Mountain Mahogany, Plate 32.

156 SHRUBBY CREAMBUSH, *Holodiscus dumosus.* Rose Family. Uncom., SN Rims, Wood. and For. Shrub to 10'. Lvs. to 2" long, velvety below. Bark on older branches red, later gray and peeling in thin strips. Flrs. clustered in feathery, terminal racemes or panicles. May–September.

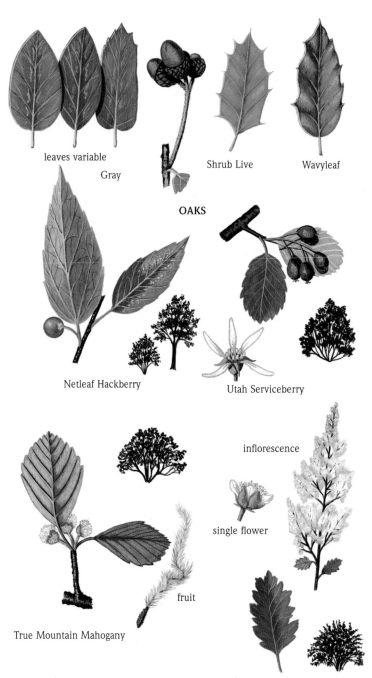

leaves variable

Gray

Shrub Live

Wavyleaf

OAKS

Netleaf Hackberry

Utah Serviceberry

inflorescence

single flower

True Mountain Mahogany

fruit

Shrubby Creambush

Plate 37

Leaves Simple and Alternate, with Toothed or Scalloped Margins

CHOKECHERRY, *Prunus virginiana.* Rose Family. N Rim, For. Shrub or tree to 15' or more. Lvs. to 4" long. Flrs. about ½" Diam., in racemes to 4" long. Fruit very bitter. April–June. Desert Almond, *P. fasciculata,* is a spiny shrub of the Gorge.

BIRCHLEAF BUCKTHORN, *Frangula betulaefolia.* Buckthorn Family. SN Rims and Can., Ripar. and other damp places, U Son. and Tran. Shrub to 8'. Lvs. to 5" long. Flrs. tiny. Fruit a 3-seeded, berrylike drupe, bitter but edible.

BIG SAGEBRUSH, *Artemisia tridentata.* Aster Family. Com., SN Rims and Can. above 5000', Scrub, Wood., and pine For. Shrub to 4', rarely more. Lvs. mostly 3-toothed at tip, to 1½" long, silver-hairy, aromatic. Flrs. small, composite, heads in panicles. July–September. Black Sagebrush, *A. arbuscula subspecies nova,* and Bigelow Sagebrush, *A. bigelovii,* are much smaller shrubs (to 16") with silver-hairy twigs.

SEEP-WILLOW, *Baccharis salicifolia.* Aster Family. Com., Can., Ripar. Shrub to 10' or more, often forming thickets along river. Lvs. to 3½" long, slightly sticky, 3-veined. Flrs. composite, heads clustered in compact terminal panicles. Fruits fuzzy tufts of silky-haired achenes. February–May.

DESERT BRICKELLBUSH, *Brickellia atactyoides.* Aster Family. Uncom., Can., mostly rocky places of Gorge. Shrub to 12", intricately branched, with shredding bark. Lvs. stiff, to ⅝" long. Flrs. tiny, composite, about 50 in heads about ½" Diam. One of 8 *Brickellia* species in canyon.

fruit

flower

Chokecherry

Birchleaf Buckthorn

fruit

flower

flower

Big Sagebrush

flower

Seep-Willow

Desert Brickellbush

Plate 38

Leaves Simple and Opposite

FENDLER BUSH, *Fendlera rupicola.* Saxifrage Family. Uncom., SN Rims; Com., Can. above Gorge, Scrub and Wood. Shrub to 9'. Stems smooth to downy, becoming gray with shredding bark. Lvs. to 1½" long, smooth or stiff-hair on both sides, margins sometimes rolled under. Flrs. showy, about 1" Diam. Fruit a 3-parted, persistent woody capsule. March–June.

FENDLERELLA, *Fendlerella utahensis.* Saxifrage Family. SN Rims and Can., U Son. and Tran., mostly open Wood. Shrub to 40". Twigs covered with stiff hairs. Lvs. numerous, sometimes bundled, to ⅝" long, 3-veined. Flrs. tiny, in sparse clusters at ends of branches, 5 petals. June–September.

MOCK ORANGE, *Philadelphus microphyllus.* Saxifrage Family. SN Rims and Can., dry rocky slopes. Shrub to 7'. Bark reddish brown or tan, peeling. Lvs. about 1" long, downy below. Flrs. fragrant, about 1" across, 4 petals. May–August.

BIGTOOTH MAPLE, *Acer grandidentatum.* Maple Family. Moist, shady places just below rims, especially N Rim. Shrub or tree to 30'. Lvs. deciduous, to 4" long, with a few blunt teeth on margins. Flrs. inconspicuous. Fruit a winged samara. April. Cf. Boxelder, Plate 41.

ROCKY MOUNTAIN MAPLE, *Acer glabrum.* Maple Family. Uncom., N Rim, sunny places in For. Shrub or tree to 30'. Lvs. deciduous, to 3" long and wide, 3- to 5-lobed, with numerous sharp teeth. Fruit a winged samara. May. Cf. Boxelder, Plate 41.

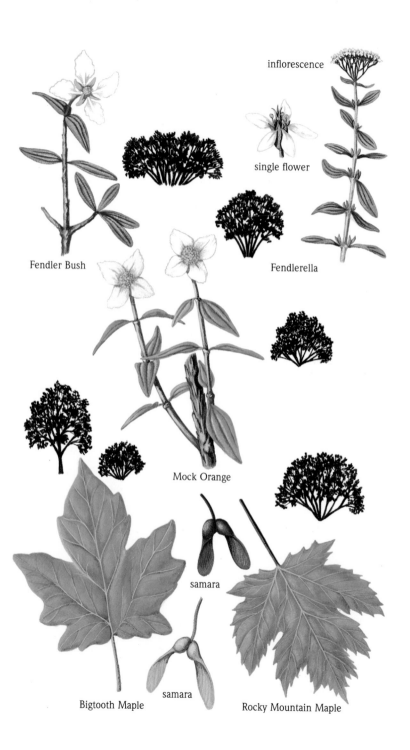

inflorescence

single flower

Fendler Bush

Fendlerella

Mock Orange

samara

samara

Bigtooth Maple

Rocky Mountain Maple

Plate 39

Leaves Simple and Opposite

BLACKBRUSH, *Coleogyne ramosissima.* Rose Family. Com., Can., Scrub, forming nearly pure stands on Tonto Platform. Shrub to 6'. Branches tangled, often spine-tipped. Lvs. to ½", with rolled margins, in bundles. Flrs. ½" Diam., solitary, with petallike sepals. March–May.

YELLOWLEAF SILKTASSEL, *Garrya flavescens.* Dogwood Family. Can., Wood., dry, rocky places. Shrub to 12'. Lvs. entire, to 2½" long. Male and female catkins on separate plants. Fruit berrylike, about ½" long, in long, drooping clusters. Lvs., Flr. bracts, and fruit covered with silky hairs. January–April. Wright Silktassel, *G. wrightii,* lacks hairs on fruit and mature Lvs.

SINGLELEAF ASH, *Fraxinus anomala.* Olive Family. SN Rims and Can., U Son. and lower Tran. Shrub or tree to 26'. Lvs. simple or sometimes compound with 3 or more leaflets, entire or scalloped, to 2" long. Flrs. inconspicuous, in panicles. Fruit a winged achene.

DESERT-WILLOW, *Chilopsis linearis.* Bignonia Family. Uncom., Can., Ripar. below 5000'. Shrub or tree to 30'. Alternate and opposite Lvs. on same plant, latter toward base, former above. Lvs. deciduous, entire, to about 5" long. Flrs. about 1" long, showy, in racemes at ends of leafy branches. Fruit a podlike capsule to 10" long. April–August.

LONGFLOWER SNOWBERRY, *Symphoricarpos longiflorus.* Honeysuckle Family. SN Rims and upper elevations of Can., Wood. and For. Shrub to 4'. Lvs. lance-shaped to elliptical, entire, smooth or sparsely downy. Flrs. tubular, to ½" long or more, single or in pairs in upper leaf axils. Older stems gray and shredding; younger stems brown. Fruit white, waxy, berrylike. May–June. Mountain Snowberry, *S. oreophilus,* is similar, but Lvs. broader, sometimes toothed, and older stems brown. Roundleaf Snowberry, *S. rotundifolius,* has nearly round, downy Lvs. and downy young stems.

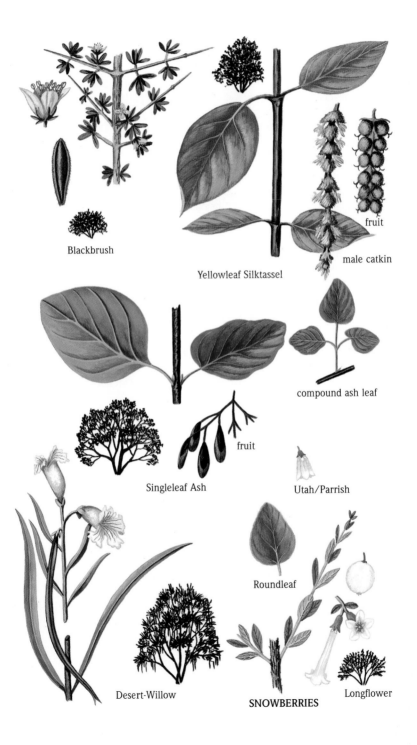

Blackbrush

Yellowleaf Silktassel

fruit

male catkin

compound ash leaf

fruit

Singleleaf Ash

Utah/Parrish

Roundleaf

Desert-Willow

SNOWBERRIES

Longflower

Plate 40

Leaves Compound

ARIZONA WALNUT, *Juglans major.* Walnut Family. Uncom., Havasu Canyon, Ripar. Tree to 50'. Lvs. alternate, pinnate, to 12" long, with 9–13 leaflets, each toothed and to 4" long. Male Flrs. in drooping catkins; female Flrs. solitary or few in a cluster. Nuts about 1" Diam.

CREEPING BARBERRY, *Mahonia repens.* Barberry Family. Com., N Rim, For., mostly above 5000'; Uncom., S Rim. Prostrate shrub to 6" high, with creeping stems. Stems root where they touch the ground. Lvs. pinnate, with 3–7 hollylike leaflets to ¾" long. Flrs. tiny, clustered. April–June. Desert Barberry, *B. fremontii,* an erect shrub to 9', with dry, blue berries, is Com. in shady places in Can.

FERN BUSH, *Chamaebatiaria millefolium.* Rose Family. Com., SN Rims and Can., Wood., Scrub, and For., 4500–8000'. Shrub to 6'. Lvs. fernlike, aromatic, sticky-hairy. Flrs. to ½" Diam., in dense panicles at branch ends. August–September.

CATCLAW ACACIA, *Acacia greggii.* Legume Family. Com., Can., L and U Son., Ripar. Shrub or tree to 20', often forming thickets along river, streams, and dry washes. Branches with curved spines ("catclaws"). Lvs. bipinnate, with numerous tiny leaflets. Young twigs and leaflet stems are minutely hairy. Flrs. tiny, in fluffy spikes to 1½" long. Pods flat and twisted, to 5" long. April–October. Cf. Mesquite, below.

HONEY MESQUITE, *Prosopis glandulosa.* Legume Family. Com., Gorge and side canyons at or just upstream from Gorge, Ripar. and sandy bottoms. Shrub to 20'. Branches with straight thorns in pairs at leaf axils. Lvs. bipinnate, 2-stemmed, with numerous slender leaflets, but longer than those of Catclaw Acacia. Young twigs and leaflet stems are smooth. Flrs. fragrant, tiny, in fluffy spikes to 3" long. Pods rounded and straight, to 6" long. April–August. Cf. Catclaw Acacia, above.

walnut

Creeping Barberry

fruit

Arizona Walnut

flower

Fern Bush

Catclaw Acacia

fruit

Honey Mesquite

fruit

Plate 41

Leaves Compound

NEW MEXICAN LOCUST, *Robinia neomexicana.* Legume Family. Com., N Rim, in thickets with Gambel Oak (see Plate 31); Uncom., S Rim and Can. Shrub or tree to 25'. Bark and twigs armed with thorns. Lvs. pinnate, leaflets entire, to $3/4$" long. Flrs. fragrant, about $3/4$" long. May–July.

PALE HOPTREE, *Ptelea trifoliata.* Rue Family. Com., SN Rims and Can., U Son. Large shrub or small tree to 20'. Branches and Lvs. unpleasantly pungent. Lvs. with 3 leaflets, each thick, firm, downy or with a whitish bloom below, smooth above. Terminal leafletseldom 3 times longer than wide. Bark of twigs straw- to olive-colored. Flrs. about $1/2$" Diam. April–June. Narrowleaf Hoptree, *P. angustifolia,* is similar, but bark of twigs is dark brown or purple.

SQUAW BUSH, *Rhus trilobata.* Sumac Family. Com., S Rim and Can., brushy and rocky areas below 7500'. Shrub to 7'. Lvs. of plants on rim have 3 leaflets, each to 1" long and 3-lobed with scalloped margins. Can. plants have only one leaflet per leaf. Flrs. tiny, in spikelike clusters appearing before Lvs. Fruit sticky-hairy. Plant ill-smelling. April.

BOXELDER, *Acer negundo.* Maple Family. Uncom., mostly N Rim, also S Rim and Can., Tran. For., moist sunny places. Tree to 60'. Lvs. with 3 leaflets, each to 4" long, entire, coarsely toothed or 3-lobed. Twigs downy when young, later smooth. Flrs. either male or female, on separate trees. Fruit a 2-winged samara. April.

166   CREOSOTEBUSH, *Larrea tridentata.* Caltrop Family. Com., Gorge, Scrub below 5000', and west of Havasu Canyon. Shrub to 8'. Lvs. evergreen, strong-scented, with 2 leaflets fused at the base and growing in opposite pairs. Flrs. to $1/2$" Diam., with petals twisted like the vanes of a windmill. April–May.

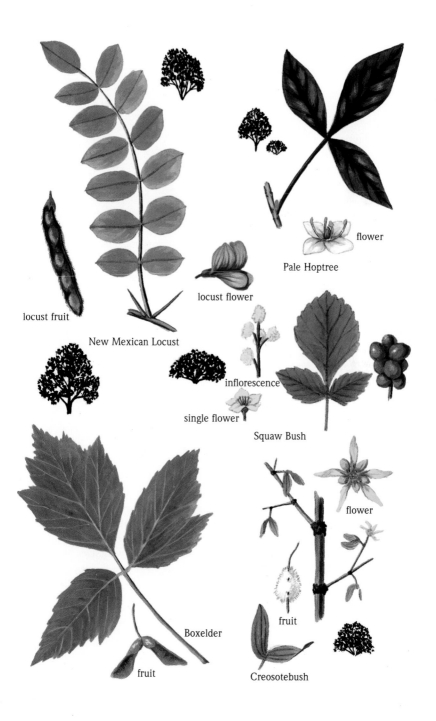

locust fruit

locust flower

New Mexican Locust

Pale Hoptree

flower

inflorescence

single flower

Squaw Bush

Boxelder

fruit

flower

fruit

Creosotebush

Plate 42

Leaves Basal, Inconspicuous or Absent

MORMON TEA, *Ephedra viridis*. Joint-fir Family. A conifer. Com., SN Rims and Can., Scrub and Wood. below 7000' to Tonto Platform. Shrub to 3'. Stems jointed, much branched to form broomlike clumps. Lvs. inconspicuous and scalelike, in opposing pairs at stem joints. Male cones have tiny Flrs. on stalks emerging from between scales. Female cones stemless, on different plants from male cones. In Gorge, *E. nevadensis* and *E. torreyana,* both very similar to the above, are the more common species.

BANANA YUCCA, *Yucca baccata.* Agave Family. Com., S Rim and Can. above Gorge, especially Tonto Platform, Wood. and Scrub; N Rim, only in dry places at canyon brink; along the river only in Marble Canyon. Shrub to 30" except when flowering, at which time the flowering stem may grow to 4'. Lvs. 16–30" long, about 2" wide, with coarse fibers along margins, forming rosette at base. Flr. stalk rises from among basal Lvs. and is often branched. Fruit fleshy and bananalike. April–May. Fineleaf Yucca, *Y. angustissima,* has much shorter, narrower Lvs. with finer fibers along the margins; a mostly unbranched Flr. stalk rising at or just above basal Lvs.; and erect, dry seed pods for fruit. Our Lord's Candle, *Y. whipplei,* found along the Colorado River in the western Grand Canyon, has long, narrow Lvs. with serrated rather than fibrous margins and a sharp terminal spine. Its Flrs., sometimes tinged purple, grow on a stalk to 12'.

CENTURY PLANT, *Agave utahensis*. Agave Family. Com., SN Rims and Can., Scrub, Wood., and pine For. Shrub with rigid, fleshy, daggerlike Lvs. to 15" long, with terminal spines to 2" long and shorter, curved marginal spines. Flrs. on stalk 3–14', in spike covering upper $2/3$ of stalk. Plants often clustered, each one blooming only once, usually after 15–25 years, thereafter dying. May–July.

TURPENTINE BROOM, *Thamnosma montana*. Rue Family. Uncom., Can. below Redwall, Scrub. Shrub to 24". Stems much-branched, broomlike, spine-tipped, glandular. Lvs. alternate, entire, about ½" long, succulent, glandular and soon deciduous. Most of the year plant is leafless. When crushed, it gives off a strong, pungent odor not unlike citrus or turpentine. Flrs. to ⅝" long. Fruit a glandular, fleshy, 2-lobed capsule. February–April.

OCOTILLO, *Fouquieria splendens*. Ocotillo Family. Com., Gorge, Scrub, from Havasu Canyon westward. Canelike shrub to 23'. Canes several to numerous, erect, usually leafless, mostly unbranched and crowded with thorns. Lvs. appear only for a short time following rains. They are alternate or in bundles, succulent, to 1" long. Flrs. to 1" long, in long terminal panicles. April–June.

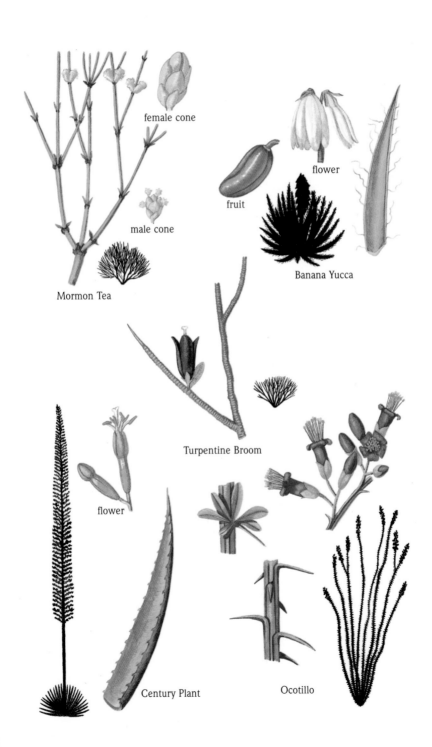

female cone

male cone

Mormon Tea

flower

fruit

Banana Yucca

Turpentine Broom

flower

Century Plant

Ocotillo

PART III

THE ANIMALS

6

Mammals

ammals are four-legged, fur-bearing animals that suckle their young. Like birds, their body temperature is regulated internally. Most mammals escape excessive daytime heat by seeking shelter in burrows, caves, rock crevices, tree cavities, and similar cool retreats. Protection from cold is provided by both body fat and the fur coat, or pelage, which consists of durable outer guard hairs and short, soft inner fur that provides insulation.

The young are born live and are thereafter nourished by milk secreted from the mother's mammary glands. The young of some species, notably rabbits, rodents, and most carnivores, are born naked, blind, and helpless. Those of jackrabbits (which are hares rather than true rabbits) and hoofed mammals, however, are fully active and alert shortly after birth.

Most mammals have acute senses of smell, hearing, and vision. Many species also possess sensitive facial whiskers that convey information through touch. Along with excellent night vision and a sharp sense of smell, these vibrissae, as they are called, are adaptations to nocturnal activity.

Many mammals are wholly or partly nocturnal and therefore are rarely seen. Small mammals, with the notable exception of most squirrels, tend to be nocturnal because at night they are less conspicuous to predators. In response, predatory mammals are usually at least partly nocturnal as well. And since nocturnality is also an excellent way to beat the heat, mammals are preadapted, so to speak, to desert conditions.

A large desert mammal, such as the desert bighorn or mountain sheep, is able to range widely for water. Ground squirrels, mice, and rats, however, are too small to make the long journeys that often would be necessary to obtain water in the Inner Canyon. Instead, they are able to derive sufficient moisture from their food. A few small rodents, such as kangaroo rats, are able to subsist on the small amounts of water produced as a normal byproduct of food metabolism. Most, however, require green vegetation or some surface water, such as vernal pools or even dewdrops clinging to plants. The northern grasshopper mouse obtains most of the water it needs from its prey, which are chiefly insects but also may include other mice.

Antelope ground squirrels are highly specialized desert rodents. Though mostly vegetarian, they supplement their diet with insects, thereby increasing their moisture supply. Although antelope ground squirrels occupy the hottest, most arid parts of the Grand Canyon, they may be seen abroad even on the hottest days. They keep cool by foraging in the shade of rocks and shrubs and by retreating to their burrows for short rests. Their light-colored fur tends to reflect heat. The bottom of their tail, which they often hold over their back like a parasol, is white. When overheated, the antelope ground squirrel slobbers onto its chest fur, where the saliva cools the animal through evaporation.

Kangaroo rats escape intense heat by spending the day in their burrows. Because of the insulative qualities of soil, a burrow even a few inches below ground is substantially cooler than at the surface. By plugging the burrow opening, the kangaroo rat prevents hot air and predators from entering and cool, relatively moist air from escaping. The rodent derives metabolic water from its food, which mostly consists of seeds. Since its diet contains little protein, it urinates infrequently.

Heat and drought do not pose problems for mammals living on the Kaibab Plateau. Instead, large mammals must contend with winter food shortages brought on by cold weather and deep snow. Some small mammals such as voles and pocket gophers continue to forage under the protective insulation of the snow cover. They encounter difficulty only when extreme cold combined with a lack of snow cover (or when it rains and freezes) either prevents them from foraging or allows them to forage only by expending a great deal of energy. Cold by itself, however, is rarely a problem, for most mammals are protected by their fur from all but extreme cold.

Some mammals, such as the mule deer, cope with winter food shortages by migrating downslope into the pinyon-juniper woodland, where food is more plentiful. In spring the mule deer follow the retreating snow line upslope, feeding on newly sprouted grasses and shrubs. Their constant, though unwelcome, companion in this semiannual trek is the mountain lion, which feeds chiefly on deer and must therefore go where they go.

Most tree squirrels cope with winter food shortages by living off caches of seeds stored during the summer. The Abert and Kaibab squirrels, however, feed in winter off the soft inner tissue (the cambium layer) of twigs. Ground squirrels and chipmunks hibernate, living off layers of fat put on for that purpose during the late summer. When hibernating, their body temperature and overall metabolism are reduced to maintenance levels, thereby reducing the need for food and water.

The black bear also sleeps away much of the winter, living off body fat in the manner of chipmunks. This is not true hibernation, though, since the bear's body temperature remains near normal. During warmer periods, male bears may even venture abroad for a spell. Female bears, who give birth and suckle their young in the winter, wake up frequently but remain with the cubs in their shared den.

Most carnivores are active throughout the winter, though some migrate downslope if food becomes too scarce. Even at higher elevations, however, prey species such as tree squirrels, rats, and mice, as well as numerous small birds, remain active throughout the winter, holing up only during nasty weather.

Mammal Distribution

More than seventy species of mammals have been observed in Grand Canyon National Park. Several others may be present at least part of the time, though their presence has not been substantiated by specimens or photographs. Mammals occupy every life zone and plant community. Large mammals tend to range freely from one zone or community to another, though each species usually has a preferred habitat for bearing and suckling young. Small mammals are more restricted, though many appear in more than one community or zone.

The canyon itself and perhaps the river in particular have posed a barrier to the movement of some species from one rim to the other. Eleven species are restricted to the north side of the river, nine to the south. Of the former, at least four are absent from the south for lack of suitable habitats. The remainder, however, are missing despite the existence of such habitats. Apparently, they were unable to bridge either the canyon or the river. Mammals restricted to particular geographic areas at the Grand Canyon are listed in Table 5.

Of the mammals restricted to one or the other of the rims, the most famous are the two tassel-eared squirrels, which are quite similar except for the coloration of their undersides and tails. The Kaibab squirrel of the North Rim pine forest occurs nowhere else in the world. The Abert squirrel, which inhabits the pine forest of the South Rim, occurs as far north as Colorado and as far south as Mexico. It seems likely that the Abert squirrel managed to cross over to the North Rim at a time when pines were more widespread. Later, as the climate became more arid and the pine forests retreated to higher elevations, the squirrels on the North Rim were isolated from their kin. Mammalogists differ as to whether the Abert and Kaibab squirrels should be treated as separate species or as races of a single species. The former classification is used here largely as a practical device for illustration and discussion.

Identifying Mammals

The plates in this guide depict forty species of mammals found at the Grand Canyon. These include most of the mammals one is likely to see plus a few that are uncommon but especially interesting. Many of the smaller mammals can be distinguished with certainty only by an expert holding a specimen in hand. Of such groups, one or two species are selected for illustration. Bats, which are well represented at the Grand Canyon, are nonetheless not illustrated because their small size, mostly nocturnal habits, and rapid, erratic flight make them very difficult to distinguish. For a complete roster of species known to occur in the Grand Canyon area, and for the common names used in this guidebook, see Butterfield, Kathy et al., *Checklist of the Mammals of the Grand Canyon Area* (Grand Canyon: Grand Canyon Natural History Association, 1981). Abbreviations used in the species descriptions appear in Table 1.

Since most mammals come in shades of brown or gray, color is usually less important to identification than it is for, say, birds. Instead, such characteristics as overall size and shape; posture; shape and size of head, body, and tail; and patterns of light and dark fur are more helpful. For this reason mammals are

176

Table 5.
Mammal Distribution

Found Only North of the River	Found Only South of the River	Found Only in the Canyon	Found Only near the Colorado River or Its Tributaries
Dwarf Shrew	Spotted Squirrel,	California Myotis	Raccoon
Nuttall Cottontail	Whitetail, or Gunni-	Spotted Skunk	Beaver
Golden-Mantled	son's Prairie Dog,	White-Tailed Antelope	
Ground Squirrel	Ground Squirrel	Ground Squirrel	
Least Chipmunk	Abert Squirrel	Rock Pocket Mouse	
Uinta Chipmunk	Silky Pocket Mouse	Long-Tailed	
Kaibab Squirrel	Rock Pocket Mouse	Pocket Mouse	
Red, or Spruce,	Stephens Wood Rat	Canyon Mouse	
Squirrel	White-Throated	Cactus Mouse	
Northern Pocket	Wood Rat	Desert Wood Rat	
Gopher	Mexican Wood Rat		
Long-Tailed	Mexican Vole		
Pocket Mouse			
Bushy-Tailed Wood Rat			
Long-Tailed Vole			

(From Hoffmeister: *Mammals of Grand Canyon*, 1971)

depicted in black and white line drawings. Pelage coloration is noted in the species descriptions.

The best times to see mammals are at dawn and dusk, when both nocturnal and diurnal types may be abroad. The worst time is midday, when even diurnal mammals may hole up. The most likely places to find mammals are near water sources or in areas where burrows, dens, or nests are located. An observer who waits patiently and quietly in a concealed spot downwind from the observation area stands the best chance of success.

More often, one sees only signs of the beast: tracks, scat, nests, and the like. Tracks are shown on each plate. Other distinctive signs are mentioned in the text.

Plate 43

BLACK BEAR, *Ursus americanus.* Bear Family. Rare, SN Rims, Wood. and For. Lgth. about 5'. Tail 5" long. Black or dark brown. Sign: scratch marks on trees; large black or brown droppings. Mostly nocturnal.

MOUNTAIN LION, *Puma concolor.* Cat Family. Rare., SN Rims and Can., most habitats. Lgth. 6'. Tail 2–3' long. Tawny, slightly paler below. Sign: large catlike droppings. Abroad day and night.

BOBCAT, *Lynx rufus.* Cat Family. Com., SN Rims and Can., most habitats. Lgth. 28³/₄–33". Tail 5–6" long. Yellowish brown or yellowish gray above, white below, rusty spots on sides, black on legs, face, back, tail, ears, and below. Sign: catlike droppings. Abroad day and night.

COYOTE, *Canis latrans.* Dog Family. Com., SN Rims and Can., all terrestrial habitats. Lgth. 41½–49". Tail 7³/₄" long. Gray or buff above, whitish below, legs rusty. Sign: doglike tracks and droppings. Abroad day and night.

GRAY FOX, *Urocyon cinereoargenteus.* Dog Family. Uncom., SN Rims, all terrestrial habitats. Lgth. 36½–41". Tail 15³/₈–17³/₈" long. Dark gray above, white below; sides, ears, and underside of tail reddish. Sign: doglike droppings. Abroad day and night.

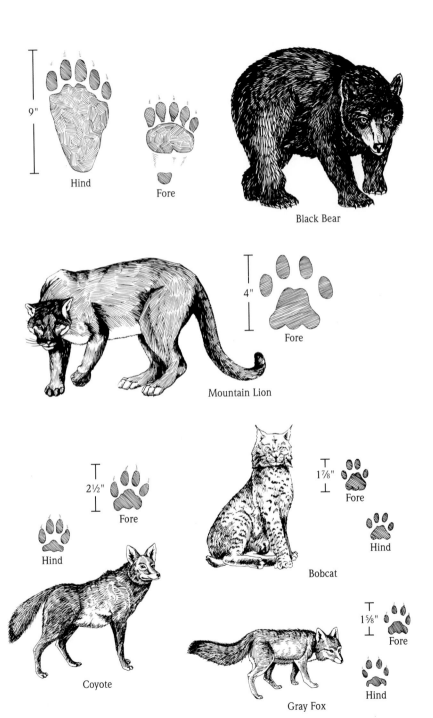

9"

Hind

Fore

Black Bear

4"

Fore

Mountain Lion

2½"

Fore

Hind

Coyote

1⅞"

Fore

Hind

Bobcat

1⅝"

Fore

Hind

Gray Fox

Plate 44

LONG-TAILED WEASEL, *Mustela frenata.* Weasel Family. Uncom., SN Rims and Can., Ripar., Grass., Wood. and For. Lgth. 11¾–14¾". Tail 4–6" long. Brown above, orangish below, black-tipped tail, white mouth and chin. Partly nocturnal.

WESTERN SPOTTED SKUNK, *Spilogale gracilis.* Weasel Family. Com., Can. below 4500', Ripar., Scrub, and all habitats. Lgth. 15¼–17⅛". Tail 5½–6½" long. Black and white. Sign: odor! Abroad at night.

STRIPED SKUNK, *Mephitis mephitis.* Weasel Family. Com., S Rim and probable on N Rim, Wood. and For. Lgth. 23¾–26¾". Tail 10–12¾" long. Black and white. Sign: odor! Mostly nocturnal.

RIVER OTTER, *Lutra canadensis.* Weasel Family. Rare, Can., Aquat. and Ripar. Lgth. about 50". Tail 18" long. Dark brown above, lighter below, some gray on head and neck. Abroad day and night.

AMERICAN BADGER, *Taxidea taxus.* Weasel Family. Uncom., SN Rims, Scrub, Grass., Wood., and For. Lgth. 23¼–31½". Tail 4½–6¼" long. Gray tinged with yellowish brown, undersides and tail pale yellow, face black and white. Sign: large burrow openings. Abroad day and night.

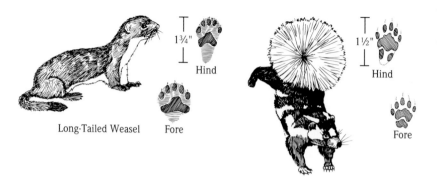

Long-Tailed Weasel

1¾"
Hind

Fore

1½"
Hind

Fore

Western Spotted Skunk

2½"
Hind

Fore

Striped Skunk

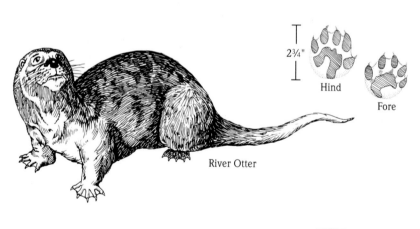

2¾"
Hind

Fore

River Otter

2"
Fore

Hind

American Badger

Plate 45

RACCOON, *Procyon lotor.* Raccoon Family. Rare., Can., Ripar. Lgth. 33½–37½". Tail 11½–16¼" long. Grizzled gray, black mask, tail rings black and yellowish. Abroad at night.

RINGTAIL, *Bassariscus astutus.* Raccoon Family. Com., Can., Ripar., Scrub, Wood., and rocky places. Lgth. 24¾–29¾". Tail 11¾–15" long. Grayish brown, tail rings black and white. Sign: slender, Irreg. droppings. Abroad at night.

ELK, *Cervus elaphus.* Deer Family. Rare, Grass., Wood., and For. Lgth. 81–117"; Ht. 4½–5' at shoulders. Brown or reddish brown, darker beneath and on neck and head; rump and tail yellowish; large, many-tined antlers to 5' long on male. Abroad day and night.

MULE DEER, *Odocoileus hemionus.* Deer Family. Com., SN Rims, most habitats; Rare, Can. Lgth. 5½–6'. Tail about 7" long. Reddish in Sum., gray in Win., white tail tipped in black. Female lacks antlers. Usually in small bands. Sign: black, elliptical droppings to ½" long. Abroad day and night.

PRONGHORNED ANTELOPE, *Antilocapra americana.* Deer Family. Rare., S Rim, Scrub, Grass., and Wood. Lgth. about 4½'. Tail about 6" long. Mostly tan, with white on rump, flanks, and throat. Horn coverings shed annually. Abroad during the day.

DESERT BIGHORN, *Ovis canadensis.* Deer Family. Uncom., Can., rocky areas and cliffs. Seldom visits rims. Lgth. about 5¾'. Tail about 4" long. Pale brown, with creamy rump. Sign: cylindrical droppings to ½" long, somewhat pointed at one end. Abroad during the day.

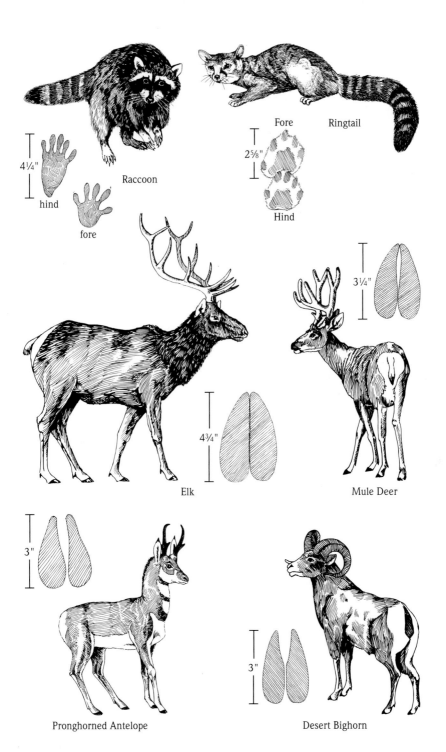

4¼"

hind

fore

Raccoon

Fore   Ringtail

2⅝"

Hind

3¼"

4¾"

Elk

Mule Deer

3"

Pronghorned Antelope

3"

Desert Bighorn

Plate 46

PORCUPINE, *Erithizon dorsatum.* American Porcupine Family. Com., SN Rims, Wood. and For.; Rare, Can. Lgth. 26–33". Tail 7–9" long. Grayish. Sign: conifers partly stripped of bark; tooth marks on trees. Abroad during the day.

BEAVER, *Castor canadensis.* Beaver Family. Com., Can., Aquat. and Ripar. Lgth. 40–48". Tail 15–21" long. Pale orangish brown in the Grand Canyon. Sign: dams and lodges of brush and mud in tributary streams; gnawed or felled trees and brush. Abroad at night.

BLACK-TAILED JACKRABBIT, *Lepus californicus.* Hare Family. Uncom., SN Rims, Grass., Wood. and Scrub. Lgth. 20–23". Tail 2½–4" long. Gray-brown with black on tip of ears and top of tail. Active near dawn and dusk.

DESERT COTTONTAIL, *Sylvilagus audubonii.* Hare Family. Com., S Rim and adjacent part of Can., Scrub, Grass., and Wood. Lgth. 14½–16". Tail 2–3" long. Gray-brown above, white below. Sign: droppings—flattened pellets. Active near dawn and dusk. The very similar Mountain, or Nuttall's, Cottontail, *S. nuttallii,* inhabits N Rim and adjacent Can.

VALLEY POCKET GOPHER, *Thomomys bottae.* Pocket Gopher Family. Com., S Rim and western N Rim, Grass., Scrub, Wood., and For. Rarely appears above ground. Lgth. 6¾–9½". Tail 2–2¾" long. Brown all over. Sign: mounds of loose dirt piled near tunnel opening. Nocturnal/diurnal. Northern Pocket Gopher, *T. talpoides,* is similar but has white chin. It is Com. on the Kaibab Plateau, where the Common, or Valley, Pocket Gopher is rare.

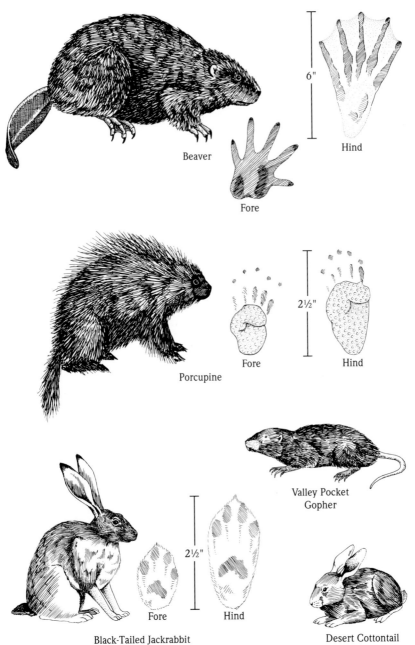

6"

Beaver

Fore

Hind

Porcupine

2½"

Fore

Hind

Valley Pocket
Gopher

2½"

Black-Tailed Jackrabbit

Fore

Hind

Desert Cottontail

Plate 47

RED, or SPRUCE, SQUIRREL, *Tamiasciurus hudsonicus.* Squirrel Family. Com., N Rim, fir and spruce-fir For.; rare, pine For. Lgth. 12½–14". Tail 4¾–6¼" long. Rusty gray above, white below, black band where flanks meet belly. Sign: a feeding stump littered with nuts or dismantled pine cones. Abroad during the day.

ABERT'S SQUIRREL, *Sciurus aberti.* Squirrel Family. Com., S Rim, Wood. and For. Lgth. 19–21". Tail 7¼–9¾" long. Bluish gray head, flanks, and top of tail; reddish back; white on breast, belly, and underside of tail; black band where flanks meet belly. Sign: globular nest of twigs placed high in pines; remains of pine cones dismantled for their seeds. Abroad during the day.

KAIBAB SQUIRREL, *Sciurus kaibabensis.* Squirrel Family. Com., N Rim, pine For. Unique to the Kaibab Plateau. Same size as above. Color similar to Abert Squirrel, but belly dark gray and tail entirely white. Sign same as above. Abroad during the day.

ROCK SQUIRREL, *Spermophilus variegatus.* Squirrel Family. Com., SN Rims and Can., rocky areas, most habitats. Lgth. 17½–20". Tail 7½–9½" long. Much larger than other Grand Canyon ground squirrels. Mottled gray, lower back often rusty. Abroad during the day.

WHITETAIL PRAIRIE DOG, *Cynomys gunnisoni.* Squirrel Family. Rare and local, S Rim, open sandy areas in Scrub and Grass. Lgth. 13–14½". Tail 1¾–2¾" long. Buffy above, white below and on tail. Sign: prairie dog "towns," with numerous burrows and radiating paths. Abroad during the day.

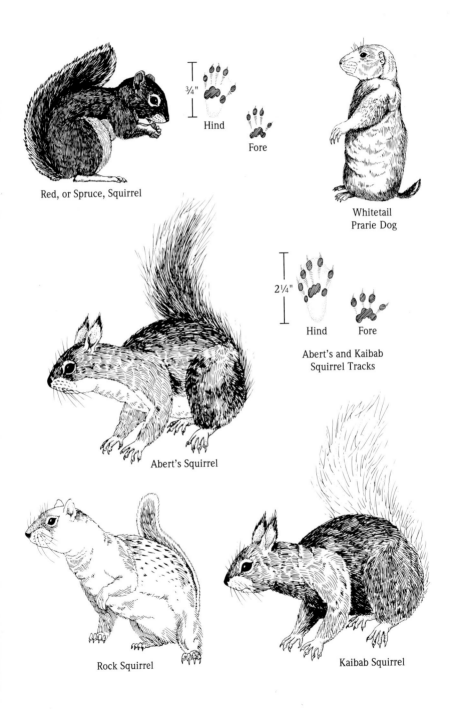

Red, or Spruce, Squirrel

¾"
Hind

Fore

Whitetail
Prarie Dog

2¼"
Hind   Fore

Abert's and Kaibab
Squirrel Tracks

Abert's Squirrel

Rock Squirrel

Kaibab Squirrel

Plate 48

SPOTTED GROUND SQUIRREL, *Spermophilus spilosoma*. Squirrel Family. Rare, S Rim, open sandy areas in Scrub and Grass. Lgth. 7½–9". Tail 3¼" long. Reddish brown and spotted above, paler below. Abroad during the day.

WHITE-TAILED ANTELOPE SQUIRREL, *Ammospermophilus leucurus*. Squirrel Family. Com., S Rim and Can., most habitats. Lgth. 7¾–9". Tail 2½–3½" long. Pale reddish or sandy gray above, white below and on underside of tail, 2 white back stripes not bordered with black. Sign: burrows with radiating paths. Abroad during the day. Harris' Antelope Squirrel, *A. harrisii,* is a rare Can. Res. in Scrub and Ripar.

GOLDEN-MANTLED GROUND SQUIRREL, *Spermophilus lateralis*. Squirrel Family. Com., N Rim, For. Lgth. 9½–11½". Tail 3–4½" long. Rusty gold with black and white stripes on back, but not head (Cf. to chipmunks, below); tail brown below. Sign: burrows near rocks and logs. Abroad during the day.

CLIFF CHIPMUNK, *Tamias dorsalis*. Squirrel Family. Com., SN Rims and Can., cliffs and rocky places. The only chipmunk on the S Rim. Lgth. 7¾–9". Tail 3⅜–4" long. Reddish gray with indistinct back stripes and bolder face stripes; tail dark above and rusty below. Abroad during the day.

LEAST CHIPMUNK, *Tamias minimus*. Squirrel Family. Com., N Rim, Scrub, open Wood., and For. Lgth. 7¼–8". Tail 3¼–3¾" long. Yellowish gray above, buff below, with 9 distinct, narrow back stripes, tail yellowish below. Abroad during the day.

UINTA CHIPMUNK, *Tamias umbrinus*. Squirrel Family. Com., N Rim, Wood., For., and rocky places. Lgth. 8–9¼". Tail 3½–4¼" long. Bright rusty gray above, white below, with broad back stripes, the lowest on each side white. Abroad during the day.

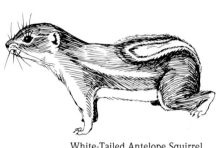

White-Tailed Antelope Squirrel

Spotted Ground Squirrel

Golden-Mantled Ground Squirrel

Uinta Chipmunk

Cliff Chipmunk

Least Chipmunk

3/4"

Hind

Fore

Plate 49

DEER MOUSE, *Peromyscus maniculatus.* New World Mice Family. Com., SN Rims; Uncom. and local, Can. Lgth. 5¾–7". Tail 2¼–3¼" long. Reddish to yellowish brown above, white below, tail short and furred. Abroad at night. One of 5 species of very similar white-footed mice found in the park. **Warning:** Deer Mice in the Southwest have been found to carry the deadly Hanta virus and under no circumstances should be handled. In any event, it is illegal to handle any animals within the park.

BUSHY-TAILED WOOD RAT, *Neotoma cinerea.* New World Mice Family. Com., N Rim, Wood. and For. Lgth. 13¼–16⅞". Tail 5½–7½" long. Sandy brown above, darker on tail; feet and underside of body and tail white. Note bushy, squirrellike tail. Sign: collections of sticks and woody debris among rocks; black cylindrical droppings. Abroad at night. One of 5 species of very similar wood rats (or pack rats) in the area. The other species all have hairy but not bushy tails.

NORTHERN GRASSHOPPER MOUSE, *Onychomys leucogaster.* New World Mice Family. Uncom., SN Rims, Scrub, Wood., and rocky places. Lgth. about 6". Tail 1½–2⅛" long. Brownish gray above, white below and on tip of tail. Abroad at night.

WESTERN HARVEST MOUSE, *Reithrodontomys megalotis.* New World Mice Family. Com., SN Rims and Can., Grass.; Uncom. in other habitats. Lgth. 5–6". Tail 2½–3" long. Reddish brown above, white below. Sign: spherical fiber nests in grass. Abroad at night.

LONG-TAILED VOLE, *Microtus longicaudus.* New World Mice Family. Com., N Rim, Ripar., Grass., and For. Lgth. 6½–7½". Tail 2–2½" long. Dark brown above, gray below. Sign: runways in grass. Abroad both day and night. Mexican Vole, *M. mexicanus,* similar but only found on S Rim.

ROCK POCKET MOUSE, *Chaetodipus intermedius.* Pocket Mouse Family. Com., Can. south of river and S Rim, rocky places and Scrub. Lgth. 6–7". Tail 3⅜–4" long. Buff to gray above, white below. Abroad at night. Silky Pocket Mouse, *P. flavus,* similar but rare. Long-Tailed Pocket Mouse, *P. formosus,* similar but only found north of river.

ORD'S KANGAROO RAT, *Dipodomys ordii.* Pocket Mouse Family. Rare, S Rim, sandy places in Scrub and Grass. Lgth. 9–10". Tail 5¼–6" long. Buffy above, white below. Abroad at night. The similar Merriam's Kangaroo Rat, *D. merriami,* is rare in Can. Scrub.

MERRIAM'S SHREW, *Solex merriami.* Shrew Family. Rare, SN Rims, Grass., Wood., and For. Lgth. 3½–4¼". Tail about 1½" long. Brownish gray above, white below. One of 3 species in area, all exceedingly difficult to distinguish in the field.

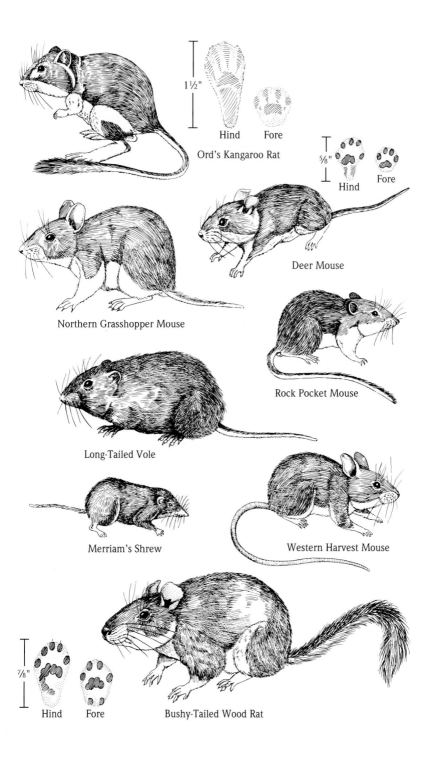

1½"

Hind   Fore

Ord's Kangaroo Rat

⅝"

Hind   Fore

Deer Mouse

Northern Grasshopper Mouse

Rock Pocket Mouse

Long-Tailed Vole

Merriam's Shrew

Western Harvest Mouse

⅞"

Hind   Fore

Bushy-Tailed Wood Rat

Birds

Bird life at the Grand Canyon is extremely diverse. Altogether, more than 300 species have been observed in the Grand Canyon region. Of these, more than 136 are known to nest in the area. Some forty species live in the area year-round. This large, varied avian population reflects the diversity of habitats found in the park, a diversity produced mainly by extreme changes in elevation over relatively short distances. In addition, the Colorado River attracts a large number of species that otherwise would be scarce or absent in the area.

For obvious reasons, the immense gulf of the Grand Canyon poses no barrier to birds, which occur on either side of the river wherever suitable habitat exists. The rims, however, are migratory barriers to some lowland species, largely because their preferred or essential habitats are not present at higher elevations.

Bird Distribution

The birds found within the Grand Canyon are mostly desert species that are widely distributed throughout the arid regions of the West. As a group, however, birds are preadapted, as it were, to survival in desert conditions. Though active during the day, the ability to fly allows birds to escape the heat. They can journey to watering places for a drink and a bath, migrate upslope during hot weather, ride thermals to altitudes where the air is cooler, or retreat to cool, shady roosts located well above the ground where temperatures are highest. In addition, birds have higher body temperatures than mammals: 104–108°F for most species. As a result, they can tolerate higher air temperatures. Since birds can fly to water, the region's aridity seldom poses a problem. Though some species rely on open water for moisture, many others obtain sufficient amounts from the consumption of insects and other animal prey. Moreover, birds secrete relatively dry uric acid crystals rather than true urine, thereby conserving moisture.

At the other extreme, birds are also well adapted to the cold, snowy conditions found on the Kaibab Plateau during the winter. Feathers provide good insulation against cold and may be fluffed up to create additional loft. In effect, birds have their own built-in down parkas. Cold poses a problem largely to the extent that it limits food supplies. The same is true of snow.

Most species nesting on the Kaibab Plateau leave the area at or before the onset of winter. Many are summer residents that migrate out of the region to winter quarters where food is readily available. Other species remain in the park but winter in the Inner Canyon or on the generally warmer, less snowy South Rim. A surprisingly large number of species remain on the Kaibab Plateau throughout the winter, surviving on various types of food—conifer seeds and dormant insects, to cite but two examples—that remain available throughout the season. And since most of the summer residents have left the plateau, competition for these foods is greatly reduced.

In this century human activities at the Grand Canyon have created new habitats that have attracted birds that were formerly uncommon or absent in the area. The most dramatic alteration has occurred along the Colorado River. Before the completion of Glen Canyon Dam in 1963, seasonal flooding prevented the establishment of riparian vegetation. Since then, regulation of the river's flow has permitted a distinctive woodland community to develop quickly along its banks. This new riparian woodland provides nesting opportunities for such species as Lucy's warbler, Bell's vireo, willow flycatcher, hooded oriole, blue grosbeak, and others, none of which were formerly common in the area. Bald eagles, which were rarely sighted in the Grand Canyon before 1986, are now common winter residents along the river. The river and its perennial tributaries also attract a large number of waterfowl and other aquatic or semiaquatic species including grebes, herons, egrets, coots, rails, gulls, and shorebirds.

When the Park Service expanded the South Rim sewage lagoons in 1976, they became a popular resting place for migrants, including a number of species seldom found elsewhere in the area. These artificial ponds are among the best birding spots at the Grand Canyon.

Identifying Birds

193

More than 125 species of birds are depicted in this guide, including most nesting species and all fairly common to common visitors and migrants. Omitted for reasons of space are uncommon or rare visitors and transients. The species shown here are those that an average park visitor is most likely to see. For a complete roster of species known to occur in the Grand Canyon area, and for the common names used in this guidebook, see Brown, Bryan T. et al., *Checklist of the Birds of the Grand Canyon Region,* 1993. The common and scientific names for species that are used in this book conform to the *Checklist of the Birds of the Grand Canyon Region* by Bryan T. Brown et al. (Grand Canyon: Grand Canyon Association, 1983). Because the two publications have different formats, common family names used in this book do not exactly match those of the checklist. The names used in the two publications are close enough, however, that readers using either publication should have no trouble locating corresponding family names in the other. The checklist in turn derives its nomenclature from the sixth edition of the American Ornithologist Union's *Checklist of North American Birds* (Lawrence, Kansas: American Ornothologist Union, 1983), and subsequent supplements. The "A.O.U. Checklist," as it is known, is the standard arbiter among both professional and amateur ornithologists for bird classification and nomenclature.

Birds are grouped on the plates by family, though for various reasons the taxonomic order preferred by ornithologists is not consistently followed here. Where males and females of a species have significantly different plumage, that of the female, which is usually much drabber than her mate, is either shown as well or briefly described in the text. Several species either come in more than one color phase or exhibit markedly different plumage during the nesting season than they do thereafter. Such species are usually shown only in the plumage they most commonly exhibit during their residence or sojourn at the Grand Canyon. In addition, birds of a single species often exhibit minor individual differences. Finally, colors and markings may appear different according to available light. The illustrations portray typical individuals seen at close range in direct, bright light.

In addition to plumage, features of importance to identification include general shape and posture; overall size; manner of flight; shape and color of bill, legs, and feet; and habitat. Species descriptions indicate preferred habitats and point out those features by which one species can be readily told from similar types. Size is indicated directly on the plates.

Experienced birders also rely on behavior and song, as well as physical characteristics. For the inexperienced it is usually a handful simply to sort out field marks, so information on behavior and song is in most cases omitted here. In any event, attempts to render bird songs phonetically are rarely successful and are of limited use to most observers.

For successful birding, a pair of good, preferably lightweight binoculars is essential. A notebook for jotting down field marks or behavior is often useful for later reference.

Species descriptions indicate only the preferred habitats of each species for the season indicated. Since birds are the most mobile of creatures, they wander widely and may often be found outside their normal haunts. This is particularly true after the nesting season. In addition, the seasonal status given for each species refers only to those times when it is fairly common or common in the Grand Canyon region. Many species also occur in other habitats and seasons in lesser numbers, and one should therefore not be overly surprised to encounter a particular species at a time or place not indicated in the descriptions. Abbreviations used in the species descriptions appear in Table 1.

Plate 50

DOUBLE-CRESTED CORMORANT, *Phalacrocorax auritis.* Cormorant Family. Com. Res., Aquat. Lgth. 30–40". Note large size, black body, long neck, and yellow pouch beneath hooked bill. Immatures (not shown) are brown with white neck and breast.

GREAT BLUE HERON, *Ardea herodias.* Heron Family. Com. Res., Ripar. and Aquat. Lgth. 40–52". Recorded all months but June. Note large size, daggerlike bill, long legs, and blue-gray plumage.

CANADA GOOSE, *Branta candadensis.* Waterfowl Family. Com. Win. Vis., Aquat. Lgth. 25–43". Note large size, long black neck, and white chin patch on otherwise black head.

MALLARD, *Anas platyrhynchos.* Waterfowl Family. Com. Res., Aquat. Lgth. 20–28". Note male's green head and white collar; female's mottled brown plumage, orange bill, white on tail, and iridescent blue wing patch.

GADWALL, *Anas strepera.* Waterfowl Family. Com. Win. Vis., Aquat. Lgth. 19–23". Note male's gray body and black rump; female's white wing patch.

BLUE-WINGED TEAL, *Anas discors.* Waterfowl Family. Com. Sum. Res., Aquat. Lgth. 15–16". Note male's white crescent on head and gray wing patch; female's pale blue wing patch.

Canada Goose

Double-Crested Cormorant

male

female

Blue-Winged Teal

female

male

Gadwall

Great Blue Heron

female

male

Mallard

Plate 51

REDHEAD, *Aythyra americana.* Waterfowl Family. Com. Win. Vis., Aquat. Lgth. 18–23". Note male's reddish head and neck; female's pale area near bill.

LESSER SCAUP, *Aythyra affinis.* Waterfowl Family. Com. Win. Vis., Aquat. Lgth. 15–18". Note male's black breast, rump, and head, the latter with purple sheen; female's white band encircling bill.

AMERICAN WIGEON, *Anas americana.* Waterfowl Family. Com. Win. Vis., Aquat. Lgth. 18–23". Note male's white crown and green eye patch; female's gray head and neck.

COMMON GOLDENEYE, *Bucephala clangula.* Waterfowl Family. Com. Win. Vis., Aquat. Lgth. 16–20". Note male's striking black and white plumage, green sheen on head, and white spot before the eye; female's brown head and white collar.

BUFFLEHEAD, *Bucephala albeola.* Waterfowl Family. Com. Win. Vis., Aquat. Lgth. 13–16". Note male's white body and head patch; female's white ear patch.

COMMON MERGANSER, *Mergus merganser.* Waterfowl Family. Com., Aquat. Lgth. 22–27". Note male's white body and green head; female's crested, rusty head. Both have narrow, hooked, serrated bills.

AMERICAN COOT, *Fulica americana.* Rail Family. Com. Res., Ripar. and Aquat. Lgth. 13–16". Note black body and white bill.

SPOTTED SANDPIPER, *Actitis macularia.* Sandpiper Family. Com. Sum. Res., near water. Lgth. 7–8". Note spotted underparts and bobbing walk. Spots absent in Win. plumage. Nests on ground.

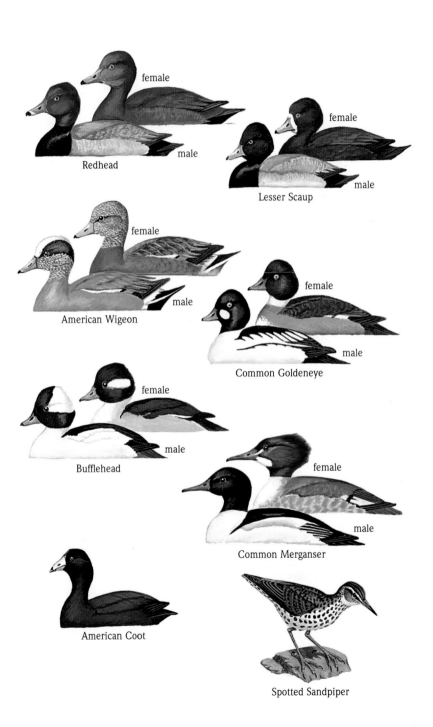

Redhead
female
male

Lesser Scaup
female
male

American Wigeon
female
male

Common Goldeneye
female
male

Bufflehead
female
male

Common Merganser
female
male

American Coot

Spotted Sandpiper

Plate 52

TURKEY VULTURE, *Cathartes aura.* New World Vulture Family. Com. Sum. Res., L and U Son. and Tran., most habitats. Lgth. 26–32". Usually seen soaring. Nests in cliff crevices, among rocks, on ground. Note naked red head and uniform black plumage.

NORTHERN GOSHAWK, *Accipiter gentilis.* Hawk Family. Uncom. Res., Tran. and Bor., For. Lgth. 20–26". Note light breast, gray back, and red eye; immature's (not shown) brown backs and spotted breasts.

SHARP-SHINNED HAWK, *Accipiter striatus.* Hawk Family. Uncom. Sum. Res., Wood. and For. Lgth. 10–14". Note notched tip of tail. Cooper's Hawk, *A cooperii,* is similar to the Sharp-Shinned Hawk but larger and its tail is rounded at the tip rather than notched.

SWAINSON'S HAWK, *Buteo swainsoni.* Hawk Family. Uncom. Vis., most habitats. Lgth. 19–22". Highly variable species. Note dark breast band and light, barred tail of typical birds; wings also more pointed than those of Red-Tailed Hawk.

RED-TAILED HAWK, *Buteo jamaicensis.* Hawk Family. Com. Res., most habitats. Lgth. 19–25". The most common of the several buteo hawks found in the Grand Canyon area. Usually seen soaring. Note rusty tail. Some birds darker than shown. Ferruginous Hawk, *B. regalis,* has a white tail. Rough-Legged Hawk, *B. lagopus,* has pale tail with broad black band near tip.

BALD EAGLE, *Haliaetus leucocephalus.* Hawk Family. Com. Win. Vis., along river; may be seen overhead in areas away from the river. Lgth. 30–43". Note large size and adult's white head, neck, and tail; patches of white in young.

GOLDEN EAGLE, *Aquila chrysaetos.* Hawk Family. Uncom. Res., U Son. through Bor., most habitats. Nests on cliffs. Lgth. 30–40". Usually seen soaring. Note very large size and dark, uniform color.

PRAIRIE FALCON, *Falco mexicanus.* Falcon Family. Rare Res. below Bor., most habitats but prefers open country. Lgth. 14–18". Nests in cliffs. Note pale plumage, pointed wings, and black in "wingpits."

PEREGRINE FALCON, *Falco peregrinus.* Falcon Family. Com. Res. below Bor., most habitats but prefers open country. Lgth. 15–20". Nests in cliffs. Note gray back, black and white head, pointed wings, and absence of black in "wingpits."

AMERICAN KESTREL, *Falco sparverius.* Falcon Family. Com. Res., most habitats, but prefers open areas with shrubs or rocks for vantage points. Lgth. 9–12". Note small size, pointed wings, rusty coloration. Female (not shown) similar, but has rusty wings and banded tail. Most common "hawk" along river.

Northern Goshawk

Sharp-Shinned Hawk

Red-Tailed Hawk

Swainson's Hawk

Golden Eagle

Bald Eagle

male

Peregrine Falcon

male

Prairie Falcon

male

American Kestrel

Turkey Vulture

Plate 53

GREAT HORNED OWL, *Bubo virginianus.* Owl Family. Com. Res., SN Rims and Can., most habitats. Lgth. 18–25". Note large size, ear tufts, and barred undersides. Nests in trees, on cliffs, even on ground. Abroad at night.

SPOTTED OWL, *Strix occidentalis.* Owl Family. Rare Res., Wood. and For. Lgth. 16–19". Note large size, dark eyes, round tuftless head, and heavily spotted and streaked underparts. Nests in tree cavities or caves and crevices in cliffs. Abroad at night.

NORTHERN PYGMY OWL, *Glaucidium gnoma.* Owl Family. Rare Res., Tran. and Bor., Wood. and For. Lgth. 7–8". Nests in tree cavities. Note songbird size, black patches at nape of neck, and streaked sides. Mostly abroad at night; sometimes during the day.

NORTHERN SAW-WHET OWL, *Aegolius acadicus.* Owl Family. Irreg. Sum. Res. and Win. Vis., For. Lgth. 7–9". Note songbird size, lack of ear tufts, and streaked underparts; immature's (not shown) white V marking above eyes. Abroad at night.

WESTERN SCREECH OWL, *Otus kennicottii.* Owl Family. Uncom. Res., U Son. and Tran., Ripar., Wood., and For. Lgth. 6–8". Note small size and ear tufts. Nests in tree cavities. Abroad at night.

FLAMMULATED OWL, *Otus flammeolus.* Owl Family. Com. Sum. Res., For. Lgth. 6–7". Note small size, dark eyes, and inconspicuous ear tufts. Nests in tree cavities. Abroad at night.

COMMON POORWILL, *Phalaenoptilus nuttallii.* Goatsucker Family. Com. Sum. Res., L and U Son., Ripar., Grass., and Scrub. Lgth. 7–8". Note rounded wings without white bars and short, rounded tail with white outer corners. Abroad at night. Rests during the day in shady places on or near the ground.

COMMON NIGHTHAWK, *Choldeiles minor.* Goatsucker Family. Com. Sum. Res., Wood. and For. Lgth. 8–10". Note pointed, swept-back wings with white bar on each. Usually seen flying at twilight in the manner of swifts or swallows, but much larger. Utters a sharp nasal call during flight. Lesser Nighthawk, *C. acutipennis,* very similar, but rare.

gray phase

Western Screech Owl

Flammulated Owl

Great Horned Owl

Northern Saw-Whet Owl

Northern Pygmy Owl

Spotted Owl

Common Poorwill

Common Nighthawk

Plate 54

BLUE GROUSE, *Dendragapus obscurus.* Grouse Family. Uncom. Res., N Rim, For. Lgth. 15–21". Note chickenlike appearance and dark coloration.

CHUKAR, *Alectoris chukar.* Pheasant Family. Uncom. Res., Scrub. Lgth. 13". Note red legs and lack of topknot. Native to Old World. Introduced to area in 1960.

GAMBEL'S QUAIL, *Calipepla gambelii.* Pheasant Family. Com. Res., U Son., Grass., Scrub, and Wood. Lgth. 10–12". Note bold markings and topknot. Female (not shown) is similar. Nests on ground among brush.

GREATER ROADRUNNER, *Geococcyx californianus.* Cuckoo Family. Uncom. Res., L and U Son., Grass., Scrub, and Wood. Lgth. 20–24". Note long tail, streaked plumage, slight crest. Feeds on lizards, snakes, insects. Nests in low trees, brush, and cactus.

WILD TURKEY, *Meleagris gallopavo.* Pheasant Family. Com. Res., SN Rims, pine For. Lgth. 36–48". Note bare bluish head with red wattles. Females smaller, slimmer, less iridescent. Introduced to Kaibab Plateau in 1950. Though once possibly native to region, S Rim birds may be escaped domestic birds.

BAND-TAILED PIGEON, *Columba fasciata.* Pigeon Family. Uncom. Sum. Res., Wood. and pine For. Lgth. 14–16". Similar to Rock Dove (domestic pigeon), but slimmer, with white crescent at nape of neck and light band on tail.

MOURNING DOVE, *Zenaida macroura.* Pigeon Family. Com. Sum. Res., Scrub, Wood., and pine For. Lgth. 11–13". Note slim build, pale plumage, and long pointed tail bordered with white (especially noticeable in flight).

Blue Grouse

Chukar

Gambel's Quail

Greater Roadrunner

Wild Turkey

Band-Tailed Pigeon

Mourning Dove

Plate 55

NORTHERN FLICKER, *Colaptes auratus*. Woodpecker Family. Com. Res., Tran. and Bor., Wood. and For. Lgth. 12–14". Note red streak (absent in female) on gray cheek and orange on underside of wings and tail. Nests in tree cavities, but feeds on ground, mostly on ants.

ACORN WOODPECKER, *Melanerpes formicivorus*. Woodpecker Family. Uncom. Res., Wood. and pine For. Lgth. 8–10". Note clownlike face and black back. Feeds on acorns, which it stores in holes drilled in trees, utility poles, etc.

LEWIS' WOODPECKER, *Melanerpes lewis*. Woodpecker Family. Rare Sum. Res. and Win. Vis., N. Rim, Wood. and For. Lgth. 10–12". Note red face, pink underparts, green head and back.

RED-NAPED SAPSUCKER, *Sphyrapicus varius*. Woodpecker Family. Com. Sum. Res., Wood. and For.; Win. Vis., Ripar. Lgth. 8–9". Note red crown and chin (partly white in females), black patch on breast, white wing patch, and barred back. Feeds on sap and bark insects. Note rows of holes circling tree trunks.

WILLIAMSON'S SAPSUCKER, *Sphyrapicus thyroideus*. Woodpecker Family. Uncom. Sum. Res., N Rim. Bor. For. Lgth. 8–9". Nests in aspens. Note black back and breast, black crown, red chin, and white wing patch. Female (not shown) has brown head, barred back and wings, and yellow belly.

HAIRY WOODPECKER, *Picoides villosus*. Woodpecker Family. Com. Res., Wood. and For. Lgth. 8–11". Note clear white back and large black bill. Female (not shown) lacks red on head.

DOWNY WOODPECKER, *Picoides pubescens*. Woodpecker Family. Rare Res., For., often wandering to lower elevations. Lgth. 6–7". Very similar to preceding species, but smaller overall and with slimmer bill. Female (not shown) lacks red on head.

LADDER-BACKED WOODPECKER, *Picoides scalaris*. Woodpecker Family. Rare Res., L and U Son., Ripar., Scrub, Grass., and Wood. Lgth. 6–8". Note striped face and barred back. Female lacks red cap.

THREE-TOED WOODPECKER, *Picoides tridactylus*. Woodpecker Family. Rare Res., For. Lgth. 8–10". Note yellow cap of male and barred sides of both sexes.

Northern Flicker

male

Acorn Woodpecker

Lewis' Woodpecker

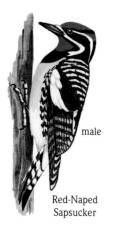

male

Red-Naped
Sapsucker

male

Williamson's
Sapsucker

male

Hairy Woodpecker

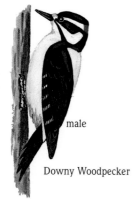

male

Downy Woodpecker

male

Ladder-Backed
Woodpecker

male

Three-Toed
Woodpecker

Plate 56

BLACK-CHINNED HUMMINGBIRD, *Archilochus alexandri.* Hummingbird Family. Com. Sum. Res., most habitats below Bor. Lgth. 3–4". Note male's black chin, iridescent purple throat, and white breast patch; female's lack of rust-colored plumage.

BROAD-TAILED HUMMINGBIRD, *Selasphorus platycercus.* Hummingbird Family. Com. Sum. Res., For. Lgth. 4–5". Note male's rosy throat, green back, and dark tail; female's rusty tail and sides.

RUFOUS HUMMINGBIRD, *Selasphorus rufus.* Hummingbird Family. Com. Fall Vis. and rare Spr. Vis., most habitats. Lgth. 3–4". Note male's rusty head, back, sides, and tail. Female (not shown) is virtually identical to—but slightly smaller than—female Broad-Tailed Hummingbird.

COSTA'S HUMMINGBIRD, *Calypte costae.* Hummingbird Family. Com. Sum. Res., Ripar. and Scrub. Lgth. 3–4". Note male's purple throat and crown.

WHITE-THROATED SWIFT, *Aeronautes saxatalis.* Swift Family. Com. Sum. Res. below Bor., usually seen swooping and diving over Can. Lgth. 6–7". Distinguished from swallows by black-and-white plumage; long, narrow, swept-back wings; more erratic flight; and "twinkling" wing movements in flight. Nests on cliffs, but spends most of life in the air.

VIOLET-GREEN SWALLOW, *Tachycineta thalassina.* Swallow Family. Com. Sum. Res., cliffs and For. Lgth. 5–6". Note white rump patches and white around eye. Flight steadier than swift's and wings not swept back.

CLIFF SWALLOW, *Petrochelidon pyrrhonota.* Swallow Family. Irreg. Sum. Res., nesting on cliffs. Lgth. 5–6". Note pale rump, unforked tail, and reddish brown throat.

NORTHERN ROUGH-WINGED SWALLOW, *Stelgidopteryx serripenis.* Swallow Family. Com. Sum. Res., Ripar. and Aquat. Lgth. 5–6". Note brown back and throat.

PURPLE MARTIN, *Progne subis.* Swallow Family. Uncom. Sum. Res., For., nesting in tree cavities. Lgth. 7–9". Note uniform, dark coloration and forked tail. Female (not shown) has pale gray breast.

male

male

male

female

female

female

Black-Chinned Hummingbird

Broad-Tailed Hummingbird

Rufous Hummingbird

male

female

Costa's Hummingbird

White-Throated Swift

Violet-Green Swallow

Northern Rough-
Winged Swallow

Cliff Swallow

Purple Martin

Plate 57

WESTERN KINGBIRD, *Tyrannus verticalis.* New World Flycatcher Family. Uncom. Sum. Res., Ripar., Scrub, and Wood. Lgth. 8–10". Note pale breast, poorly defined white patch on throat, and white border on tail. Cf. Cassin's Kingbird, below.

CASSIN'S KINGBIRD, *Tyrannus vociferans.* New World Flycatcher Family. Com. Sum. Res., Ripar., Scrub, and Wood. Lgth. 8–9". Note dark breast, well-defined white throat patch, and lack of white border on tail. Cf. Western Kingbird, above.

ASH-THROATED FLYCATCHER, *Myiarchus cinerascens.* New World Flycatcher Family. Com. Sum. Res., most habitats. Lgth. 7–9". Note cinnamon wings and tail.

BLACK PHOEBE, *Sayornis nigricans.* New World Flycatcher Family. Com. Res., Ripar. Lgth. 6–7". Note black breast. Rarely found away from water. From perch amid or near a stream or puddle, it repeatedly sallies forth for flying insects. This habit is common to all tyrant flycatchers.

SAY'S PHOEBE, *Sayornis saya.* New World Flycatcher Family. Com. Res., most habitats below Bor. Lgth. 7–8". Note rusty belly.

GRAY FLYCATCHER, *Empidonax wrightii.* New World Flycatcher Family. Com. Sum. Res., S Rim, Wood. Lgth. 5–6". Note small size, two white wing bars, fly-catching habit. Virtually impossible to distinguish in the field from the Willow Flycatcher, *E. traillii,* rare or extirpated Sum. Res., Ripar.; and the Cordilleran Flycatcher, *E. occidentalis,* rare Sum. Vis., For. Even experts have trouble with these and related species.

WESTERN WOOD-PEWEE, *Contopus sordidulus.* New World Flycatcher Family. Com. Sum. Res., U Son., Wood. Lgth. 6–7". Similar to preceding species, but larger (sparrow size), with darker back and breast, no eye ring, and longer wings in proportion to body.

OLIVE-SIDED FLYCATCHER, *Cantopus cooperi.* New World Flycatcher Family. Uncom. Sum. Res., For. Lgth. 7–8". Note lack of wing bars and olive "vest" over white breast. More often heard than seen: song "Hip, Three Cheers" uttered from upper branches of conifers.

Western Kingbird

Cassin's Kingbird

Ash-Throated Flycatcher

Say's Phoebe

Black Phoebe

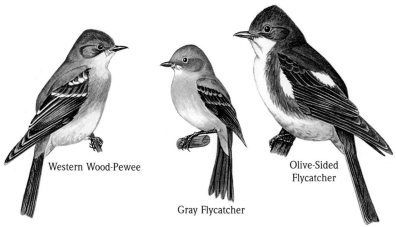

Western Wood-Pewee

Gray Flycatcher

Olive-Sided
Flycatcher

Plate 58

CLARK'S NUTCRACKER, *Nucifraga columbiana.* Crow Family. Com. Res., Bor. For. Wanders widely in Win. Lgth. 12–13". Note large, black, awl-shaped bill and black-and-white wings and tail.

PINYON JAY, *Gymnorhinus cyanocephalus.* Crow Family. Com. Res., Wood. Wanders widely in Win. Lgth. 9–12". Distinguished from following species by uniform blue-gray color. Often in flocks. Preferred food is pinyon nuts.

WESTERN SCRUB JAY, *Aphelocoma californica.* Crow Family. Com. Res., Grass. and Wood. Lgth. 11–13". Distinguished from preceding species by white throat, dark necklace, and olive-gray back. Seldom in flocks. Prefers brush and small trees to For.

STELLER'S JAY, *Cyanocitta stelleri.* Crow Family. Com. Res., Wood. and For. Lgth. 12–14". Note dark blue body and black, crested head. Nearly twice the size of the Phainopepla (see below), the only other dark, crested bird in the area.

COMMON RAVEN, *Corvus corax.* Crow Family. Com. Res., most habitats, but usually seen indulging in aerial acrobatics along SN Rims and over Can. Lgth. 21–27". Distinguished from American Crow, *C. brachyrhynchos,* Irreg. Sum. Vis., by large size, thick bill, shaggy throat feathers, wedge-shaped tail, and deeper, harsher call.

PHAINOPEPLA, *Phainopepla nitens.* Silky Flycatcher Family. Uncom. Res., Ripar., and Uncom. Sum. Vis., U Son. and Tran., Scrub. Lgth. 7–8". Note dark plumage with crest and white wing patches in flight. Note female's gray plumage, lighter wings, and dark tail. Red eye of both sexes is distinctive.

Clark's Nutcracker

Pinyon Jay

Western Scrub Jay

Steller's Jay

female

male

Phainopepla

Common Raven

Plate 59

MOUNTAIN CHICKADEE, *Poecile gambeli.* Titmouse Family. Com. Res., U Son. through Bor., Wood. and For. Lgth. 5–6". Note black bib and white stripe over eye. Gleans insects from outer branches of conifers, often hanging upside-down in the process.

JUNIPER TITMOUSE, *Baeolophus ridgwayi.* Titmouse Family. Com. Res., U Son., Scrub and Wood. Lgth. 5–6". Note plain gray plumage and crest. Distinguished from female Phainopepla (Plate 58) by dark eye, eye ring, lighter tail.

COMMON BUSHTIT, *Psaltriparus minimus.* Bushtit Family. Com. Res., U Son. Wood., and Win. Vis., Ripar. Lgth. 3–4". Note tiny size, long tail, and brown cheek. Occurs in loose, chattering flocks.

HORNED LARK, *Eremophila alpestris.* Lark Family. Com. Res., U Son., Grass. Lgth. 7–8". Note black bib, face patch, and "horns"; yellow face; and pale underparts. Immatures (not shown) lack horns and show little or no black. Usually seen in flocks, feeding on open ground.

AMERICAN DIPPER, *Cinclus mexicanus.* Dipper Family. Com. Res. along permanent tributaries in Can.; Com. Win. Vis. along the river. Lgth. 7–9". Note slate color, stubby tail, and constant bobbing motion. Rarely far from running water. Feeds in stream shallows and even dives beneath the surface after insects.

WHITE-BREASTED NUTHATCH, *Sitta carolinensis.* Nuthatch Family. Com. Res., U Son. and Tran., Wood. and For.; Vis., Ripar. Lgth. 5–6". Distinguished from following species by black eye on white face. Nuthatches typically hang upside-down on branches and head-down on tree trunks.

RED-BREASTED NUTHATCH, *Sitta canadensis.* Nuthatch Family. Uncom. Res., N Rim, Wood. and For. Lgth. 4–5". Note pinkish underparts and white stripe over eye. Behavior similar to that of White-Breasted Nuthatch, above.

PYGMY NUTHATCH, *Sitta pygmaea.* Nuthatch Family. Com. Res., SN Rims, Wood. and For. Lgth. 4–5". Note brown cap and black eye stripe. Behavior similar to that of White-Breasted Nuthatch, above.

BROWN CREEPER, *Certhia americana.* Creeper Family. Com. Sum. Res., N Rim, For.; Win. Vis., Wood. Lgth. 5–6". Note curved beak, rusty, pointed tail, and streaked brown back. Spirals head-first up tree trunks searching for bark insects, then flies to the base of nearby tree and repeats the process. Easily overlooked.

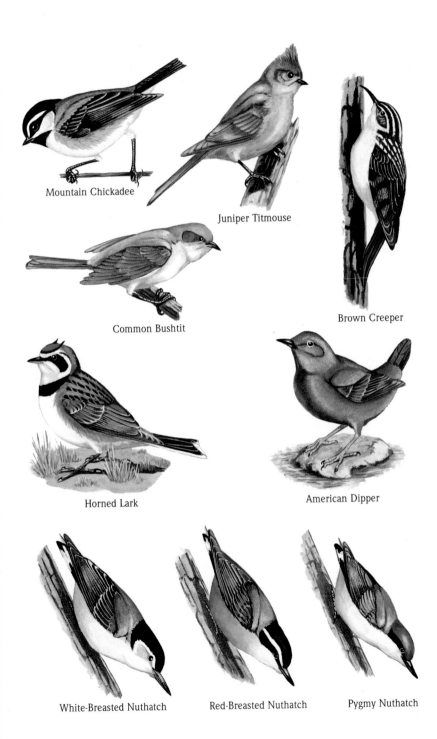

Mountain Chickadee

Juniper Titmouse

Brown Creeper

Common Bushtit

Horned Lark

American Dipper

White-Breasted Nuthatch

Red-Breasted Nuthatch

Pygmy Nuthatch

Plate 60

HOUSE WREN, *Troglodytes aedon.* Wren Family. Com. Sum. Res., N Rim, Bor. For. Lgth. 4–5". Note plain gray-brown plumage and lack of eye stripe.

BEWICK'S WREN, *Thryomanes bewickii.* Wren Family. Com. Sum. Res., Wood. and Ripar.; Win. Vis., other habitats. Lgth. 5–6". Note white underparts, white in tail, bold white stripe over eye, and plain brown back.

CANYON WREN, *Catherpes mexicanus.* Wren Family. Com. Res., most habitats. Lgth. 5–6". Note contrasting white breast and brown belly. The song of this bird—a rich, cascading series of whistles, descending in pitch and slowing toward the end—is one of the most common sounds in the Can.

ROCK WREN, *Salpinctes obsoletus.* Wren Family. Com. Res., most habitats. Lgth. 5–6". Note buffy corners of tail, lightly streaked breast, and faint white stripe over eye.

CACTUS WREN, *Campylorhynchus brunneicapillus.* Wren Family. Uncom. Sum. Res., Scrub and Grass. Lgth. 8–9". Note large size, heavy spotting on breast and throat, white stripe over eye, and white spots on outer tail feathers.

MARSH WREN, *Cistothorus palustris.* Wren Family. Uncom. Res., Aquat. Lgth. 4–5". Note white stripe over eye and white streaks on upper back.

EUROPEAN STARLING, *Sturnus vulgaris.* Starling Family. Introduced species. Com. Res. near human habitations. Lgth. 7–9". Note yellow bill and short tail of breeding adult; black bill and spotted plumage of Win. birds.

HOUSE SPARROW, *Passer domesticus.* Old World Sparrow Family. Introduced species. Com. Res. near human habitations. Lgth. 5–6". Note male's black bib and gray crown. Female (not shown) has pale gray breast and light eye stripe.

House Wren

Bewick's Wren

Cactus Wren

Canyon Wren

Marsh Wren

Rock Wren

House Sparrow

winter

European Starling

summer

Plate 61

LOGGERHEAD SHRIKE, *Lanius ludovicianus.* Shrike Family. Uncom. Res., L and U Son., Grass., Scrub, and Wood. Lgth. 8–10". Note black mask and hooked, hawklike bill. A predatory songbird, feeding on small rodents and birds as well as insects. Called "butcherbird" because it impales prey on thorns for later use.

NORTHERN MOCKINGBIRD, *Mimus polyglottos.* Mimic Thrush Family. Uncom. Sum. Res., U Son., Grass., Scrub, and Wood. Lgth. 9–11". Note conspicuous white tail margins and wing patches. An accomplished mimic of other birds, with a large repertoire of songs.

AMERICAN ROBIN, *Turdus migratorius.* Old World Flycatcher Family. Com. Res., For. Lgth. 9–11". Note rusty breast and dark back.

HERMIT THRUSH, *Catharus guttatus.* Old World Flycatcher Family. Com. Sum. Res., For. Lgth. 6–8". Note spotted breast, rusty tail, and beautiful flutelike song. The Sage Thrasher, *Oreoscoptes montanus,* Uncom. Sum. Vis., is somewhat similar, but has a longer, curved bill and longer tail.

WESTERN BLUEBIRD, *Sialia mexicana.* Old World Flycatcher Family. Com. Res., Wood. and For.; widespread Win. Vis. Lgth. 6–7". Note male's bright blue head, wings, and tail; rusty back and breast. Female (not shown) is similar, but far paler.

MOUNTAIN BLUEBIRD, *Sialia currucoides.* Old World Flycatcher Family. Com. Sum. Res., Tran. and Bor., Grass. and other open places in For.; wanders widely in Win. Lgth. 6–8". Note uniform turquoise color. Female (not shown) resembles female Western Bluebird, above, but has a gray, rather than rusty, breast.

TOWNSEND'S SOLITAIRE, *Myadestes townsendii.* Old World Flycatcher Family. Com. Res., For.; Win. Vis., Wood. and Scrub. Lgth. 8–10". Note white eye ring, white tail margins, and buffy wing patches.

Loggerhead Shrike

Northern Mockingbird

Hermit Thrush

American Robin

male

male

Western Bluebird

Mountain Bluebird

Townsend's Solitaire

Plate 62

BLUE-GRAY GNATCATCHER, *Polioptila caerulea.* Old World Flycatcher Family. Com. Sum. Res., Can., Ripar., Scrub, and Wood.; Uncom. Sum. Res., SN Rims. Lgth. 4–5". Note blue-gray crown, white eye ring, and predominance of white on underside of tail.

BLACK-TAILED GNATCATCHER, *Polioptila melanura.* Old World Flycatcher Family. Rare Res. or Vis., western Grand Canyon region, L Son., Ripar. Lgth. 4–5". Note Sum. male's black cap, lack of eye ring, and predominance of black on underside of tail. Female and young have gray-brown head and back. Win. male duller, without black cap.

GOLDEN-CROWNED KINGLET, *Regulus satrapa.* Old World Flycatcher Family. Uncom. Sum. Res., N Rim, Bor. For. Lgth. 3–4". Note male's yellow, red, and black crown. Female similar, but lacks red on crown.

RUBY-CROWNED KINGLET, *Regulus calendula.* Old World Flycatcher Family. Com. Sum. Res., N Rim, Bor. For. Lgth. 3–5". Red crown patch of male often hidden. Female (not shown) lacks red crown patch but otherwise similar. Note lack of yellow on crown, broken eye ring, and habit of constantly fluttering its wings.

BELL'S VIREO, *Vireo bellii.* Vireo Family. Com. Sum. Res., Can., Ripar. Lgth. 4–5". Note olive color, pale yellow sides, and usually 2 wing bars. Does not twitch tail, flutter wings, or sally forth after flies (Cf. tyrant flycatchers, Plate 57).

GRAY VIREO, *Vireo vicinior.* Vireo Family. Uncom. Sum. Res., U Son., Scrub and Wood. Lgth. 5–6". Note gray color, gray or buffy sides, obscure white "spectacles," and 1 faint wing bar. Twitches tail, but does not flutter wings or sally forth after flies.

PLUMBEOUS VIREO, *Vireo plumbeus.* Vireo Family. Com. Sum. Res., For. Lgth. 5–6". Note white "spectacles," snow-white throat, and prominent wing bars. Cassin's Vireo, *V. cassinii,* is similar but plumage more olive than grey.

WARBLING VIREO, *Vireo gilvus.* Vireo Family. Com. Sum. Res., Tran. and Bor. For. Lgth. 4–6". Note faint eye stripe and whitish breast.

Blue-Gray
Gnatcatcher

female

male

Black-Tailed Gnatcatcher

Bell's Vireo

male

female

Golden-Crowned Kinglet

female

male

Ruby-Crowned Kinglet

Gray Vireo

Plumbeous Vireo

Warbling Vireo

Plate 63

VIRGINIA'S WARBLER, *Vermivora virginiae.* New World Sparrow Family: Wood Warbler Subfamily. Com. Sum. Res., U Son. and Bor. Wood. and For. Lgth. 4–5". Note yellowish rump and breast.

LUCY'S WARBLER, *Vermivora luciae.* New World Sparrow Family: Wood Warbler Subfamily. Com. Sum. Res., L and U Son., Ripar. Lgth. 4–5". Note reddish brown rump and whitish breast. The most common warbler along the Colorado River.

YELLOW WARBLER, *Dendroica petechia.* New World Sparrow Family: Wood Warbler Subfamily. Com. Sum. Res., L and U Son., Ripar. Lgth. 4–6". Note yellow tail spots and rusty streaks on breast. Streaks faint or missing in female.

YELLOW-RUMPED WARBLER, *Dendroica coronata.* New World Sparrow Family: Wood Warbler Subfamily. Com. Sum. Res., N Rim, For.; Com. Vis., most other habitats. Lgth. 5–6". Note yellow throat and rump, black breast, and white wing patches. In Spr. and Sum., female (not shown) brown with two white wing bars. Win. birds brownish, streaked, white below, with yellow throats.

BLACK-THROATED GRAY WARBLER, *Dendroica nigrescens.* New World Sparrow Family: Wood Warbler Subfamily. Com. Sum. Res., U Son., Scrub and Wood. Lgth. 4–5". Note black crown, cheeks, and throat. Female (not shown) duller and lacks black throat patch.

GRACE'S WARBLER, *Dendroica graciae.* New World Sparrow Family: Wood Warbler Subfamily. Com. Sum. Res., N Rim, For. Lgth. 4–5". Note striped flanks and yellow throat and breast.

COMMON YELLOWTHROAT, *Geothlypis trichas.* New World Sparrow Family: Wood Warbler Subfamily. Com. Sum. Res., L and U Son., Ripar. Lgth. 4–6". Note male's black mask and yellow throat; female's white belly and buffy sides.

YELLOW-BREASTED CHAT, *Icteria virens.* New World Sparrow Family: Wood Warbler Subfamily. Com. Sum. Res., L and U Son., Ripar. Lgth. 6–8". Note large size, thick bill, yellow breast, and white belly. Very unwarblerlike.

WILSON'S WARBLER, *Wilsonia pusilla.* New World Sparrow Family: Wood Warbler Subfamily. Com. Vis. below Bor. Lgth. 4–5". Note black cap of male. Female lacks cap, wing bars, or other conspicuous markings.

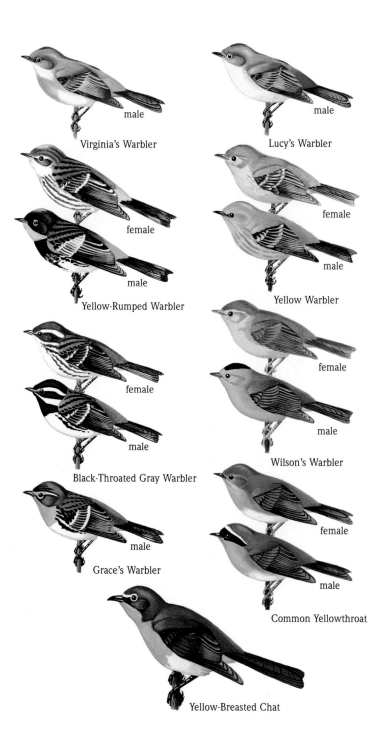

male

Virginia's Warbler

male

Lucy's Warbler

female

Yellow-Rumped Warbler

male

female

male

Yellow Warbler

female

Black-Throated Gray Warbler

male

female

male

Wilson's Warbler

male

Grace's Warbler

female

male

Common Yellowthroat

Yellow-Breasted Chat

Plate 64

WESTERN MEADOWLARK, *Sturnella neglecta.* New World Sparrow Family: Oriole Subfamily. Com. Res., U Son., Grass. and Scrub. Lgth. 8–11". Note yellow underparts and black V-shaped necklace. Eastern Meadowlark, *Sturnella magna,* is Uncom. Sum. Res., U Son., Grass. and Scrub. The two meadowlarks are difficult to distinguish visually, but their songs are quite different. The Western Meadowlark has a bubbling, flutelike song; the Eastern Meadowlark has a song consisting of two clear, sustained flutelike notes.

RED-WINGED BLACKBIRD, *Agelaius phoeniceus.* New World Sparrow Family: Oriole Subfamily. Com. Res., Ripar. Lgth. 7–10". Note male's red shoulder patches and female's streaked underparts.

BREWER'S BLACKBIRD, *Euphagus cyanocephalus.* New World Sparrow Family: Oriole Subfamily. Com. Sum. Res., N Rim; Irreg. Sum. Res., S Rim. Lgth. 8–10". Nest in bush or tree; usually forages in open areas. Note male's yellow eye, dark bill, and iridescent black plumage; female's gray plumage, long, pointed bill, and black eye.

BROWN-HEADED COWBIRD, *Molothrus ater.* New World Sparrow Family: Oriole Subfamily. Com. Sum. Res., SN Rims, all habitats. Lgth. 6–8". Note male's brown head and sparrowlike bill. Female (not shown) is gray, with sparrowlike bill.

HOODED ORIOLE, *Icterus cucullatus.* New World Sparrow Family: Oriole Subfamily. Com. Sum. Res., Ripar. Lgth. 7–8". Note male's yellow-orange crown and black throat; female's yellowish underparts.

SCOTT'S ORIOLE, *Icterus parisorum.* New World Sparrow Family: Oriole Subfamily. Com. Sum. Res., U Son., Scrub and Wood. Lgth. 7–8". Note male's lemon yellow and black plumage; female similar to female Hooded Oriole, but underparts yellow-green and back streaked.

NORTHERN ORIOLE, *Icterus galbula.* New World Sparrow Family: Oriole Subfamily. Uncom. Sum. Res., Ripar., especially cottonwoods. Lgth. 7–9". Note male's black crown, orange cheek, and white wing patch. Female similar to female Hooded Oriole, but belly white.

WESTERN TANAGER, *Piranga ludoviciana.* New World Sparrow Family: Tanager Subfamily. Com. Sum. Res., Tran. and Bor., For. Lgth. 6–8". Note male's red head, yellow breast, and black wings and tail; female's thick bill and conspicuous wing bars.

SUMMER TANAGER, *Piranga rubra.* New World Sparrow Family: Tanager Subfamily. Rare Sum. Res., Ripar. Lgth. 7–8". Note male's uniform rosy plumage. Female (not shown) similar to female Western Tanager, but lacks wing bars.

Western Meadowlark

female

Red-Winged Blackbird

male

female

Brewer's Blackbird

male

male

Brown-Headed
Cowbird

female

male

Hooded Oriole

female

male

Western Tanager

male

Scott's Oriole

male

Summer Tanager

male

Northern Oriole

Plate 65

BLACK-HEADED GROSBEAK, *Pheucticus melanocephalus.* New World Sparrow Family: Cardinal Subfamily. Com. Sum. Res., U Son. and Tran., Wood. and For. Lgth. 6–8". Note male's black head, ocher to rusty breast, and white wing spots; female's large size, striped head, thick bill.

BLUE GROSBEAK, *Passerina caerulea.* New World Sparrow Family: Cardinal Subfamily. Com. Sum. Res., Ripar. Lgth. 6–8". Note both sexes' thick bills and tan wing bars.

INDIGO BUNTING, *Passerina cyanea.* New World Sparrow Family: Cardinal Subfamily. Uncom. Sum. Res. and Vis., Can., Ripar. Lgth. 5–6". Note male's uniform blue plumage; female's faintly streaked underparts and lack of wing bars.

LAZULI BUNTING, *Passerina amoena.* New World Sparrow Family: Cardinal Subfamily. Com. Sum. Res., Can., Ripar. Lgth. 5–6". Note male's rusty breast, white belly, and white wing bars; female's unstreaked underparts and white wing bars.

CASSIN'S FINCH, *Carpodacus cassinni.* Finch Family. Com. Res., N Rim, Bor. For. Lgth. 6–7". Note male's brownish neck and lack of side streaks.

HOUSE FINCH, *Carpodacus mexicanus.* Finch Family. Com. Sum. Res., most habitats below Bor. Lgth. 5–6". Note male's streaked sides. Female very similar to female Cassin's Finch. Male Purple Finch, *C. purpureus,* Irreg. Vis. to Bor. For., lacks streaked sides and brown neck. Cf. Cassin's Finch, above.

PINE SISKIN, *Carduelis pinus.* Finch Family. Com. Res., N Rim, Bor. For. Lgth. 4–5". Note heavy streaking and yellowish wings and tail. In flocks.

LESSER GOLDFINCH, *Carduelis psaltria.* Finch Family. Com. Res., Ripar., and Sum. Vis., U Son. and Tran., Scrub, Wood., and For. Lgth. 4–5". Note male's black back and head; female's olive green rump.

GREEN-TAILED TOWHEE, *Pipilo chlorurus.* New World Sparrow Family: Sparrow Subfamily. Com. Sum. Res., N Rim, Bor.; Com. Vis., other zones and habitats. Lgth. 6–7". Note rusty cap and white throat. Call a catlike mew.

SPOTTED TOWHEE, *Pipilo maculatus.* New World Sparrow Family: Sparrow Subfamily. Com. Sum. Res., Tran. and Bor. For., and Win. Vis., U Son., Scrub and Wood. Lgth. 7–8". Note white underparts, rusty sides, and black head, breast, back, and tail. Female (not shown) similar, but with brown head and back.

male

female

female

male

Black-Headed
Grosbeak

Indigo Bunting

female

male

Blue Grosbeak

female

male

Lazuli Bunting

Pine Siskin

female

male

female

male

Cassin's Finch

Lesser
Goldfinch

male

male

House Finch

Green-Tailed
Towhee

male

Spotted
Towhee

Plate 66

VESPER SPARROW, *Pooecetes gramineus.* New World Sparrow Family: Sparrow Subfamily. Uncom. Sum. Res., U Son. Grass., occasionally Tran. Lgth. 5–7". Note streaked breast and white outer tail feathers.

LARK SPARROW, *Chondestes grammacus.* New World Sparrow Family: Sparrow Subfamily. Com. Sum. Res., U Son., Grass. and Scrub; Sum. Vis., throughout area. Lgth. 5–7". Note bold head stripes and black spot on white breast.

RUFOUS-CROWNED SPARROW, *Aimophila ruficeps.* New World Sparrow Family: Sparrow Subfamily. Uncom. Res., U Son., Scrub and Wood. Lgth. 5–6". Note rusty cap and black streak near bill.

BLACK-THROATED SPARROW, *Amphispiza bilineata.* New World Sparrow Family: Sparrow Subfamily. Com. Sum. Res., L and U Son., Ripar., Grass., and Scrub. Lgth. 5". Note white head stripes and black throat.

DARK-EYED JUNCO, *Junco hyemalis.* New World Sparrow Family: Sparrow Subfamily. A highly variable species with two prominent forms regularly occurring in the Grand Canyon region: Gray-Headed Junco, Com. Res., For.; and Oregon Junco, Com. Win. Vis., various habitats. A third form, the Slate-Colored Junco, is a rare Win. Vis. to Wood. and For. Lgth. 5–6", all forms. Note Oregon Junco's black or gray hood, brown back, pale brown sides; Gray-Headed Junco's gray sides and hood and brown back; the rare Slate-Colored Junco's dark gray hood, breast, and back.

CHIPPING SPARROW, *Spizella passerina.* New World Sparrow Family: Sparrow Subfamily. Com. Sum. Res., SN Rims, Wood. and For., especially open, grassy areas. Lgth. 5–6". Note rusty crown and white "eyebrow."

BLACK-CHINNED SPARROW, *Spizella atrogularis.* New World Sparrow Family: Sparrow Subfamily. Rare Sum. Res., L and U Son., Scrub and Wood. Lgth. 5–6". Note gray head and breast, with pink bill surrounded by black. Female lacks black chin.

WHITE-CROWNED SPARROW, *Zonotrichia leucophrys.* New World Sparrow Family: Sparrow Subfamily. Com. Sum. Res., For., and Win. Vis., most habitats. Lgth. 5–7". Note white crown, gray throat, and pink bill. Immatures have striped gray and brown crowns.

LINCOLN'S SPARROW, *Melospiza lincolnii.* New World Sparrow Family: Sparrow Subfamily. Uncom. Vis., throughout region. Lgth. 5–6". Note streaked, buffy breast.

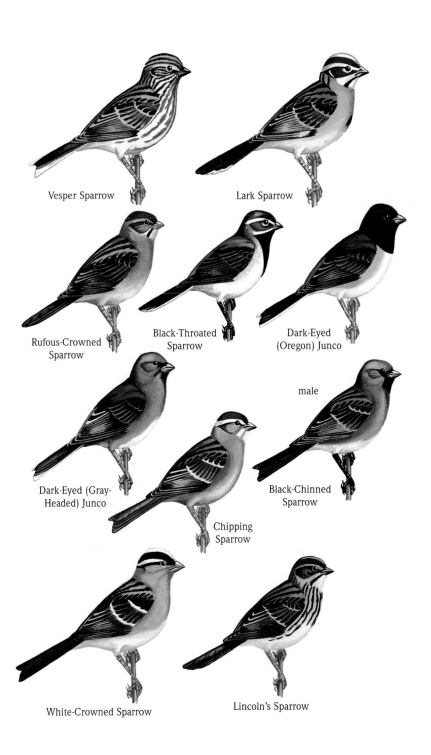

Vesper Sparrow

Lark Sparrow

Rufous-Crowned
Sparrow

Black-Throated
Sparrow

Dark-Eyed
(Oregon) Junco

Dark-Eyed (Gray-
Headed) Junco

male

Black-Chinned
Sparrow

Chipping
Sparrow

White-Crowned Sparrow

Lincoln's Sparrow

8

Amphibians and Reptiles

Amphibians and reptiles constitute two distinct classes of vertebrate animals. Except that both are cold-blooded, with body temperatures that vary with their surroundings, they have little in common. They are lumped together here because there are too few species of amphibians at the Grand Canyon—only seven in all—to warrant a separate chapter.

Amphibians

Amphibians are partly aquatic, partly terrestrial. As a rule they spawn in water, which is scarce at the Grand Canyon. Eggs are deposited in jellylike masses or strings. Fertilization is external. They begin life as larvae (tadpoles) equipped with gills and tail. The larvae transform into adults, a process called metamorphosis, developing limbs and, in most cases, lungs. Metamorphosis usually takes place in a single season.

Frogs rarely venture from water even as adults and may be seen abroad during the day. Toads and salamanders are more terrestrial, returning to water largely to spawn. They spend much of the day holed up in burrows and other damp retreats, seldom appearing except on warm nights during or following rains. At the Grand Canyon, suitable conditions for activity and spawning occur from spring through fall. The rest of the year is largely spent in hibernation.

Most amphibians have moist skin produced by a thin coating of mucus secreted from numerous glands. Some also secrete a toxic substance distasteful to predators and irritating to the eyes and mucous membranes of humans. The mucous coating makes amphibians slippery prey, retards loss of body moisture, and aids in respiration—for, though all Grand Canyon amphibian species possess lungs, most also breathe to some extent through the skin.

Salamanders superficially resemble lizards but are readily distinguished by their smooth, moist skin and clawless toes. Toads and frogs are usually tailless, have moist skin—warty in toads, smooth in frogs—enlarged hind legs, webbed feet, and clawless toes.

Reptiles

Reptiles are well suited to desert environments and, in the Grand Canyon, are distributed through all life zones. Their tough skin retards moisture loss, while replacement water is obtained through their food. Though fairly tolerant of hot weather, reptiles must also avoid the heat of summer. Most snakes will die if exposed for prolonged periods to temperatures much more than 100°F. Lizards tend to have higher limits—often much higher—but within the canyon even these limits are often exceeded. In hot weather most reptiles are active only in the morning and early evening and seek shelter during the hottest part of the day. Several species at the Grand Canyon are wholly or partly nocturnal.

Reptiles tend to be intolerant of cold weather. Most Grand Canyon species hibernate during the winter, which may bring freezing temperatures even to the Inner Gorge. Where winters are long and cold, as on the Kaibab Plateau, reptiles are uncommon or absent. At the Grand Canyon they are most abundant in the Sonoran zones.

Reptiles maintain remarkably constant body temperatures by moving back and forth between sunny and shady locations. During early morning, many snakes and lizards warm up by basking on rocks or open ground exposed to the sun. At dusk they commonly seek out rocks or pavement, which retain the day's heat long after sundown.

Most reptiles hatch from hard- or leathery-shelled eggs buried in warm, sandy ground. Some are born live: horned lizards, garter snakes, and rattlesnakes, for example. In either case fertilization occurs through copulation. The young are born fully active and alert.

Identifying Amphibians and Reptiles

Amphibians are seldom seen because they are scarce as a group, largely nocturnal, and of local occurrence. The best way to see them is to explore along streams and ponds on warm summer nights after a rain. With the single exception of the tiger salamander, which is distinctive, identification may be difficult in the dark. A flashlight, of course, is essential.

Lizards and snakes are also rarely seen by the casual visitor. Rattlesnakes in particular are uncommon in the area and are of a retiring disposition. As a result, visitors more often worry about them than encounter them. Most reptiles in the Grand Canyon are fairly easy to identify. Some groups, however, consist of several quite similar species, and some species vary widely in coloration, with the result that it may not always be possible, without actually holding the animal, to make a positive identification. Do not, however, disturb or handle any reptile within the park. To do so is not only illegal, but may result in a painful bite or possible harm to the animal.

Of the forty-eight species of amphibians and reptiles found at the Grand Canyon region, eighteen of the more common and conspicuous species are shown in this guide. The following unpictured species are uncommon or rare in appropriate habitats within the region:

Leopard Frog, *Rana pipiens pipiens.*
Desert Banded Gecko, *Coleonyx variegatus variegatus.*
Arizona Night Lizard, *Xantusia vigilis arizonae.*
Zebra-Tailed Lizard, *Callisaurus draconoides.*
Banded Gila Monster, *Heloderma suspectum cinctum.*
Western Blind Snake, *Leptotyphlops humilis humilis.*
Red Racer Snake, *Masticophis flagellum piceus.*
Mojave Patch-Nosed Snake, *Salvadora hexalepis mojavensis.*
Sonoran Lyre Snake, *Trimorphodon biscutatus lambda.*
Utah Mountain Kingsnake, *Lampropeltis pyromelana infralabialis.*
Western Ground Snake, *Sonora semiannulata gloydi.*
Utah Black Headed Snake, *Tantilla planiceps utahensis.*

For a complete roster of species known to occur in the Grand Canyon area, and for the common and names used in this guidebook, see Miller, Donald, et al., *Checklist of the Reptiles and Amphibians of the Grand Canyon Area* (Grand Canyon: Grand Canyon Natural History Association, 1981). Abbreviations used in the species descriptions appear in Table 1.

Plate 67

Amphibians

ARIZONA TIGER SALAMANDER, *Ambystoma mavortium.* Ambystoma Family. Com., Tran. and Bor. 6–13³/₈". Dark gray or olive with dusky spots on back and sides. Recently transformed adults may also have yellow blotches. Breeds in ponds and "tanks," rests in crevices, decayed logs, or burrows of other animals. Usually abroad only on warm nights during or after a rain.

GREAT BASIN SPADEFOOT TOAD, *Spea intermontana.* Spadefoot Toad Family. Com., N Rim, Tran. and Bor. 1½–2". Olive or gray-green with light stripes on flanks, hump between eyes, and wedge-shaped "spade" on each hind foot. Breeds in ponds, pools, and quiet streams.

RED-SPOTTED TOAD, *Bufo punctatus.* Toad Family. Abun., Can., near water. 1–2½". Olive green to gray-brown, with numerous red warts. Song a high-pitched trill. Most active at twilight. Breeds in pools and streams, rests in rock crevices. Rocky Mountain Toad, *B. woodhousei,* also Com., Can., near water, 2½–5", has numerous dark spots on pale tan or reddish ground. Its song is a wheezy trill.

CANYON TREE FROG, *Hyla arenicolor.* Tree Frog Family. Com., Can., perennial tributary streams. 1³/₄–2¼". Olive, tan, or gray, with darker blotches. Male's throat black or gray. Note large toe pads. Breeds in streams and pools, rests in rock crevices.

Lizards

WESTERN CHUCKWALLA, *Sauromalus ater.* Iguana Family. Com., Can., Ripar. and Scrub. 11– 16½". Male with black head, forelegs, and forward part of trunk, becoming gray, yellowish, or reddish toward rear. Female and young (not shown) often crossbanded. Rests in crevices. Abroad during the day, sometimes seen sunning on rocks.

MOUNTAIN SHORT HORNED LIZARD, *Phrynosoma hernandesi.* Iguana Family. Com., U Son. and Tran., Grass., Wood., and For. 2½–5⁷/₈". Gray or brownish, with 2 rows of darker spots down back. Note flat body and prominent, reddish, horizontal spines on head. Desert Horned Lizard, *P. platyrhinos,* Rare Res., L and U Son., Grass. and Scrub, is very similar, but with somewat longer head spines, wavy crossbands on sides of head, and dark splotches on neck.

Arizona Tiger Salamander

Great Basin Spadefoot Toad

Red-Spotted Toad

Canyon Tree Frog

Western
Chuckwalla

Mountain Short Horned Lizard

Plate 68

EASTERN COLLARED LIZARD, *Crotaphytus collaris.* Iguana Family. Com., L and U Son., Scrub and Wood. 8–14". Note black-and-white collar, rounded tail, and dark mouth lining. Body color of males mostly green. Many individuals drabber than shown. Females may have orange bands or spots on sides. Young often crossbanded. Desert Collared Lizard, *C. bicinctores* is similar, but mostly tan, with pale yellow crossbands. Throat of male blue with dark blotch.

TREE LIZARD, *Urosaurus ornatus wrightii.* Iguana Family. Com., L and U Son., Ripar. 4½–6¼". Note blue, orange, or yellowish throat and male's blue belly patches.

SIDE-BLOTCHED LIZARD, *Uta stansburiana.* Iguana Family. Com., L and U Son., most habitats. 4–6³⁄₈". Note dark blotch behind forelimb. Color and patterns variable. Mostly ground-dwelling.

PLATEAU LIZARD, *Sceloporus undulatus.* Iguana Family. Com., U Son. and Tran., Wood. and For. 3½–7½". Prefers open, rocky areas. Note blue patch on each side of throat, yellow on back of legs, and lateral striping. Northern Sagebrush Lizard, *S. graciosus graciosus*—Com., U Son., Grass.—has entirely blue throat and white on back of legs. Yellow-Backed Spiny Lizard, *S. magister uniformis*—Com., L and U Son., most habitats—has black shoulder patches and coarse, pointed scales.

NORTHERN WHIPTAIL, *Cnemidophorus tigris.* Whiptail Family. Com., L and U Son., most habitats. 8–12". Prefers open areas. Color variable, stripes sometimes faded or replaced by mottling. Plateau Whiptail, *C. velox,* similar, but tail light blue and pale stripes separated by dark bands without spots. Tails of immatures are bright blue in both species.

VARIABLE SKINK, *Eumeces mulitivirgatus.* Skink Family. Com., For. 5–7⁵⁄₈". Note short limbs and numerous narrow stripes. Immatures have bright blue tails. Great Basin Skink, *E. skiltonianus utahensis,* has a broad brown stripe down the middle of the back.

Eastern
Collared Lizard

Tree Lizard

Side-Blotched Lizard

Plateau Lizard

Northern Whiptail

Variable Skink

Plate 69

GREAT BASIN WHIPSNAKE, *Masticophis taeniatus.* Racer Family. Com., along streambeds. 40–72". Hunts among rocks, trees, and shrubs.

GOPHER SNAKE, *Pituophis catenifer.* Racer Family. Com., U Son. through Bor., most habitats. 48–100". When molested, mimics a rattlesnake, but is not poisonous. Distinguished from rattlesnakes by narrow, tapering (not triangular) head and lack of rattles.

WESTERN LONG-NOSED SNAKE, *Rhinocheilus lecontei.* Racer Family. Com., U Son., Ripar., Scrub, and Wood. 22–41". Most active at dawn and dusk. Note pointed, protruding snout and partial banding. Utah Mountain Kingsnake, *Lampropeltis pyromelana infralabialis,* has white bands encircling body. Note: the venomous and somewhat similar Arizona coral snake does not occur at the Grand Canyon.

CALIFORNIA KINGSNAKE, *Lampropeltis getulus.* Racer Family. Com., L and U Son., Ripar., Scrub, and Wood., often among rocks and brush. 36–82".

WANDERING GARTER SNAKE, *Thamnophis elegans vagrans.* Racer Family. Com., Can. and SN Rims, Ripar., Wood., and For. 18–42". Color variable; may appear greenish from a distance.

GRAND CANYON RATTLESNAKE, *Crotalus viridis.* Pit Viper Family. Uncom., most habitats below Bor. 16–64". Venomous and dangerous. Note triangular, rather than slender, head; heat-sensing pit between nostril and eye; and rattles. Related Hopi Rattlesnake, pinkish, greenish, or grayish, but splotches well defined—Can. and S Rim; and Great Basin Rattlesnake, *C. oregonus,* light brown or gray, with dark, well-defined, narrow splotches— Can. and N Rim. Southwestern Speckled Rattlesnake, *C. mitchelii pyrrhus,* conspicuously speckled, with muted crossbands or blotches. Northern Black-Tailed Rattlesnake, *C. molossus molossus,* has sharply contrasting black tail. Both species are rare.

Great Basin Whipsnake

Gopher Snake

Western Long-Nosed Snake

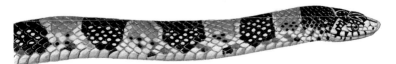

California Kingsnake

Wandering Garter Snake

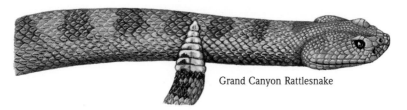

Grand Canyon Rattlesnake

9

Butterflies

The insect order Lepidoptera includes moths, butterflies, and related types. In North America there are about 9000 species of moths and 800 species of butterflies. There is no single feature that separates all moths and butterflies, but moths tend to have stouter, hairier bodies and feathery rather than club-shape antennae. In addition the fore and hind wings of most moths are held together in flight by a small, curved spine or set of bristles called a frenulum. Butterflies lack this device. Most moths are nocturnal, while butterflies are more often abroad during the day. Moths therefore attract less notice and for this reason are not included in this guide.

Life Cycle

Ninety percent of all insects, including butterflies, moths, beetles, flies, and bees among others, undergo radical transformations as they develop into adults. This process is called complete metamorphosis to distinguish it from the less dramatic anatomical changes (simple metamorphosis) experienced in the course of development by grasshoppers, true bugs, and certain other insects. Complete metamorphosis includes four separate stages: egg, larva, pupa, and adult.

All insects hatch from eggs. Those of butterflies vary greatly in size and shape and are usually ornamented with grooves, pits, ribs, knobs, or other sculpturing. Each female butterfly deposits her eggs in a manner and pattern characteristic of her species. In most cases the eggs are placed on the particular type of plant or plants preferred or required by the larvae of each species. Within a few days the larvae—caterpillars—emerge from the eggs to begin feeding on the host plant.

Caterpillars are primarily eating machines. When not resting, they are ravenously consuming leaves or other parts of their host plants. Many caterpillars are serious agricultural pests, but the larvae of butterflies more often feed on deciduous trees or wild herbaceous plants. Like bees, however, adult butterflies and moths play an important, sometimes essential role in pollinating various plants.

In the wild, caterpillar populations are usually kept in balance by a large number of predators, including spiders and their kin, other insects, amphibians, reptiles, birds, and even mammals. In response, caterpillars have evolved a variety of defenses. Some caterpillars make themselves inconspicuous by mimicking the leaves, twigs, and other parts of the plants on which they feed. Others have developed a variety of feeding and resting habits designed to evade predators. For example, it is not uncommon for caterpillars to consume each leaf completely before going on to another. In this way they do not betray their presence through partly chewed foliage. Others are not so tidy, but are careful not to rest on the same shoots where they have been feeding. Other defenses evolved by various species include acrid or toxic body fluids, poisons stored in their shell-like body walls, and stinging or poisonous hairs or spines. Caterpillars so equipped often display gaudy colors to advertise their undesirable qualities, a strategy called aposematic coloration. At the same time, a number of perfectly tasty species hide the fact by mimicking the acrid or poisonous types. This type of mimicry also exists among adult butterflies.

Butterfly larvae come in a great variety of sizes and shapes, but most are smooth-skinned. The caterpillar of each species may be more distinctly marked than the adult, but since caterpillars are usually shy and inconspicuous, they are not depicted in this guide.

As a caterpillar grows it molts several times, sloughing off its old skin in favor of a new, roomier suit. When the larva reaches full size, it typically attaches itself to a firm support, such as the stem of its host plant, by means of silky thread generated by its spinarets. Then, during a final molt, it transforms into a pupa by developing a hard, mummylike case called a chrysalis. Moth pupae are in addition usually encased in a densely woven shroud of silken strands called a cocoon. During the pupal stage, the insect is inactive while it undergoes the radical transformation into an adult. This transformation is timed and directed by hormones, but external factors such as air temperature, length of day, or humidity may trigger the process. Depending on the species, the change from pupa to adult may take from a few days to several months. Many species pupate in the fall, spend the winter in this fashion, and emerge as adults in the spring. Butterfly pupae, like the larvae, can be distinctive, but are not depicted in this guide.

Butterflies and all other insects have bodies composed of three segmented sections: head, thorax, and abdomen. In butterflies the head includes the following parts: (1) two segmented antennae, which are typically slender and terminate in an enlarged "club"; (2) two compound, hemispherical eyes, each consisting of thousands of hexagonal simple eyes; (3) two jointed sensory organs called palpi located one on each side of the mouth; and (4) a coiled tubular proboscis which, when extended, may be longer than the body.

The thorax is the stout, middle section of the body. It consists of three segments, each bearing a pair of five-jointed legs. In addition, the middle and rear segments each bear a pair of wings. The abdomen is the slender, rear portion of the body extending backward from the legs. It consists of eleven segments, not all of which may be visible to the naked eye. Butterflies breathe through spiracles, a series of tiny openings located along the body. Oxygen passes into the blood and circulates through veins to all parts of the body, including the wings. Attached to the end of the abdomen are the genitalia: the ovipositor of the female and the claspers of the male.

Butterfly wings are membranous and densely coated with overlapping scales, which come off as "dust" when the insect is carelessly handled. The scales determine the color of the wings. Some scales may contain pigments, while others create the impression of color through the refraction of light. Other scales are modified into hairs. In male butterflies some of the scales also produce scents that probably play important roles in recognition and courtship.

Adult butterflies feed largely on flower nectar, which is obtained by uncoiling the proboscis and inserting it into the throat of a flower. Some butterfly species are quite selective, visiting only certain types of plants, often not the same type on which their larvae are found. Other species have rather catholic tastes. Adult butterflies drink nectar to sustain themselves, but they are usually short-lived compared to their larvae, and do not grow in size. Their function is not to eat but to reproduce. Normally there are one or two broods a year, and sometimes a brood may contain insects of only one sex. The flight season given for various species refers to the period after the adults emerge from their pupae.

Butterfly Distribution

The Grand Canyon influences butterfly populations ecologically in several ways. It can act as a barrier that prevents movement between the rims; it can act as a channel between the Great Basin Desert of Utah and Nevada, and the Sonoran and Mojave Deserts of Arizona and California; and it can act as a refugium (an area to which a species is restricted) for native species or subspecies.

The Grand Canyon is not as effective a barrier to flying or drifting organisms as it is to strictly terrestrial species. Butterflies are not particularly strong fliers and are more subject to wind dispersion than are many other insects. Blown off course, butterflies may end up at the bottom of the canyon or on the opposite rim.

Thus, it is rare for a species to be restricted to one side of the canyon; yet this is the case for the Grand Canyon Ringlet, which inhabits only the south side of the park. Because of great differences in daily temperatures between the rims and the canyon floor, some butterflies may be active along the Colorado River during the early spring and late fall, at times which are far from optimal for them at higher elevations.

The most noted North American migrant butterfly is the monarch. From late summer through autumn it can be seen floating through the gorge along the river. It uses the Inner Gorge as a channel for its seasonal movements. Other species, searching for food plants which grow along the river, also use the canyon as a channel.

Several subspecies of butterflies are endemic to the Grand Canyon. These include the Pegala satyr and the Grand Canyon ringlet. Another subspecies, Shellbach's fritillary, is only rarely found outside the park. These butterflies show that the Grand Canyon can serve not only as a barrier and a channel, but also as an ecological sanctuary for its inhabitants.

Identifying Butterflies

Although a fair number of Grand Canyon butterflies can be easily identified "on the wing," as it were, the majority are readily distinguished only through the careful examination of handheld specimens. Such features as genitalia, the vein pattern of wings, or the presence or absence of hairs in one place or another may be essential to positive identification. Close examination, however, is not possible in Grand Canyon National Park, because collecting specimens is forbidden except by special permit. Therefore, the casual observer must be content to identify only the large, distinctively marked types that fly slowly, alight often, and frequent habitats accessible to people. Smaller, drabber, more elusive species can usually be assigned to a particular family or occasionally a single genus, but rarely distinguished beyond that.

Plate 70

MONARCH, *Danaus plexippus.* Milkweed Butterfly Family. Abun., SN Rims, Can., and Gorge., Sum. and Fall. Similar to the Striated Queen, *D. gilippus,* but larger, lighter in color, and more distinctly marked. A renowned migrant. Food: milkweeds.

GRAND CANYON RINGLET, *Coenonympha ochracea furcae.* Satyr Family. Com., S Rim and Can. south of river, late Spr. and early Sum. Endemic to the Grand Canyon. Food: grasses.

ARIZONA SISTER, *Adelpha bredowii.* Brush-footed Butterfly Family. Com., SN Rims, Can., and Gorge. Late Spr. through Sum. Glides with wings held at slight angle below horizontal. Food: oaks.

WEIDEMEYER'S ADMIRAL, *Limenitis weidemeyerii.* Brush-footed Butterfly Family. Com., N Rim, Sum. Adults attracted to dung. Food: aspen, willows.

THE SATYR, *Polygonia satyrus.* Brush-footed Butterfly Family. Com., SN Rims, streamsides, Spr. and Sum. Food: nettles.

WEST COAST LADY, *Vanessa annabella.* Brush-footed Butterfly Family. Com., N Rim, Sum. Similar to the American Painted Lady, *V. virginiensis.* Food: lupines, nettles, mallows.

MOURNING CLOAK, *Nymphalis antiopa.* Brush-footed Butterfly Family. Abun., SN Rims, Can., and Gorge, streamsides, Spr. and Sum. Overwinters as an adult and is often the first butterfly seen in Spr. Food: willows, cottonwood, hackberry.

SHELLBACH'S FRITILLARY, *Speyeria electa shellbachi.* Brush-footed Butterfly Family. Com., N Rim, secluded draws. Adults attracted to thistle flowers. First discovered at Grand Canyon.

SNOUT BUTTERFLY, *Libytheana bachmannii.* Snout Butterfly Family. Uncom., S Rim, Can., and Gorge, streamsides and side canyons, Spr. through Fall. Note extra-long palpi, which resemble a snout or beak. Food: netleaf hackberry.

Monarch

Grand Canyon Ringlet

Arizona Sister

Weidemeyer's Admiral

The Satyr

Mourning Cloak

West Coast Lady

Snout Butterfly

Shellbach's Fritillary

Plate 71

MORMON METALMARK, *Apodemia mormo.* Metalmark Family. SN Rims, Can., and Gorge. Widespread Sum. flier. Prefers bright sunlight. Food: wild buckwheats.

COLORADO HAIRSTREAK, *Hypaurotis crysalus.* Hairstreak, Copper, and Blue Family. Uncom., SN Rims and Can., Sum. One of the largest, showiest hairstreaks. Food: oaks.

NEVADA COPPER, *Lycaena arota.* Hairstreak, Copper, and Blue Family. Com., U Son. through Bor., early to midsummer. Food: gooseberries.

ALFALFA BUTTERFLY, *Colias eurytheme.* White Family. Abun., SN Rims, Can., and Gorge, early to midsummer. Food: deervetch, clover, alfalfa, and other members of the Legume Family.

INGHAM'S ORANGE-TIP, *Anthocharis sara inghami.* White Family. Com., S Rim and Can. Early fliers. Food: wild mustards.

WESTERN TIGER SWALLOWTAIL, *Papilio rutulus.* Swallowtail Family. Com., SN Rims, Can., and Gorge, streamsides, Sum. Two-Tailed Swallowtail, *P. multicaudautus,* is larger, with 2 tails. Also Cf. light form of Baird's Swallowtail. Food: willows, aspen.

BAIRD'S SWALLOWTAIL, *Papilio bairdii.* Swallowtail Family. Com., SN Rims, Can., and Gorge, Sum. Note light and dark forms. Food: sagebrush.

YUCCA SKIPPER, *Megathymus streckeri.* Giant Skipper Family. Uncom., S Rim, Can., and Gorge, late Spr. and Sum. Large, stout, swift, and elusive mothlike butterfly. Food: yuccas.

SILVER-SPOTTED SKIPPER, *Epargyreus clarus.* Skipper Family. Uncom., SN Rims, Can., and Gorge, Sum. Largest, most conspicuous member of this well-represented family. Food: New Mexican locust.

Mormon Metalmark

Colorado Hairstreak

Nevada Copper

Alfalfa Butterfly

Ingham's Orange-Tip

Western Tiger Swallowtail

Baird's Swallowtail

dark phase

light phase

Yucca Skipper

underside, hind wing

Silver-Spotted Skipper

Suggested References

General

Anderson, Bette Roda. *Weather in the West.* Palo Alto, Calif.: American West, 1975.

Braun, Ernest. *Grand Canyon of the Living Colorado.* San Francisco: Sierra Club/Ballantine, 1970.

Brown, David E., ed. *Biotic Communities: Southwestern United States and Northwestern Mexico.* Salt Lake City: University of Utah Press, 1994.

Carothers, Stephen W., and Bryan T. Brown. *The Colorado River Through Grand Canyon: Natural History and Human Change.* Tucson: University of Arizona Press, 1991.

Crampton, C. Gregory. *Land of Living Rock; The Grand Canyon and the High Plateaus: Arizona, Utah, Nevada.* New York: Knopf, 1972.

Fletcher, Colin. *The Man Who Walked Through Time.* New York: Knopf, 1968.

Hamblin, W. Kenneth, and Joseph R. Murphy. *Grand Canyon Perspectives.* Provo, Utah: Brigham Young University Printing Service, 1969.

Kirk, Ruth. *Desert: The American Southwest.* Boston: Houghton Mifflin, 1973.

Krutch, Joseph Wood. *Grand Canyon, Today and All Its Yesterdays.* New York: William Sloan Associates, 1958.

Lamb, Susan, ed. *The Best of Grand Canyon Nature Notes, 1926–1935.* Grand Canyon: Grand Canyon Association, 1994.

Lowe, Charles H. *Arizona's Natural Environment.* Tucson: University of Arizona Press, 1964.

Price, Grier, *Grand Canyon: The Story Behind the Scenery,* rev. ed. Las Vegas, Nev.: KC Publications, 1995.

Schmidt, Jeremy. *Grand Canyon National Park.* Boston: Houghton Mifflin, 1993.

Sellers, William D., and Richard H. Hill, eds. *Arizona Climate.* Tucson: University of Arizona Press, 1974.

Sutton, Ann, and Myron Sutton. *The Wilderness World of the Grand Canyon.* New York: Lippincott, 1970.

United States Geological Survey. *The Colorado River Region and John Wesley Powell.* Professional Paper 669-C, Washington, D.C.: Government Printing Office, 1969.

Wallace, Robert, and the editors of Time-Life Books. *The Grand Canyon.* New York: Time-Life, 1972.

Geology

Baars, Donald L. *Red Rock Country: the Geologic History of the Colorado Plateau.* Garden City, N.Y.: Doubleday/Natural History Press, 1972.

Beal, M. D. *Grand Canyon: The Story behind the Scenery.* Las Vegas: KC Publications, 1978.

Beus, Stanley S., and Michael Morales, eds. *Grand Canyon Geology.* New York: Oxford University Press and the Museum of Northern Arizona, 1990.

Breed, William J., George H. Billingsly, Jr., and Peter W. Huntoon. *Geologic Map of the Eastern Part of the Grand Canyon National Park, Arizona.* Grand Canyon: Grand Canyon Association and Museum of Northern Arizona, 1986.

Breed, William J., and E. C. Road, eds. *Geology of the Grand Canyon.* Flagstaff: Museum of Northern Arizona/Grand Canyon Natural History Association, 1974.

Carothers, Steven W., and Bryan T. Brown. *The Colorado River Through Grand Canyon: Natural History and Human Change.* Tucson: University of Arizona Press, 1991.

Collier, Michael. *An Introduction to Grand Canyon Geology.* Grand Canyon: Grand Canyon Natural History Association, 1980.

McKee, Edwin D. *Ancient Landscapes of the Grand Canyon Region,* 28th ed. Flagstaff: Northland Press, 1978.

Thayer, David. *A Guide to Grand Canyon Geology Along Bright Angel Trail.* Grand Canyon: Grand Canyon Natural History Association, 1986.

United States Geological Survey. *The Colorado River Region and John Wesley Powell.* Professional Paper 669-C, Washington, D.C.: Government Printing Office, 1969.

Plants

Arnberger, Leslie P. *Flowers of the Southwest Mountains,* 5th ed. Globe, Ariz.: Southwest Parks and Monuments Association, 1974.

Benson, Lyman. *The Cacti of Arizona,* 3d ed. Tucson: University of Arizona Press, 1969.

Benson, Lyman, and Robert A. Darrow. *The Trees and Shrubs of the Southwestern Deserts.* Tucson and Albuquerque: University of Arizona Press and University of New Mexico Press, 1954.

Cronquist, Arthur et al. *Intermountain Flora: Vascular Plants of the Intermountain West, USA,* vol. 1. New York: Hafner, 1972.

Dittmer, Howard J. et al. *The Ferns and Fern Allies of New Mexico.* Albuquerque: University of New Mexico Press, 1954.

Dodge, Natt N. *Flowers of the Southwest Deserts,* 9th ed. Globe, Ariz.: Southwest Parks and Monuments Association, 1985.

Elmore, Francis H. *Shrubs and Trees of the Southwest Uplands.* Globe, Ariz.: Southwest Parks and Monuments Association, 1976.

Kearney, Thomas H., and Robert H. Peebles. *Arizona Flora,* 2d ed. with supplement. Berkeley: University of California Press, 1960.

Little, Elbert L., Jr. *Southwestern Trees.* Agriculture Handbook no. 9, reprint. Washington, D.C.: Government Printing Office, 1968.

Patraw, Pauline. *Flowers of the Southwest Mesas,* 6th ed. Globe, Ariz.: Southwest Parks and Monuments Association, 1977.

Phillips, Arthur M., III, and John Richardson. *Grand Canyon Wildflowers.* Grand Canyon: Grand Canyon Natural History Association, 1990.

Phillips, B. G., Arthur M. Phillips, and M. A. S. Bernzott. *Annotated Checklist of Vascular Plants of Grand Canyon National Park.* Grand Canyon Natural History Association Monograph no. 7. Grand Canyon: Grand Canyon Natural History Association, 1987.

Phillips, W. S. "A Checklist of the Ferns of Arizona," *American Fern Journal* 36 (1946): 97–108; 37 (1947): 13–20, 39–51.

Rickett, Harold W. *Wildflowers of the United States,* vol. 4, pts. 1, 2 and 3, *The Southwest States.* New York: McGraw-Hill, 1970.

Stockert, John W., and Joanne W. Stockert. *Common Wildflowers of the Grand Canyon,* 5th ed. Salt Lake City: Wheelwright Press, 1979.

Taylor, Therean E., and Karen L. Taylor. *Checklist of Selected Plants of the Grand Canyon Area.* Grand Canyon: Grand Canyon Association, 1992.

Venning, Frank D. *Cacti.* New York: Golden Press, 1974.

Vines, Robert A. *Trees, Shrubs and Woody Vines of the Southwest.* Austin: University of Texas Press, 1960.

Animals

Bailey, Vernon. *Mammals of the Grand Canyon Region.* Natural History Bulletin no. 1. Grand Canyon: Grand Canyon Natural History Association, 1935.

Brown, Bryan T. et al. *Birds of the Grand Canyon Region: An Annotated Checklist.* Grand Canyon: Grand Canyon Natural History Association, 1978.

Brown, Bryan T., Steven W. Carothers, and R. Roy Johnson. *Grand Canyon Birds.* Tucson: University of Arizona Press, 1987.

Brown, Bryan T., Steven W. Carothers, R. Roy Johnson, and Lawrence E. Stevens. *Checklist of the Birds of the Grand Canyon Region.* Grand Canyon: Grand Canyon Association, 1993.

Butterfield, Kathy, Bryan T. Brown, R. Roy Johnson, and Nick Czaplewski. *Checklist of the Mammals of the Grand Canyon Area.* Grand Canyon: Grand Canyon Association, 1981.

Cornett, James W. *Wildlife of the North American Deserts.* Palm Springs, Calif.: Nature Trails Press, 1987.

Dodge, Natt N. *Amphibians and Reptiles of Grand Canyon National Park.* Natural History Bulletin no. 9. Grand Canyon: Grand Canyon Natural History Association, 1938.

Garth, John S. *Butterflies of Grand Canyon National Park.* Natural History Bulletin no. 11. Grand Canyon: Grand Canyon Natural History Association, 1950.

Hoffmeister, Donald F. *Mammals of the Grand Canyon.* Urbana: University of Illinois Press, 1971.

Johnson, R. R. et al. *Grand Canyon Birds Field Check List.* Grand Canyon: Grand Canyon Natural History Association, 1976.

Miller, Donald, Robert A. Young, Thomas W. Gatlin, and John A. Richardson. *Amphibians and Reptiles of the Grand Canyon.* Grand Canyon Natural History Association Monograph no. 4. Grand Canyon: Grand Canyon Natural History Association, 1982.

Miller, Donald, and Robert A. Young. *Checklist of the Reptiles and Amphibians of the Grand Canyon Area.* Grand Canyon: Grand Canyon Association, 1981.

Minckley, W. L. *Fishes of Arizona.* Phoenix: Arizona Game and Fish, 1973.

Olin, George, and Dale Thompson. *Mammals of the Southwest Deserts,* rev. ed. Tucson: Southwest Parks and Monuments Association, 1982.

Phillips, A. R. et al. *The Birds of Arizona.* Tucson: University of Arizona Press, 1964.

Tomko, D. S. *Grand Canyon Amphibians and Reptiles Field Check List.* Grand Canyon: Grand Canyon Natural History Association, 1976.

Wagner, Frederic H. *Wildlife of the Deserts.* New York: Abrams, 1980.

Acknowledgments

I am indebted to many individuals for their generous and skilled assistance in the preparation of this natural history guidebook. I am grateful in particular to Greer Price and Anita Davis of the National Park Service staff at the Grand Canyon for reviewing the revised manuscript and alerting me to various errors and omissions. I am also in debt to a number of individuals who assisted me in preparing the first edition of this book, including Stewart Aitchison, Karen Brantley, Bryan T. Brown, Kathy Butterfield, Nick Czaplewski, Louise Hinchliffe, Donald Keller, William Kemsley, Jr., John C. O'Brien, Arthur Phillips III, T.J. Priehs, Mark Sinclair, Larry Stevens, and Joe Wiesczyk.

The efforts of the above reviewers greatly improved the clarity and accuracy of this book. Any factual errors that may remain are, of course, solely my responsibility.

I am also grateful to the staff of The Mountaineers Books for their careful, professional handling of this project. Their attention to detail and patience with my authorial quirks are much appreciated. Special thanks go to Cindy Bohn, Managing Editor; Helen Cherullo, Prepress Manager, Margaret Foster, Editor-in-Chief; Uma Kukathas, Project Editor; Alice Merrill, Art Director; Ani Rucki, Production Editor.

Copyeditor Kris Fulsaas deserves special thanks for her extremely careful and highly sensitive editing of the manuscript. I greatly appreciate her skill and professionalism. I also want to thank my friend graphic designer Nick Gregoric for his beautiful, simple design, which represents a quantum leap in quality from that of the first edition. Thanks as well to cover designer Elizabeth Watson and indexer Linda Robinson.

Index

267

About the Author

Stephen Whitney is the author of seven books on natural history and outdoor recreation, including *A Field Guide to the Cascades and Olympics, Nature Walks in and Around Seattle, A Sierra Club Naturalist's Guide: The Sierra Nevada, A Sierra Club Naturalist's Guide: The Pacific Northwest,* and *Western Forests.* He is a former managing editor of the *Sierra Club Bulletin,* now *Sierra,* associate editor of *The Mother Earth News,* and contributing editor of *Backpacker.* In addition, Whitney was editorial manager of The Mountaineers Books for six years. He lives in Seattle, Washington.

THE MOUNTAINEERS, founded in 1906, is a nonprofit outdoor activity and conservation club, whose mission is "to explore, study, preserve, and enjoy the natural beauty of the outdoors...." Based in Seattle, Washington, the club is now one of the largest such organizations in the United States, with seven branches throughout Washington State.

The Mountaineers sponsors both classes and year-round outdoor activities in the Pacific Northwest, which include hiking, mountain climbing, ski-touring, snowshoeing, bicycling, camping, kayaking and canoeing, nature study, sailing, and adventure travel. The club's conservation division supports environmental causes through educational activities, sponsoring legislation, and presenting informational programs. All club activities are led by skilled, experienced volunteers, who are dedicated to promoting safe and responsible enjoyment and preservation of the outdoors.

If you would like to participate in these organized outdoor activities or the club's programs, consider a membership in The Mountaineers. For information and an application, write or call The Mountaineers, Club Headquarters, 7700 Sand Point Way NE, Seattle, Washington 98115; 206-521-6001.

The Mountaineers Books, an active, nonprofit publishing program of the club, produces guidebooks, instructional texts, historical works, natural history guides, and works on environmental conservation. All books produced by The Mountaineers Books fulfill the club's mission.

Send or call for our catalog of more than 500 outdoor titles:

The Mountaineers Books
1001 SW Klickitat Way, Suite 201
Seattle, WA 98134
800-553-4453
mbooks@mountaineersbooks.org
www.mountaineersbooks.org

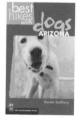